With best wishes!
Loren Kruse

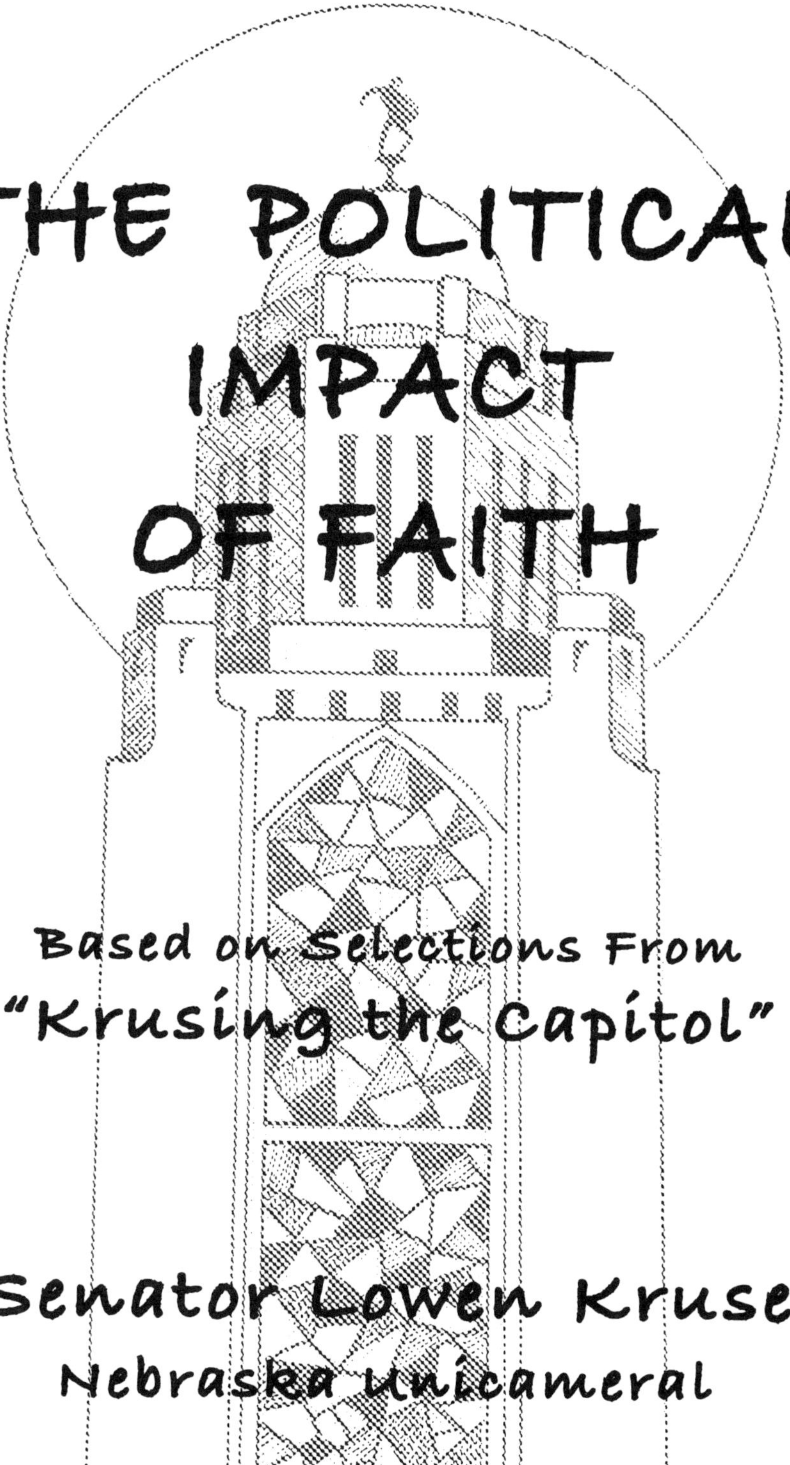

THE POLITICAL IMPACT OF FAITH

Based on Selections From

"Krusing the Capitol"

Senator Lowen Kruse

Nebraska Unicameral

THE POLITICAL IMPACT OF FAITH

Based on Selections From
The "Krusing the Capitol" Journal

Senator Lowen Kruse

Nebraska Unicameral, 2001-2009

Published 2009
Published by: Paradise Publishing
5404 North 50 Avenue
Omaha Nebraska

Artwork by: Tim Fickenscher
Paul Fell
Chris Nielsen

Printed by: Augstums Printing Service, Inc.
Lincoln, Nebraska

Library of Congress Cataloging-in-Publication Data
Reference notes, Index
1. Nebraska – legislature 2. Christian – Jewish – Moslem
3. Politics – legislation 4. Faith advocacy in politics
5. Church/State

Library of Congress Catalog Card Number: 2009936021

ISBN: 978-0-9616821-4-0

DEDICATION

This book is dedicated to my fellow senators, colleagues on the floor during my eight years in the Unicameral. They, with members of our legislative staffs, created a special ambiance of friendship, diversity and responsibility.

We Senators were strikingly different, and certainly represented all Nebraskans. We were committed to making decisions which would be a true benefit to our state, even when citizens could not understand that. Those legislators, every one of them, have a special place in my life. We came to a consensus on what was best more often than I would have expected.

We have footprints started,
and miles to go before we sleep

Contents

Contents

Contents

Contents

Prelude

A symphony orchestra/choir concert is the ultimate experience of community. In the community concert, we complement each other's contribution, while not drowning out other voices. The weakest voice is a gift to all. A group of persons with a mutual goal and with a distinct variety of voices, listens and responds to each other for a shared action which is of benefit to them and to others. Let us add to that the thought that when someone is out of harmony the rest have to adjust to accommodate the discord in their journey together.

Consider this the Prelude to one concert and to an examination of how religion, and the religious experiences of past generations, influence legislative decisions in that concert. What do Nebraska senators hear as they listen to each other? How do they identify and accommodate passion as they craft statutes which will benefit the total community? To be specific, we will consider formative key historic legislative actions through the last four centuries in England and the United States, the application of those (unconscious) memories, and the very conscious impact of current religious thought in the Nebraska Legislature from 2001 to 2009.

State senators are persons of faith, which affects their lives and decisions. As a pastor who served eight years in the Nebraska Legislature, I do not see religion controlling the legislature, though religious institutions do have an undue influence on a few subjects. This book is a summary of my observations of the effect of the combination of spirit-led senators and religious groups in the legislature's task of developing public policy.

Up front, I can not present every religious philosophy or all the thoughts religious folks had on legislation. This book is one pastor's perspective, looking at all legislation and reflecting on the variety of ideas which come from a faith perspective. It is a product of my pastoral career and what I experienced in the Nebraska Legislature. As a senator, I did not represent a church and very seldom thought or spoke as a pastor. As an author, now I can review my journal on those experiences and am back to being a pastor, commenting on how our work appears in the eye of faith.

"Persons of faith" is my term for religious groups I dare to claim to represent. When used, the thoughts following that phrase are representative of Christian, Jewish and Muslim "mainline" thought. Not included are the opinions of left or right wings in any group.

That assertion sounds bold, but it is not. Every faith named has at its center the Golden Rule in some form, has the expectation of care for one's neighbor as oneself, and rejects hatred or harm to a neighbor. God in our many faiths is universally a God of love, is creator of each of us, and is directing us about how to live in community. "How to live in community" is a simple definition of the task of the legislature!

To identify my specific perspective, I am a Methodist/United Methodist pastor with over 50 years experience in Nebraska. I have been a pastor of 15 churches, from 20 to 3,000 in membership, and have served on bishops' cabinets for 13 of those years. I was for years our denomination's contact for networking with most Christian denominations in Nebraska, and for 20 years was a delegate or alternate to our national body which writes our *Discipline*, our book of law.

My duties included helping local congregations do long range planning, supervising pastors and churches, and administering large budgets which were developed through a wide range of committees and debate. One gratefully recalls an interesting, fulfilling career, with an enjoyable populist base!

It has been my privilege to participate in interfaith activities, including Jewish, Muslim, Hindu, Buddhist, and Native American religions, and to be asked to speak for several of them on occasion.

My religious understanding is also influenced by my wife, Ruth, who is a minister in the United Methodist Church and has a Masters degree from seminary. For 15 years, Ruth served the residents of an integrated community, through the church, on North 24th Street in Omaha.

We both are forever changed by her experiences with wonderful people who cared about hurting and desperate neighbors, who made good things happen, and who recognized the marks of a healthy community. Without Ruth's perspective I would not have tried for the legislature or understood some of the complex personal issues there. I am grateful to her beyond words.

My seminary tranining centered on how to research what a scripture passage meant in its original language and setting,. Special research included the subject of homosexuality in the scriptures (teaching it), and the aspects of salvation. For most subjects, we depend on the combined witness of many full time scholars. Hopefully, all of us approach the scriptures with humility, knowing the mystery of God is beyond what we can know.

Also for perspective, I am now a Democrat, was active in the Nebraska Republican party for 41 years and have been an active Democrat for 18 years. I have a deep respect and appreciation for both parties, but reject the partisan "fundamentalists" that can be found in each. These doctrinaire types divide us into saints and sinners politically, which simply is not the real world.

My final personal note is reference to my three books on Nebraska history: Paradise on the Prairie (Nebraska settlers' stories), We Are the Church (Collection of Nebraska stories from church members, from a 150 year period), and Omaha: the Prairie Blossoms (History of the creation of the Nebraska Territory and its early development, plus an account of how faith groups responded to the evolving critical needs in the development of the Omaha community).

Respecting each other's faith is tough to do, but is essential in a free-speech society. My target audience in writing about religion in a public setting is persons who try to follow that principle and are committed to discussion on how we do it best. **My central purpose** is to help persons of faith to become bold as they better understand the issues. Senators need thoughtful concerns clearly expressed.

I frankly ignore the radicals on the left and the right. Their minds are made up and discussion is useless. They clearly have the right to their opinion, but meanwhile the rest of us have difficult work to do.

My experience is that all state senators are spiritual persons and over 90% belong to a Christian congregation. With one exception, which is identified, we do not put down one another's faith, even when that matter of belief is a point of contention. The respect is genuine.

Senators are far more alike than different. I have never voted for a bill that would specifically help my legislative district. Some have. However, when it comes to the bottom line, the majority will vote for what is best for the state as a whole. We are state senators. What best represents moral conviction as a whole? What best delivers necessary services to every type of citizen in the state? What best represents careful use of the funds citizens have entrusted to our management? What values are we expressing in legislation?

Someone is always trying to get us into a "rural/urban" split. That is bogus, even on a geographical issue like roads. Our family has lived across this state, from Scottsbluff to Norfolk to Omaha. We love every part of it. I am impressed with how often western senators have voted for an Omaha project, saying it is good for the state, and how often eastern senators have voted for a project in sparsely populated areas, for the same reason.

We are also nonpartisan. The political parties and a few of the public try to stamp us, but I frankly do not know the political party of every senator and do not want to. In eight years I have never seen a caucus of my party or met in a caucus of our city.

"Krusing the Capitol" was the title of my weekly newsletter/journal while we were in session. It is my quirky but serious view of what was going on in senators' minds as we did our work that week -- "News the papers will not print." I quickly found an enthusiastic reception for simple, common sense reflections.

The letter went to several thousand persons -- I have no idea how many received it by forwarded mail. At times the forwarding included the Central Committee of both major parties, which creates an intriguing audience. I write for those who are interested in more information and who are open to forming new thoughts. When the legislature was not in session, I published a brief paper each month on a current issue, and continue to do that by email.

Comments from my journal are interwoven in the text, without quotes but sometimes with a dating at the end of the piece (4-6 is the 2004 session, week 6). References to published sources are connected by a letter -- A -- to the "Notes" appendix.

Without considerable help, a book simply could not happen. I am grateful to readers/editors: Richard Carter, Iola Mullins, Doug Rose, and Ruth Kruse. The delightful cartoons which add interest to the copy and cover are from Paul Fell. Tim Fickenscher designed the jacket for the book. Chris Nielsen provided line drawings. Rabbi Ayreh Azriel, Senator Bill Avery, Marilyn Meacham, Dr. Charlie Harper, and Jim Cavanaugh have added comments to the jacket, along with their supportive ideas.

Their thoughts help me and their comments allow the reader to have an idea of what to look for. I would not have attempted this work if it were not for the encouragement of these and many others. Thank you, thank you!

My intent in this book is to describe religious values which are timeless, and not to dwell on dated current events and opinions which illustrate those values. The book is based on the beginning of the 21st century and hopefully will be relevant at the end of the century. Parts of our basic written scriptures are, after all, over 30 centuries old and we have centuries of books by pastors/scholars on how the scriptures relate to life, law, and the times.

May this book be helpful in private reflection, in public or congregational discussion on faith and its effects, in considering the proper role of faith in developing public policy <u>and</u> to encourage persons of faith to step up and be heard.

Lowen Kruse

November 1, 2009

The capitol renovation included scaffolding all the way to the top. For one week in 2002, senators were allowed to make the climb, inspect the work, learn the foreman's perspective on the tasks, and even sit on the shoulders of the sower.

Senator Kruse referred to the sower as "Olaf," since he is obviously Greek and Egyptian in artistic style and needs a Nebraska farmer name. The cast bronze sower is 19 feet tall, weighs nine ton, and has lead inside his legs up to his knees, to allow movement in the wind. Amazingly, when a person presses a thumb on Olaf's forehead, he will easily move half an inch. More description of capitol art begins on page 124.

1. Establishment of Religion?

The Nebraska legislature is remarkable for its members' agreement to courteously disagree on matters of religion. Far from indifference, this represents good listening. We have an intense interest in the effects of faith values on legislative debate and do not doubt that faith affects votes. However, personal faith is seldom mentioned and standing in for a religious body is deeply resented. That is the way we are. Most of this book will examine how we think and vote as persons of faith. But first, it is appropriate to ask, "How did we get the way we are?"

"Establishment" and "disestablishment" are the key heavy words in church/state history. We must recover these concepts to understand who we are. The founders of our nation set out a radical new and unusual premise: the government may not establish churches and churches may not control the government. Clear enough, but we are still not there. Our ideals and attitudes on church/state relations are not so clear, and for good reason: differing, deep streams of passionately held, conflicting ideals influence our thoughts.

"This I believe. I can do no other." Our experiences of tense debate have identified diverse attitudes about the role of church and other religions. Unconsciously, we mirror the assumptions from thousands of years of so-called "divine" rulers. We especially reflect the tensions developed over the last 400 years, from the beginning time of the Plymouth settlement and the colonies, with events in both England and the New World colonies.

Do moral arguments have a place in a legislature? Do we assume these moral arguments are the product of faith? Our colonial founders were witness to bitter arguments, and to passionate rhetoric in divisive events. We are their legislative children.

Part of the reason we are not as conscious of the tensions as we could be is that we do not examine the church/state issue or talk about it. Religion and politics cannot mix, right? Wrong. That is easy avoidance. They do mix continuously, but we seldom analyze it.

Separation of church and state should not be confused with separation of religious influence from politics. That was Hitler's plan. Faith was removed from public discussion. That was the Pharaoh's plan for Hebrew religion. The Exodus, the signal event of Jewish history, was to escape from that spiritually sterile life and all it implied and to become a people of true justice. Both religion and the state have a vested interest in justice. If each does its mission well the result may be justice for diverse peoples.

The purpose of this chapter is to remind us of our fascinating checkered history on the role of religion in governing society.

The influence of religion on government is very old!

From the beginning of recorded history, religion and government have impacted each other. Why should anyone be surprised at current confusing assumptions?

Most rulers of ancient governments claimed to be god, or a close relative. Pharaohs, emperors, potentates -- kings and rulers from every continent -- used their version of god to control, manipulate, inspire, punish and reward their subjects.

Our Jewish, Christian and Islamic scriptures were written by persons who lived under rulers who claimed a superior "God" as one source of their power and authority. The early church was persecuted for the first three centuries precisely because it was in competion with the religion promoted and used by the state.

One wonders how many of those ancient rulers actually believed what they said about their own divinity. Probably not many, but we cannot know. It worked. It still works for a few rulers.

What is more, the people wanted it to work. One pharaoh decided to set aside his claim to God and free the people. They rebelled and soon the kingdom was back to control by the presumed power of God.

Part of the understanding of any people's personal value is the importance of their ruler. Citizens in ancient kingdoms depended on the aura surrounding the ruler as much as on his or her wisdom or character or bravery in battle.

This leads to a primary use of religion in too many settings: to manipulate. Manipulation is easy if one is given a bit of religious authority. It develops from the mystery of belief in a higher power.

A divine ruler, a bishop, a not-so-divine pastor, a mother – each can promise reward or punishment which comes from God and not from personal opinions. "God will get you for this" was said by Old World mothers, and by kings who killed masses of 'immoral' nuisances.

Therein lies the danger and threat of any person or group who claims to speak for God to the officials of government. It is manipulation. We will find many examples in our own time. It takes persons of sound faith, with a broad perspective on community, to protect us from the foolishness of manufactured models of faith.

European Church/State

In the Middle Ages, the Roman Catholic Church controlled many European countries, for good reasons. It was an excellent organizing body, helped calm warring tribes and brought consistency to community thought. Emperor Constantine in 313 ordered that the Roman Empire be under the control of the Christian Church. In order to successfully kill his competitors and nasty relatives, he forced the baptism of his entire army. (Ironically, the mostly superstitious action did not include his own baptism until his death. He died 'clean of sin.')

Christianity then became dominant over most of life, even in the centuries with division in the original Catholic Church. Several scriptures direct that God's people (differently defined!) should have dominion over the earth. Are we owners/stewards of the world, or co-inhabitants?

A Presbyterian pastor walked into the Nebraska Territory and eloquently presented the owner view, which was well received by the first European settlers in Nebraska. He pointed out that (non-Christian) Indians obviously have not had dominion over the land and have failed to develop its potential. Witness: the prairie is still primitive. Indians did not believe in private ownership of land and they liked primitive. They saw land as sacred and we saw land as being controlled. Indians needed, in the opinion of most settlers, a good dose of Christianity. Other scripture makes it clear that those who rule do so under the authority of God. It all fit together. The theme was developed easily and often. A-p 63

To greatly oversimplify, but to sketch the diversity quickly, European political leaders found control by the church worked best for them if the government established the church! It seems bizarre when said quickly, but they soon came to a working arrangement of state churches which was experienced by most of the immigrants to the new nation forming in North America.

There was stability here but a disturbing sidelight was that the view of the king often redefined God. If a king is truly "God's representative," one will assume to know more about God by observing the king. Does a Norman king who could not forgive insults represent the nature of God? Some Brits thought so and acted on it.

Divine rulers constructed a patchwork quilt of gods, not a monolithic God. We today reject both images, even as we practice the patchwork quilt version of God.

However it was expressed, the original organizing thought of Church/State structures was that God should be involved in a government which will provide justice to the people God created. Some communities followed it as an unbending faith principle, while others were intensely angry about the abuses that grew out of decrees "in God's name." The mix of these opinions was often passionately expressed on the prairies which were the birthing place for the Nebraska Territory. The debates were not to seek consensus, but to seek control by one religious group or another.

The Czech immigrants to Nebraska are an excellent example of the view that was emotionally negative to dominance by the church. They escaped from a country in which the church, through the government, was controlling and abusive. They were belligerent and stubborn on behalf of free thought.

In the United States, the Czechs continued to believe in God and some wanted to be in a church -- but <u>not</u> associated with the government or the established church. For a group in Omaha, this meant creating a "catholic" church that was not controlled by the local Roman Catholic bishop. Under Roman Catholic polity, the diocese owns the land and church building. The Czechs bought land, refused to sign it over, and proceeded to build a "catholic" church on their property.

The details slow the story, but are available in the excellent Nebraska Catholic history. (B) The Czechs went the Baptist route (!) and called their own priest through a contact in Pennsylvania. They did it by pioneer independence! It became evident that the priest was not fully credentialed and we soon come to the strange scene of the priest, crouched down behind the altar, using a pistol to fend off the sheriff. That too is independence.

In other communities, such as Wilbur, the Czech immigrants isolated themselves from the Catholic Church and disdained participation in <u>any</u> congregation. The pattern held for several generations.

<u>***Budding denominations in England affected our revolution***</u>

The church/state events of the 1500s in England created a seedbed for religious diversity, that, when transported to the new colonies in America, exploded into active organizing. Which faith would guide the new nation? The ultimate solution: none of them, due to the separation of Church and State. That is what our Founders wrote, but we continue to debate full acceptance of the principle.

For background, in 1534 the parliament moved to replace Rome with London as the seat of the church, and to make King Charles VIII the head of the (English) Catholic Church. There were several reasons, some much overplayed. The main reason was national politics. England was not willing to go to Italy for guidance on how to do anything. The King was a devout Catholic and remained so, even though the Pope he sought to replace excommunicated him.

King Charles VIII had moved to support the Pope with a stinging putdown of one Martin Luther in the previous decade. He persecuted anti-catholics. He would allow no change in doctrine, though that was hard to enforce. Many worship services remained in Latin.

The King did want to open the church to the citizens and ordered an English translation of the Bible. The Bibles became so popular in the villages he ordered that they not be read. He feared change so much he put the Bibles under chains, for the eyes of nobility only.

However, his action against the Pope gave boldness to several religious groups, including a few moving in from the continent, such as movements like the Anabaptist and followers of Luther and Calvin. They now had Bibles. The Puritans, so named about 25 years later, objected to the king that too much Rome and not enough Bible was guiding the new Church of England. The church should be pure, be rid of vestments and of certain rituals, and should expunge practices not found in scripture – all as judged by the Puritans.

Persecutions and tension came and went, but were not resolved for 100 years. Puritans became a movement of "Pilgrims" to the new land, where they were adamant in forming congregations which followed only God and scripture. As thousands of Puritans left England, one of their own came to power there.

Oliver Cromwell proved to be a most fascinating character in the Church/State debate. He came to parliament in 1640 and soon controlled the country, even filling the role of King for a period.

As a Puritan, he knew what God wanted done, and he made that happen. When the Irish maintained a loyalty to Rome, he arranged for the slaughter of 40% of them. He knew God wanted Charles I, a weak and totally incompetent king, executed. His army beheaded the king, on behalf of God.

When you select such tidbits about a man you soon will assume you know all about him. Hold on. Cromwell ordered freedom of religion. He studied the example of Christ and decided that Jesus would not reject earnest followers. Every budding group was given the right to worship. He despised the Jehovah's Witnesses and the Roman Catholic Church (for not obeying scripture), but he used his power to protect them, on behalf of God.

This stunning open position by the most powerful man in England was brought to the colonies, where, in a quite different climate, it developed into what we have and where we are in religious freedom.

Pilgrim Witness and Reaction

The basic tenet of the Pilgrim Puritans was that God is in charge of the church and of the government. All Puritans were considered to be devout Christians, united in faith and in making decisions.

Picture a triangle, with direct lines connecting God, the individual and the government/society. God is the top point, directing both of the other points, with part of God's direction to the state coming through devout leaders. This ideal, which some of our citizens carry to this day, is that a community of persons in full covenant with God and each other will be fed by the Eucharist, be guided by scripture, and will legislate by God's will. What Puritans ordered by law God had ordered, and woe to any critic or lawbreaker.

The resulting journey of believers takes some odd turns and is considered humorous by some among us. Be assured, no one was laughing then.

The pilgrim had to be "pure" in relation to God and completely obedient to church law. That was a flawless system, except that some good people were flawed. The community considered all their citizens good people, but a few will miss communion once in a while. Or avoid one of the many rules. Or be children who are not yet in covenant. Then what? In heated debate it was recognized by all that not every person would be the ideal church member, in Full Covenant with God and the church.

So a solution was proposed: the Halfway Covenant. There would be two levels of church membership: those who were obedient in every way and those who were not quite (halfway), including children. The obedient made the laws. In this quick summary, do remember that the second group was felt to be good, upstanding citizens. No one was cast aside, except for sin.

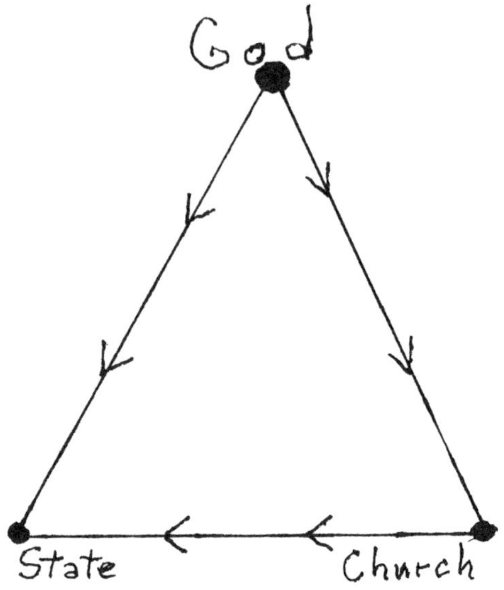

Full Member Plan

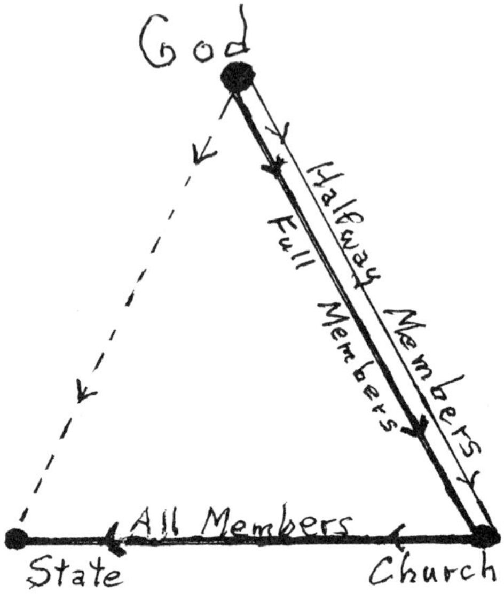

Edward's Proposal

Without describing it here, you can imagine the carping debate between Full Covenanters (makers of law) and mere members. A moment's reflection will tell you this will not work for long and certainly does not make for a cohesive membership and unruffled worship services. However, they created <u>strong towns</u> with the system and developed close communities.

Into the fray came Pastor Jonathan Edwards (1731), a famous, fluent preacher of New England. In part of his complicated path of salvation, he set out a negotiated middle ground between Full Covenant and Halfway Covenant. Edwards proposed to drop God-direct-to-government by adding all members to the governing mix. (Note: somewhat like us!) The relation between God and individual would be developed by the church on both levels of membership. Both classes of members could participate in the governing, which in turn would provide support to the church (not like us).

He insisted that the Covenant could be demanding for a limited number (the inner core) while the state (everyone) would somehow promote the church's interest. As it played out in early New England theological debate, this forced a division that left Pastor Edwards with no place to stand! It became clear that if he was correct, that the state is no longer the pure expression of God, so church and state must separate. If he was not correct in his premise that a mixed group could govern on behalf of God, the righteous in the church should run it all. The larger local group chose that position while a smaller group (Separatists) preferred the separation of church and state. C

The separatists eventually became the dominant movement and that is how we became separatists, disestablishing the church.

Consensus on government, New England style

The reader may not think about colonial history every day (!) so brief connectors to help fill in the picture can be helpful. The formative period from the Pilgrims (1620), through the development of colonies and states and through the "War for Independence" (to 1783), produced values which we continue to support.

Pilgrims were Puritans and became the Congregational church. The first to arrive at Plymouth experienced the extremely painful winter that we often recount. They came through to the spring of 1621 having lost half of their people, battered and in poor health, but stalwart in spirit. What needs to be added is that Puritans continued to come from England, with that stubborn spirit. Ten years later, in 1630, nearly 1,000 hardy immigrants took the uncertain venture in a flotilla of ships and initiated the founding of Boston.

As the Pilgrims prospered, towns were formed, moving the newcomers inland in a disciplined manner. They were a model of planning and community spirit, even cooperating to graze all of their cattle in the nearby woods with one herdsman.

They negotiated with the native Indians for more land. Our use of "Town Hall" comes from their dedication to a Town Meeting democracy in which all participated. They established a new concept, the annual election of government officers.

Their high priority on the education of their children echoes in our policies. Again, it was carefully designed. The pastor was usually the most highly educated person in the town, so he taught the children in a model brought from Europe. Harvard College was established to enhance the education of those who would be parson/teacher.

States developed with a strange but democratic hodge podge of methods, rules and churches. Usually, the Congregational or the Church of England was in charge of spiritual life. When John

Witherspoon (Presbyterian) became President of Princeton in 1768, only the Anglican clergy in that state (New Jersey) could marry a couple. He adamantly preached that it was not enough to "tolerate" other faiths, which the state claimed to do. Toleration implies superiority and condescension. Witherspoon, a signatory of the Declaration of Independence, called for a complete liberty of worship. Roger Williams, with Anne Hutchinson, escaped Massachusetts to what became Rhode Island, where he determined that democracy and right to worship included even the Indians. With similar thinking, the abolitionist movement was created by the churches of New England, where slavery was soon prohibited in every state. Condescending tolerance was not accepted. Tolerance was not tolerated.

After the war, the new U. S. constitution did not settle the church/state passions. Thomas Jefferson, who had the daunting task of urging this disparate assortment of colonies into a working system, said that his strenuous ten-year battle to change the church/state attitudes was "the severest contest" in which he was engaged. For example, Massachusetts kept Anglican/Church of England preference until 1833. Revolutionaries did not realize they were in a revolution.

Virginia sought to make a tax "assessment" for Christian churches in 1784. Jefferson was (at that time) resolute in pushing the measure. Washington intervened, strenuously objecting, and stopped the bill. Later, the federal constitution simply prohibited a religious test for elected officials, but within six months the Bill of Rights presented the new consensus: "Congress shall make no law respecting an establishment of religion, or prohibiting the free exercise thereof."

Revolutionary times

The founders who wrote our national documents had quite enough of the Pilgrim's way, plus quite enough of state control in their home countries. The "Wall of Separation" was never stated in those documents, but it became an appropriate summary of their thoughts. The church was disestablished, but the general public did not understand that and had to catch up. Obviously, many did not "catch up" and still do not agree.

In the rebelling colonies, public response to the church/state issue was dramatic. So called 'Free Church' groups which opposed the Church of England model prospered during the Revolution. The

Methodists, organized by lay preachers who moved quickly by horseback among the rebelling settlers, grew from 20 to 700 congregations during the twenty years of the revolutionary period. That is 35 times over. The Baptists, always more pointed on issues of religious liberty for individuals, grew six fold, from 150 to 850 congregations. No other denomination grew by even 50%.

The upstart new movements propelled 'disestablishment.' They did not use that word, but they knew salvation was not connected to the government.

The massive shift continued. By 1860, the "revolutionary" (free) churches outnumbered the former establishment churches 3 to 1. Castigated as antiestablishment and as outsiders, the separatists were no longer a minority. Church growth is actually a side issue, as total membership was small. The dramatic change was the rapid increase in numbers of citizens who strenuously supported the separation of church and state. Congregations gave them the place to say so.

However, constitution is one thing and practice is another. For the first 100 years, the U. S. treasury gave money to churches! A flap related to the World's Fair in 1893 called attention to the "unpatriotic ignoring" of our constitution, as some named it.

The Supreme Court, in responding to complaints about constitutional laxness, stated in 1891 churches can be supported by the government as "This is a Christian nation.". We are not and that was trouble. Con-gress felt that a "Christian nation" should close the fair on Sundays and wrapped it in the language of obeying the fourth commandment.

Then someone read the commandment. The Seventh Day Baptists said "Honoring the Sabbath" is reference to the seventh day of the week, Saturday. Then congress changed its order to (the Christian!) "First day of the week, Sunday." Then, the Baptist group came back with the charge that the feds were favoring one Christian group over another. Then someone wondered why the Roman Catholics were still getting $400,000 a year to run their churches in Cuba, when the Protestants had rejected the subsidy in recent years.

Then they decided to obey the constitution. My colleagues will be thankful that we are no longer in the business of trying to get Christians together or writing 'Christian' law. D

A shock to British thinking

However, as is always the case in heated debate on complex issues, there is more to the story. Following the revolution, a signal event in England changed the role of persons of faith and disrupted a comfortable British mentality.

William Wilberforce came to the British parliament (1780) assuming, with most, that the state/church gives the law and persons of faith should keep religion out of parliamentary discussion. His newfound religious conviction on slavery stood that assumption on its head. His "new" faith was fervent, but he expressed it in well-documented, academic argument in the parliament.

William Wilberforce, wealthy, well educated, and exceptionally gifted in mind -- carefully strategized to put his convictions into law. For our purposes in analyzing the influence of faith, it must be clear this was not action by "the church" but by individuals within the church. Historians agree that abolition of slavery in the British Empire would not have been achieved without individual believers who made their belief public.

It took nearly fifty years of continuous pressure, but Wilberforce and his supporters (from many churches and several synagogues) ended slavery in the Act of 1833, <u>thirty years before</u> our Emancipation Proclamation, and <u>before</u> our devastating Civil War which centered on the <u>same economic issues</u> that had been wrestled and settled in England. (They paid the owners for their slaves.)

Wilberforce experienced a process of conversion to a more lively faith in 1787, under the guidance of John Newton, pastor and writer of "Amazing Grace." Newton's poetic phrase "who saved a <u>wretch</u> like me" referred to his life as captain of slave ships, in which role he contributed to the horrific, cruel and degrading practices that killed one in ten Africans on board.

Key to our search for influence on legislation, if Newton had held the typical evangelical position of the day, we would have a different history. Evangelicals then held that the world is a dirty place and Christians should shun it. The parliament was among the most worldly and therefore most to be shunned. With newly found faith, Wilberforce considered becoming a priest. Newton and close friends said "No." <u>This response was a seismic shift in Christian theory</u>! "God is not calling you to church ministry. God is calling you to (ministry in) parliament, where your faith can lead you to correct a great moral wrong. You have connections, gifts and levers (!) that God can use." His "church" was to be Parliament.

After a long night of the soul, Wilberforce declared two objectives for his life and never wavered from them: 1. the abolishment of slavery and 2. the reformation of manners. The second has been criticized as a long list of picky prohibitions in the villages, but actually it changed the public attitude from acceptance of <u>terrible</u> public behavior, exceedingly course and crude, to a standard of caring about the life issues of common persons. The teachings of Jesus became a guide for personal behavior. He provided the community with a conscience. His group felt that anywhere you see suffering you are obliged to address it. "They made goodness fashionable."

The anti-slavery action began in earnest in 1787. Year after year Wilberforce brought the slave <u>trade</u> before parliament, as his strategists decided importing slaves was the place to start.

Slave trade was considered essential to the national economy, even while being judgèd a national disgrace. Wilberforce called it a national sin. Can a nation sin? Sin, it was said, is in the minds and acts of individuals, while the job of parliament is to manage the economic engine of a healthy nation. Sound familiar?

The public built such a dramatic cry over the moral issue of inhumanity through slavery that the Slave <u>Trade</u> Act eventually passed in an emotional session in 1807, by a vote of 283-16. It was early populism at its boldest. After the vote, bedlam took over the chamber and included an extended time of un-British cheering.

The Napoleonic Wars were a distraction for eight years, but the motion for abolition of slavery itself came every year until a successful vote in 1833, as Wilberforce was dying. He was proclaimed a national hero. His belief that faith can be expressed in Parliament was vindicated by that body and by the people. We in the United States were changed by it.

The next year, preparing for the emotional official day for freedom, slaves in the West Indies were up all night, singing on a hilltop where they could get the <u>earliest</u> view of the rising sun, the dawn of their first day of freedom. "Lift Every Voice," the "Black National Anthem," has lines from that drama: "Facing the rising sun, of our new day begun, Let us march on 'til victory is won." The bells ring with "the harmony of liberty." Probably the most powerful poem about freedom for slaves, the words of James Weldon Johnson were central to the benediction at President Obama's inauguration.

The "Great Awakening"

We Americans have a direct connection to that dramatic emotion. The Great Awakening (mid-1800s) was a national religious movement in the U. S. that celebrated the relevance of faith to public life, confirmed the split from the Pilgrim isolationist model and promoted a new understanding of the separation of Church and State. As noted, the primary emphasis on the individual's relation to God drove back the influence of the church hierarchies.

Persons with a conscience that was formed by their relationship with God should deliberate with others in legislation to form a just community for the people God created. Shades of Wilberforce.

That did not bring a conclusion to the debate of God's place in the legislature, but it certainly guided it. An excellent example of the ongoing faith tension in the Nebraska Territory is the issue of public education. Roman Catholics, Lutherans and Episcopalians officially opposed it, favoring a system of parochial schools without competition from public taxes. The churches which were growing the most rapidly in the Great Awakening supported public schools, which politically included favoring the vote of women.

The rhetoric was heated. It was so over the top we cannot repeat some of the statements made by religious leaders. They are too crude and offensive.

Nebraska missed a distinctive place in history when it came close to giving the women the right to vote in 1857, seventy years early! Supporters lost the women's suffrage issue, but they won public education through the new State Constitution: "The Legislature shall provide for the free instruction in the common schools of this state of all persons between the ages of five and twenty one years."
(Article VII, Sec. 1, 1875)

They knew the shape of the political argument, but did not know that sentence would become the most expensive words in the constitution. It took over 100 years before we were forced to define "all persons." Does that include mentally retarded? Yes. Developmentally disabled? Yes. Every immigrant? Yes. In

Nebraska, we are required to educate every child in the state. They did not reflect on that. They were in a religious fight.

Another strand in our thoughts on faith and the legislature came with the Populists in the 1890's. It was a political movement that centered on justice for the poor. Church leaders who failed to stand for the poor were chastised in public. Many delegates to the Populist conventions did not have money for food.

The movement which began in the Farmers Alliance quickly took root in Nebraska, with the national convention coming to Omaha in 1892. William Jennings Bryan, in his presidential campaign of 1896, thundered that "You shall not crucify mankind on a cross of gold." The campaigns were filled with Biblical images and arguments.

A review of the work of the Farmers' Alliance shows a remarkable breadth in its program, with a variety of congregations giving support. They combined education, radical political ideology, cooperative ventures and social gatherings. That strategy essentially turned Seward County into a Populist stronghold for many years.

"Populist" is a term often misused. A popular senator is not necessarily populist, though he may like to think so. The Populist movement pitted the little guy against power, as, farmers against arrogant railroads. (The railroads, with a monopoly on shipping, controlled where cattle could be sold and how far wheat could be shipped.) Populists were basically anti-Wall Street, anti-large corporations, anti-hidden control of wealth and resources, and anti-slavery of any kind. They believed the government is people and the people should control the government.

We still have not figured out the relation between the power of the people and the power of money. Teddy Roosevelt built on populist sentiment and stated that not standing against the power of money risked the future of the country. We recently proved him correct and religious voices are again rasied in protest.

The religious fervor in Populism soon died with a leadership shift to the right, leaving the public stranded. However, no short lived movement has had success comparable to the Populists. They proposed restriction of the railroads, regulation of corporations, direct election of senators, the income tax, vote of women, employee rights, protection of children, prohibition, environment conservation, civil service laws, veterans pensions, and protection of public lands -- to name a few. Every proposal was national law in a little more than twenty years -- an impressive legislative record for a movement considered dead, and a testimony to the populist effectiveness in our legislature to this day. You can pass (and enforce!) what the people want, especially when they feel powerless.

Echoes of Pilgrim Thought

In recent times, the pendulum of faith influence swung far toward the Pilgrims' position. One church network declared that persons of faith not only have the right to be politically involved but have the responsibility to control the political agenda.

Not all have agreed. Both John Kennedy and Mitt Romney, in their presidential campaigns, assured the American people they would not be tools of the church which had formed their faith. However, other Christians strongly asserted that this is the wrong attitude, that selected Christian believers should control.

Though the leaders seeking re-establishment of the church certainly have not represented a majority of Christians, the pastors quoted leave no doubt as to their intent:

James Dobson: "We voted for them and now they need to get on with it."

David Limbaugh: "We're not just in a war against terrorists ... we're in a war against the secularists ... who have tried to supplant the Judeo-Christian value base with their secular humanist value base." ("Humanist" here means "Mainline churches.")

Bishop Boone dismissed the idea of church-state separation as unbiblical and suggested that those who disagree are agents of Satan: "I know that behind you is your father the devil."

Gary Bauer, former leader in the Christian Coalition, called for control of the Supreme Court "(We cannot survive judges who use the constitution) as a weapon against everything we love and everything we hold dear."

Congressman Tom DeLay called for an IRS revision so that pastors could openly endorse candidates. He said silencing pastors removes Christians from influence of the government. "It forces Christians back into the church..... That's not what Christ asked us to do."

C

James Kennedy: "Our job is to reclaim America for Christ, whatever the cost. As the vice regents of God, we are to exercise godly dominion and influence over our neighborhoods, our schools ... government ... arts ... sports ... entertainment ... media ... science -- in short, over every aspect and institution of human society."

Pat Robertson, in his "Theology of Prosperity": "It would be terrible to think that our loving heavenly Father gave the wealth and beauty of the world to estranged sinners and insisted His own people live impoverished."

One columnist received a mailing from Robertson stating that if he were a Christian who loved his country he would vote the 'Christian' ticket and send money. Coleman's response: "I love my country and am a Christian, which I thought obliged me to love my neighbors, refrain from judging others, and, through prayer and worship, attempt to draw nearer to God."

In the happy variety of beliefs that our democracy encourages, we have persons who adamantly hold to positions similar to those above. Most believers do not. In Nebraska we do talk with one another.

However, the assumption that true believers should control legislative agendas has several examples in current issues, as we shall see in following chapters. The issue of the appropriate ways for persons of faith to engage in legislative discussion is our main subject.

Summary Thoughts by Catholic, Amish, Jewish voices

Our divergent thoughts come from modern voices as well. However, today we have lost the leaders who can speak for most persons of faith in a nonsectarian, nonpartisan manner. Michael Gerson described our dilemma well. E

> *After World War II, people cared what the Rev. Reinhold Niebuhr, Bishop Fulton Sheen and Rabbi Abraham Joshua Herschel had to say on public matters. These large figures provided the intellectual and moral ballast for a rough national crossing through the Cold War and the civil rights movement.*
>
> *Today, this cultural role seems to be filled by some mix of Oprah Winfrey and Deepak Chopra -- which is to say, not filled at all.*
>
> *In a saner, more serious time, the Rev. Richard John Neuhaus would have been a broadly familiar name. He was a*

civil rights organizer, a friend and associate of the Rev. Martin Luther King Jr., a cofounder of Clergy and Laity Concerned About Vietnam, and, with the Rev. Daniel J. Berrigan, a founding theorist of the pro-life movement and a singularly important interpreter of the teachings of Pope John Paul II.

Father Neuhaus sought out "genuine argument within the bond of civility" He defined the modern church-state argument. In his landmark book, "The Naked Public Square," he contended that American democracy depends on a robust religious life, including the sort of religiously informed public argument found in the civil rights movement. Americans must be allowed to bring their most deeply held values into the public square.

Remembering when he was a Lutheran pastor and marched with King, Neuhaus said, "At that time, people were starting to talk about the 'quality of life' with high-sounding purpose." He looked out on his impoverished parish, and not a single one had 'quality of life' by this definition. So what to do? Should they be ignored? Who do we eliminate?

Neuhaus decided to care for human lives without exception -- leading him, as one example, to oppose what he felt to be unlimited abortion license. He became a national spokesperson for that protest. We no longer have this kind of dominant leader of faith.

To summarize the journey of church/state, and to point to the Amish mark of quality in public faith, we turn to a remarkable statement by the Amish, directed toward those who admire them. It is now time for the Amish to evangelize, right? Not. Come join us -- be like us? Not.

We find none of the abominable arrogance of: "Believe like me," "We have the truth about the Bible," "God hates who we hate," "We are the way, the truth and the life." And on and on.

"The Amish culture is greatly admired, but its members would not want you to forget that they are not who they are because of the way they live, but rather they live as they do because of who they are and what they believe. They do not live as they do to be a guidepost to others (though it may also be that).

"Many of you would like to live more like the Amish. ..... So if you admire their faith -- strengthen yours. If you admire their family life -- spend more time with your family. If you admire their sense of commitment -- deepen yours. If you admire their sense of community spirit -- build one. If you admire their quality merchandise -- make quality. If you admire their humility -- be humble. If you admire their unselfishness -- put others first. If you admire their honesty -- be honest. If you admire their willingness to help those in need -- help the needy. If you admire their land stewardship -- take care of yours. If you admire their deep character and enduring values -- live them." 7-E

Rabbi Lawrence Kushner has written pointedly about our life puzzles. Each of us has a piece of someone else's puzzle. That's community. We need the gifts of others that would fit our puzzle. His metaphor has unusual food for thought. F

Each lifetime is the pieces of a jigsaw puzzle.
For some there are more pieces.
For others the puzzle is more difficult to assemble.

Some seem to be born with a nearly completed puzzle.
And so it goes.
Souls going this way and that
trying to assemble the myriad parts.

But know this. No one has within themselves
all the pieces of their puzzle --
like when they sealed jigsaw puzzles in cellophane,
insuring that all the pieces were there.

Everyone carries with them at least one and
probably many pieces to someone else's puzzle.
Sometimes they know it. Sometimes they don't.

And when you present your piece
which is worthless to you,
to another, whether you know it or not,
whether they know it or not,
You are a messenger from the Most High."

A religious book of cartoons in 1951 presented a playful look at creation and the political process. The premise: God created the world just as we now have it, with tight-fitting clothes, guns, fast food, messy beauty treatments. state borders, and on.

Humans talked and thought until they came with a better plan. They used the A-bomb to blow a large hole in the ground, put all the unnecessary items in the hole and so progressed to perfection: the Garden of Eden. And they all lived happily ever after.

2. Theologians

Statements of faith vary widely

Theology -- the study of the nature of God, and of opinions about God. Everyone who has thoughts about God is a theologian, so get used to the title – and the high wire!

This chapter was written with bias that should be stated. The writer is a Christian and a follower of Jesus, both as model for living and as a teacher for thinking. Hebrew and Christian scripture is my basic guide. All scripture, not just selected verses. This provides enough mystery for anyone! When there is conflict in scripture, which has wonderful points of tension, Jesus is the teacher. The author's perspective is a product of experience, and for him Jesus has been God's best communicator.

The writer finds wisdom in other faiths and does not doubt that God shares truth and salvation through many faiths. That is God's job. Trust God to do it well.

We are all selective. Own that, and humbly review your basis of selection. To select only hateful beliefs and ignore the evidence of an open loving God is to be plainly dishonest with scripture. "God so loved the world... " is a trustworthy theme of the Bible. 8 B

Give up the pious face. "Piety" is not pious. It is a gentle, thorough understanding that each of us is created, and is in the presence of that creator at all times. No matter what.

People of faith do not agree on all the specifics, but they should be intensely interested in each other's views. That is the way we learn. This works well and can be quite enjoyable -- until an absolutist joins the circle. That person knows what God said, or God is thinking (God thinks? God is trying to figure something out?), or what God is going to do to someone. Then learning and sharing faith is ended. Since we believe God is in each person, arrogance can block us from discovering God's message within each person.

The tension of our divisions

How do we figure faith out? For starters, fundamentalists, of any faith, are limited. They say their 'fundamentals' are set in stone, and that to even discuss another point of view is a form of blasphemy. The conservative, the traditionalist, the liberal, the modernist -- persons we define or debate -- can join with others in a spirited dialog about truth. The target audience in this book is moderates of any label who want to think about issues. The "Far Right" and the "Far Left" know it all, so dialog is useless. However, those of us in the broad middle do have to deal with the distortions they create.

Jim Wallis is a thoughtful evangelical writer:

The Christian Coalition is not in the evangelical tradition. They are fundamentalists who espouse a kind of cultural American religion that does not have much to do with Biblical faith. Martin Luther King Jr. really understood the role of the church when he said, "The church is not meant to be the master of the state." We don't take power and impose our agenda down people's throats. We don't legislate Leviticus. We are the servant of the state. We are the conscience of the state. We are prophetic interrogators. "Why are so many people and families in our shelters?" "Why?" is the prophetic question.

Abraham Lincoln had it right. Our task should not be to invoke religion and the name of God by claiming God's blessing and endorsement for all our national policies and practices - saying, in effect, that God is on our side. Rather, as Lincoln put it, we should worry earnestly whether we are on God's side.

Those are the two ways that religion has been brought into public life in American history. The first way - God on our side - leads inevitably to triumphalism, self-righteousness, bad theology, and, often, dangerous foreign policy. The second way - asking if we are on God's side - leads to much healthier attitudes, namely penitence and even repentance, humility, reflection, and accountability. We need much more of all those, because they are often the missing values of politics. G

Judeo-Christian faith

Christian and Jewish moral perspectives are so close in legislative matters we can consider them together.

Christians accept most Jewish scripture as their "Old Testament." Jews accept the teachings of Jesus as the record of teaching by a prominent Rabbi. Christians study and quote the rabbinical writings as a rich resource and commentary on their Old Testament. Jews study the New Testament letters to understand the Jewish congregations of that day and for background on moral issues which were debated.

Division of thought comes when we define Messiah, Savior, Redeemer and Son of God, which are not concepts that appropriately come before the legislature. This pastor has experienced years of direct exchange of ideas and sermons, and of leading studies between Jews and Christians. He has found no more conflict between Jews and Christians in positions on public policy than members of each side have with their own colleagues. Therefore, in only one case will the distinction between Judeo and Christian be made in this book. Following are four ways to give helpful focus to our beliefs.

What is the Judeo-Christian stance? ***The Golden Rule*** *summarizes it. Do to others as you would have them do to you.*

Jewish scripture: "What does the Lord require of you but to do justice, and love kindness, and walk humbly with your God?" -- Micah 6:8

Christian scripture: "You shall love the Lord your God with all your heart, and with all your soul, and with all your mind. This is the great and first commandment. And a second is like it. You shall love your neighbor as yourself. On these two commandments depend all the law and the prophets."

--Matthew 22:37-40

It is the gold standard and is much tougher than it sounds.

"Love" is a waffle word in our culture. It can be tough or squishy. So dig in a bit for a second word. A good test of love in scripture teaching is the **dignity** given each person.

Jesus is radical in his parable about recruiting replacement guests at a wedding banquet. Bring in <u>anyone</u> from the streets and byways, the servants are told. Give them the dignity of coming to your feast.

R

We cannot go that far. Americans cannot imagine a table they do not control. Not just anyone will come to <u>my</u> wedding banquet. We do not have enough dignity to go around. Faith will <u>stretch</u> us, but providing dignity is clearly a reach.

A third solid comprehensive concept to focus the Judeo-Christian faith is **community**. God created us for community and every one of our scriptures assumes a responsible community.

Fourth, **Micah 6:8** (above) is the base for a hymn, which summarizes the essence of the Judeo-Christian faith.

Come! Live in the light!
Shine with the joy and the love of the Lord!
We are called to be light for the kingdom,
to live in the freedom of the city of God!
We are called to act with justice,
we are called to love tenderly,
we are called to serve one another,
to walk humbly with God! Q

The Islamic faith resonates with all of these themes. The Golden Rule is central. Muslims study the Abrhamic Hebrew scripture and respect Jesus as a prophet. Unfortunately Christians and Jews do not yet study the *Koran* for insights to be gained there – are starting.

All three faiths have a central emphasis on justice, especially for the poor and those less able to care for themselves. The rest is commentary.

Put in a term so basic it is profound, Jesus centered all that he said and all that he was on the Kingdom of God. What is a kingdom? Where the king reigns. Two problems are here: we do not have many good king models, and every one of them is based on hierarchy within the kingdom. The Kingdom of God has no hierarchy.

Since we have not experienced a kingdom, there is a better image for us. "Household" is an excellent translation of the original. God's Household is here. Jesus said it is around us and behind us, and is what is to come.

God is the head of the house and is both male and female, which also fits our heads of households. What does the father or mother want for children in a household? Enough for each. That is it, across all cultures, in all of God's family. This of course is more than "enough stuff" – it includes enough respect and emotional support.

Does the father want the same for each child in the household? No, that never happens. Does he expect equal abilities, dreams, accomplishments? No, not ever. Our God plans justice for each -- enough for each. In a household, one child cannot have more than enough to eat while others starve. We have not legislated to that standard, anywhere.

In God's Household, what was the first act of the children after the Garden of Eden? A homicide. So God struck down the offender, right? Wrong. It is critical that we remember that. God's plan is for each member of the household to make better decisions and to live with the consequences of decisions.

Without question, the worst twisting of our faith we experience is the claim that God is a God of punishment and that God's prophets predict the wrath to come. Not. (In the original language, "Wrath of God" is the absence of God, not punishment.) Prophets do not predict the future, but describe the consequences of our actions within the household. "Those who live by the sword will die by the sword" is not a prediction. It is a fact of life.

The premise that God is a God of punishment and vengeance is a terrible abuse of scripture. It is used by violent people to threaten those who disagree with them with frightening futures. It is a tool of manipulation. If we were to interpret God as centered on punishing, we are all in trouble – and we would be abusing scripture.

For the first centuries, followers of Jesus never pictured him dead. They saw Jesus as healer and teacher, vibrant and lively, building a community of the joy-filled faithful.

God is love. God is the <u>head of the house</u>, expecting each child to have enough -- to experience a good life, and expecting that all of us will work with one another to become a community that plans and works so each child shall have enough.

The interfaith message is that simple, and that profound.

Both Jews and Christians have activist models in scripture for persons in politics. Jesus was aggressive in plain messages and was equal to activists of our day. He was a radical who was executed. He taught far more about caring for one's neighbor, public negligence and corruption, and participation in society than he did about the spiritual side of salvation. (Both sides are essentialin faith.) Jewish prophets Amos, Jeremiah and Isaiah, would put any modern activist in the shade. Amos was ordered into exile; Jeremiah was placed in stocks; Isaiah was executed. They were "lobbyists" in the boldest manner. The legislative floor is a quite comfortable place to be for followers of Jesus or Amos or Isaiah or Moses.

A major challenge is that Christians are in a pluralistic world and still, in our heart of hearts, want every one in it to be Christian. The "non-believers," as some call them, have figured that out. They deeply resent the attitude they see as Christian. Until we come to a negotiated settlement among ourselves we are not going to cooperate with them effectively. 4-Oct

If we are to be true to the traditions of our faiths, each of us must learn. The founder of Methodism: "Let us unite the two so long divided: knowledge and vital piety." The woman who put up the money to initiate a seminary 150 years ago said she had appreciated her Methodist pastors and their piety. However, she thought it would be a great improvement if they had more knowledge.

That thought has been in my mind so long it is taken for granted. A fellow alum of that seminary found it remarkable in retrospect that without exception faculty members demonstrated truth and piety. This graduate slowly realized, years later, his assessment is on target. Our faculty had great variety, but each clearly had piety in her/his search for truth. It is a powerful moment to realize their simple integrity has molded oneself unconsciously, all these years.

Finding the truth of Hebrew culture as you read English words is a tough go. Too many religious types abuse scripture by reading in their own opinions. In shared pastors' study, we gained protection from falling into arrogant quotes of selected scriptures. Truth is not complete in one lonely verse. More important, much of scripture is poetry, which loses its lively lesson if the words are taken as literal. Mideast story telling, a staple of Jesus and of beloved texts, is ruined with a narrow look at only literal words. We call some of our spin "prophesy," which is never literal in scripture.

Some ideas cannot be understood without lengthy study and consultation. Faith is less what you believe and more what you value. Worship centers on value. It takes time for clear thought.

One national pastor stated that what he said was from God and to be trusted but that when a candidate says the same words it is to get elected. We would like to assume each is truthful, and that each uses words chosen for a particular audience -- even as it is in scripture. In the legislature as elsewhere, words do not always have a clear meaning, because the audience keeps changing. 8-A

It is dishonest to say, when we know the other's personal language, "I know what I meant. I cannot be responsible for what he heard."

The basic bottom line to all this: clarifying thoughts requires definitions. Definitions allow communication in the search for truth. "Knowledge" is truth, not endless study. One professor wrote on a paper, alongside my extensive bibliography, "You should read less and think more." Well. Expect to be working on definitions.

"I speak for God"

Contradiction is built into faith. "This I believe" has a measure of doubt, or it is not faith. Supporting the right for others to believe is supporting the right to believe differently. Some cannot do that, because they know what God thinks. Absolutism has poisoned political dialog about faith. If I know I am right I can expect every thinking person to come to my belief -- and to my vote.

What could be more bigoted than to claim you have a monopoly on God and that any one who does not agree with you is damned? 'Tis a pity, but do not waste energy with the bigot. The rest of us can have a really good time searching together through the grains of truth each brings to the table. Only God is absolute. 8-G

Barack Obama, when he was at a book review after being elected senator, provided an excellent response when someone told him that Jesus would not vote for Obama. He responded that if someone has <u>that</u> <u>clear</u> a line to Jesus he would like to use it, because he had questions for Jesus of much greater consequence. Precisely. The guarantee to speak for Jesus could be put to greater use than to carp at each other.

A prominent TV preacher (Kennedy) regularly protested that we will not have divine rule (!) in the U. S. if we continue to hold to the separation of Church and State. Cal Thomas, a secular columnist wrote his formulation of orthodox Christianity and then boldly claimed that to even tolerate any other belief than this, which is 'God-given,' is a heresy. The Rev. James Dobson (Focus on Family) announced his plan for focus on Republicans, to mobilize congregations in eight states for that party's get out the vote campaign, with voter guides on who <u>God</u> wants them to vote for.

Gary Wills illustrates the problem of attitude. He called it blasphemy when Under Secretary of Defense Lt. Gen. William Boykin repeatedly said God made Bush president in 2000. Wills went on to state it would not remove the blasphemy for Democrats to imply that God wants Bush <u>not</u> to be president. "The institutional Jesus of the Republicans has no similarity to the Gospel figure. Neither will any institutional Jesus of the Democrats."

We have the general who claims to know who God wants elected and how our country should operate. More than one president said his presidency was an expression of divine will. We have promoters of legal action, as the so called "defense" of marriage act, who claim "God agrees with me." O Lord, deliver us.

However, God does <u>not</u> deliver us and the deception continues. Obviously, it often begins with self-deception. "If I know something for a fact, would not God know that too?" We are in a ridiculous situation. "I hate gays because God hates gays." "God did not intend choice." "God hates Muslims as much as I do." 7-11

The thoughtful Christian should be offended by several political religious protagonists. Giving example of them, Jim Wallis, evangelical theologian, points out that in the 2004 elections we heard over and over about a Christian faith summarized in four tenets: 1. This war is right. 2. Abortion is wrong. 3. God loves success. 4. Gays are bad.

Is this a summary of the Christian faith, in any version? Not in the real world, where serious Christians remember that Jesus never spoke for <u>any</u> of these "values." The Bible student knows that Jesus and the Hebrew prophets spoke in support of the poor more than any other subject. For Jesus and the Hebrew prophets the second powerful subject was justice. How can Christians possibly accept any politicized faith statement that <u>omits</u> these core values?

The "defense" of marriage (federal and Nebraska action) is a cynical expression of presumed knowledge from the true God, with the added negative of trying to trash a segment of our population. Personal opinion is to be respected. However, that God is offended by homosexual orientation is nowhere in scripture and is clearly the creation of someone's feelings. That God would be a part of the trashing of any part of God's creation is a flat denial of a core theme of scripture summarized in Genesis 1:31: "And God saw everything that God had made, and behold, it was very good."

We have a virtual basket filled with ideologies of certitude that bedevil the world today. Then they choose religion to be the fig leaf for their certitude. This is the birthplace of extremism, and we all know extremism. It labels because it cannot debate and argue. There is not room enough on certitude's mountain peak for a circle of dialog. It fights because it has forgotten how to love. It isolates and condemns because it doesn't know how to unite, to listen and to find common ground. For suicide bombers, certitude has perfected the art of dying for a cause because it cannot live for a cause.

The Nobel literature prize was recently given for the book of poems, "The Shadow of Sirius." W. S. Merlin skillfully calls our attention to Sirius, the 'Dog Star' twenty five times brighter than our sun. We cannot <u>see</u> the dark side of Sirius, but it is real! It is there.

Our best thinking reaches for the shadow, the unknown. Certitude is often a block to knowing more.

None of my statements are an objection to the variety of political opinions, or personal opinions, or religious opinions. We should welcome the expression of a multitude of opinions on marriage, personal values, sexual relations and/or one's political priorities. It is a free country, as we love to say. Our freedom is more than a cliché. Freedom includes the obligation of the rest of us to affirm our own values in public discourse. We can strongly disagree.

Fundamentalist fallacies

Religion is taking a hit. Fundamentalists of several faiths claim their strident voices and action are the true faith. Faithful people are hesitant to object. "Speaking for God" (the previous section) is simplistic and obvious, so it is easier to attack. Fundamentalism is a different game, is a distortion by selection of scripture parts. (We each have fundamentals. The fundamentalist makes a rigid religion of a few ideas, by which others are rejected.)

Fundamentalists in any religion -- Christian, Jewish and Muslim are the most common -- take a part of a faith tradition and distort it by ignoring the other parts. Each of these faith groups centers on a God of love, members living in peace, and protection of the weak. Each has fundamentalist groups who twist that to include preaching or acting on death and destruction.

Our conviction grows that fundamentalism must be confronted in public thought. Christians prefer to ignore it, and then we stridently state our strong criticism of Muslim clerics who seem to ignore their fundamentalism. We note that Fundamentalism as a movement is not basic Christianity, as some assume. Modern Fundamentalism is only 100 years old, and ignores scriptural insights which are centuries old. We can hope they all keep to themselves so we can help one another phrase new dialog. The mainline response must connect to public issues, such as standing by our court system when the right wing tries to rewrite the constitution to its opinions. 6-1

Mary Gordon, novelist, states that she finds two adversaries in her practice of faith: fundamentalism and "money is everything." She nails it. She protests giving any authority to those two forces among us. If Jesus means anything, we can see Jesus in every person. In the flesh. Not flattened out to fit a two-dimensional world created by self-centered persons who think God whispers in their ears only, or that the government is a financial playpen for them only.

We have colleagues from centuries past. Origen, Christian writer in the formative years of the church, objected to infallible claims in the third century: "The source of all heresy is a literal reading of the Bible." He went on to say that scripture is spiritual (not simply words) and that the true Word of God is Jesus (not the words).

In 1942, Claremont Lovington summarized what he could see coming. Strident voices would shout, "We are Orthodox, therefore you are not." Respond in kind? This mode of thinking gave us the Inquisition. A church or a state which believes that it rules by divine right adds to the violence in the world, which is a direct contradiction of the gospel of love. We have Christian Right speakers who openly appeal for support of Israel in order to bring on Armageddon, with the total destruction of Israel and the end of the world. This is an offense to the spirit of Jesus, and to Christians' hope and prayer for a world of peace.

Religion can abuse the Bible

Abuse of the Bible is used to mislead followers. Religion, per se, does not abuse scripture. Religious voices do that. They can twist a text to fit their purpose and to create propaganda. To be more accurate, persons with opinions and agendas gain ground by declaring what "the Bible says." Used as a club, "The Bible says" creates a barrier to discussion, reflection and prayer. The Bible has many writers, so that phrase is nearly always misleading. We read the confusing collection of modern pronouncements and know they cannot all be honest. 6-3

Righteous-minded folks can, on almost any subject, come up with scripture backing. Radicals will claim their opinion was initiated and shaped by scripture. The fallacy of that simple claim by extremists is the cause of much mischief among us. The 'believing public' is often misled by high-flown 'religious' speeches and low-level diatribes, complete with scripture.

For an example of the abuse of scripture, an email illustrates a few problems of foolish piety. The protester insisted that all Christians are required to support the death penalty because the Bible says so. Not to support the death penalty is proof positive the person is inherently not Christian! Which included this senator, of course.

It gets worse. Colossians 3:20, we were told, says that every criminal must be killed. “Politicians who are real Christians will empty the jails by executing all who are there.” Well. The state is not killing all prisoners. Absolute proof, no doubt allowed, that senators are not Christian. Next question.

The claim is so outrageous this writer did not even review Col. 3:20 at the time. There are several bloodthirsty verses in scripture, so a pastor may assume this advocate of death-dealing found one of them. Not. Upon looking at it, a fair reading could actually support an opposing opinion.

Col. 3:20: "Children, obey your parents in everything, for this pleases God." (RSV) The protester’s spin? Jail proves disobedience of parents by children, which offends God, who requires death.

Preceding and following this scripture passage are instructions to wives, husbands, fathers and slaves. Research into the original audience helps us to know that though this sounds routine to our ears it was bold indeed in the original setting. The scripture writer skillfully includes their prejudices to make a new point. They expected wives to be told to obey. But tie that with husbands are to be kind? Amazing frankness.

Children should obey, but then we read that fathers can drive children to discouragement. Centuries later, that thought is on the cutting edge. To kill a boy for a blow, a much older scripture that could support killing all criminals, is plainly set aside. Scripture gets really interesting if one is willing to learn from the original writers and audiences.

A college professor used a silly story to illustrate how scripture is abused. The story sounds manufactured. However, years of supervising preachers make it sound possible. Either way, it illustrates the key points for honest study.

The story: a pastor could not stand to see women’s hair in buns. Their crowning glory should be spread for view. He found a verse to confirm his opinion and preached his sermon: "Top Knot Come Down." He blistered the heathen with God's judgment.

His verse was Luke 17:31: "Let him who is on the house top .... not come down (to take his goods away)." (RSV) It is from an end of time scene, when those on the roof of the house would not have the time to rescue their possessions.

The abuse of scripture in the email and in this story illustrates four solid correcting principles.

1. Check your own opinions at the door when reading scripture and read for the plainest message.

2. Read the longer passage for more subtle content.

3. Remember you are reading in English, not the original language. (A play on English words – changing 'not' to 'knot' -- is hardly Greek scripture.) Check other translations to get closer to the original. Example: out of eight translations of this verse, five use "roof" instead of "top."

4. Research the original setting and the likely meaning to that audience.

This objection of abuse is directed to religious professionals, who should know better. The person next door, politicians, columnists, etc. will always create abusive quotes. Cal Thomas uses imaginative selection of scripture to "document" his opinions. Expect flawed, incomplete research. He has an agenda that raises flags. Know that.

Some leaders in a recent election dismissed others' faith as un-American! Do we have patriot measures of faith? They presume to tell us that (my) denomination, United Methodist, cannot be Christian because our beliefs counter the scriptures. Well. Methodists' first reaction is humorous, since there are few beliefs on which we ourselves completely agree, and agreement is seldom required. (Strangely, the complaint about beliefs does not question our basic beliefs about God: God is creator and redeemer, and Jesus is our authority on God.)

The second response is a groan -- for all of us. As experienced persons of faith, none of us has difficulty in understanding that some would disagree with particulars of faith. However, to assert no right to freedom of conscience is a direct assault on our humanity and our nation. The comments usually are a clumsy attempt to dismiss new ideas as being somehow unscriptural. 7-C

In Genesis, some today see an apple, the devil and original sin. Jewish people, whose story it is (!), and earliest Christians, saw far more. They made sense of a complex creation by telling a story and creating metaphors for reflecting on God's expectations of us, our inclination to ignore or even to rebel, and blessings that are the potential from acting on our role in creation. God did not create us to be sinners, but to be productive participants in a joyful, healthy creation. God does not guarantee individual rewards, but blessing in community is promised.

Scripture speaks of same sex relations. A modern assumption that the reference is to homosexual orientation is reading in to scripture what one chooses to think. *Leviticus* texts are about heterosexual fathers engaging in idol worship, a serious sin, to increase crops for their families. Idol worship was an abomination.

Or, on the other side, to imply that scripture approves various heterosexual activities is the same: reading in.

Much of scripture abuse comes from those who hate, despise, or reject. So we read/hear that God rejects Clinton, Bush, Obama, McCain, the U. S., nations who oppose the U. S., Muslims, unruly children, working wives, and on and on. God, we hear, supports death penalty/opposes death penalty. Rejects abortion/favors abortion rights. Supports war that kills enemies; rejects all violence. Those are not simple scriptural statements. They are convictions held by persons who search scripture for supporting evidence or quotes.

It is particularly offensive when anyone, of whatever political position, claims scripture as the authority for a personal opinion and then noisily claims that opponents of that opinion have abandoned the Bible. Their fresh study of scripture would be time well spent.

Abuse of scripture is not new. Slaveholders used it big time, and held "Bible believing" churches hostage for decades in the United States. They found Biblical evidence that God wants slavery and does not want women to be in charge of almost anything. Historians noted in the sidebars that women seemed to be more offended by slavery -- so it was indeed a political fit. "Do not let them vote!" Before that it was the flat earth society, when persons were burned alive for "opposing" scripture. Or, we have both those who support the use of beverage alcohol and those who oppose it .... united in quoting scripture with stern voices, proclaiming opposing messages.

The abuse has a worse, obscuring effect. Critical passages are set aside. This and all of the above examples cannot be selected and separated without ignoring hundreds of other passages. Hello, legalists?

Can we find the right words to say and thereby get into heaven? That is heresy. The Council of Nicea (325) warned against simplistic views of Jesus which become popular because they are easy. The world in which Jesus made sense involved the culture of his time. Scripture, with varied cultures, has competing views of scripture. One understands the desire to do shortcuts, but study is hard work!

"A pastor thinks like this?"

For this pastor, becoming a senator was a shift in thinking. Religious vocabulary is laid aside, church stands are trumped by citizen need, and anything like a sermon is completely out of order. Not hard to do. The problem was other senators' perceptions about pastors. As, a pastor is always out hunting for scalps for Jesus. O my. Or, a pastor is going to be more judgmental of moral failings. Actually, less than most. Or, a pastor thinks (his) denomination is better/more Biblical/more like Jesus than others. Not this pastor.

Other senators thought of a pastor simply as the friendly fellow in a neighborhood coffee shop every Wednesday morning. That worked, thin as it is. This pastor has no problem understanding that most senators have not had a pastor close at hand and that some of them have never had a serious discussion with a pastor. They have all sorts of assumptions.

The problem of perception is illustrated in an exchange on the floor with Senator Chambers, who expresses an exceedingly narrow view of Christianity. The issue was whether to increase mandatory recovery time for inebriated persons, by allowing police to hold them long enough to let them dry out and get back on food.

Chambers: "Are you a pastor?" "Yes." "So your job is to save souls." "No, it is not." "What is your job as a pastor?" "To help build community." "You just want more time with persons in jail or in treatment so that you can work them over and collect more souls to your credit." "No, I want more time for their head to clear, with real food in the stomach, so they can make better decisions. I do not decide for anyone what they should do."

God saves souls. A pastor does not. It is extreme arrogance for a pastor to claim credit for what God does. Also, ccommunity is much more than a mutual alliance to keep the peace or to provide efficiency in services. Community is caring and respect, dignity for all.

So what was my job as pastor? Simply, my job was to help provide the community where God can reign. "Thy kingdom come, thy will be done on earth..." Sometimes the helpful aid is in a sermon. More often it is an attitude and activity that reflects and demonstrates God's love in the real world. Sometimes the assist is a law that helps provide justice for the poor or respect for the outcast. The last example is exactly what Chambers tries to do. Hmmm. 7-4

Are we moral?

We dismissed for a while to go into a session on ethics. This senator was breathless. Were we actually going to talk about ethics? Public ethics? Private? What's up?

We heard from an official from Wisconsin, where several of the legislators have felonies. "That is bad." We should be honest and respectful of each other. "That is good." All of us, lobbyists included, will have public interest central in our minds. "That is hopeful."

My satirical description is not to put ethics down. We need to say these things to one another. My pet peeve is that we do not give words to what we believe. We as a society have become so sophisticated, so cool, that we do not say that shooting someone is bad and volunteering to help out is good. Mainline Christians do not talk about their faith and service clubs are embarrassed to put in a good word for something so obvious as education. Let's say what we think, out loud. Especially core values. Amen. 4-4

The ethics talk was beginning to sound like seminary. The chamber looks like a seminary chapel, so the steady debate on morals and ethics was charming. But again, in seminary we would never vote on who was wrong and therefore immoral.

Morals are difficult to debate, because folks confuse morals with ethics. Moral relates to treatment of neighbor. Nearly every bill has moral implications.

Ethics centers on trustworthy business action. It is more contract than religion. We do legislate ethics, such as the standards for integrity in public places. We are kind for moral reasons, not because of ethics. Kant defines ethics as the critiques of practical reason.

Religious principles add to the confusion with morals. They come from all over the place, with no consistent standards. There are religious principles (as, to kill a disobedient child) which are not moral. "Situation Ethics" is simply how to do the right thing.

Word of the week on the floor: turpitude n. depravity, baseness, shameful character, wickedness. (??? Those are not truly similar.)

It is fun to examine words and how persons of differing views can use them. The root word is "turpitudo," meaning nakedness or shameful. Nakedness is not necessarily shameful. Of course we developed the fig leaf industry to cover nakedness, but now the industry is going all out to design fig leaves that do not quite cover nakedness. So the spin, even in precise legal language, is endless.

We do not use that word every day, so were a bit startled when it dominated floor debate. The question was if moral turpitude should be inserted as limiting a ground for removal from office. Debate included a question as to whether a felony is evidence of turpitude. Yes. Well, not necessarily. O.K., yes. No? A person of good character could commit a felony for reasons he considered necessary. Would we agree he was not depraved?

Why would we add "moral"? Does that make it good? How about immoral turpitude? If turpitude is shameful, would inturpitude be shameless? O.K., O.K., stop having fun. Some threw in ethics, which really confuses it. We have spent entire days in academics sorting out the difference between morals and ethics. Not the same.

Moral is especially slippery when used by religionists. Immoral is what you do that I would not do, as, fifty years ago, to dance. People who claimed the Bible as their guide opposed dancing, which is praised in several Biblical passages. Christians can never claim to be consistent. We are righteous, but not consistent. 8-3

When politics steals faith

Jim Wallis summarizes these issues plainly:

Many of us feel that our faith has been stolen, and it's time to take it back. In particular, an enormous public misrepresentation of Christianity has taken place. And because of an almost uniform media misperception, many people around the world now think Christian faith stands for political commitments that are almost the opposite of its true meaning. How did the faith of Jesus come to be known as pro-rich, pro-war, and pro-American? What has happened here? And how do we get back to a historic, biblical, and genuinely evangelical faith rescued from its contemporary distortions?

Of course, nobody can steal your personal faith; that's between you and God. The problem is in the political arena, where strident voices claim to represent Christians when they clearly don't speak for most of us. It's time to take back our faith in the public square, especially in a time when a more authentic social witness is desperately needed.

Take back our faith from whom? To be honest, the confusion comes from many sources. From religious right-wingers who claim to know God's political views on every issue, then ignore the subjects that God seems to care the most about. From television preachers whose extravagant lifestyles and crass fund-raising tactics embarrass most Christians. From liberal secularists who want to banish faith from public life and deny spiritual values to the soul of politics. From liberal theologians whose cultural conformity serves to erode the foundation of faith. From New Age philosophers who want to make Jesus into a non-threatening spiritual guru. And from politicians who love to say how religious they are but who utterly fail to apply the values of faith to their public leadership and political policies.

When we reclaim faith we discover that faith challenges the 'powers that be' to do justice for the poor. We remember that faith hates violence. We see that faith creates community from racial, class and gender divisions. We are reminded that faith regards matters such as the sacredness of life and family bonds as so important that they should never be used as political pawns.

I do not ever hear them quoting the Sermon on the Mount. I'm hard pressed to think of teachings of Jesus that are being talked about in the government.

Jesus did not speak at all about homosexuality. There are about 12 verses in the Bible that touch on that question. Most of them are very contextual. There are thousands of verses on poverty. I don't hear the balance of scripture.

What you really do not hear from political leaders is Jesus saying, "Blessed are the peacemakers." Or even more, how many sermons have we heard lately on the text, "Love your enemies?" We should at least have a debate on what that means.

A talk radio host one night was yelling at me about Iraq. I said, "What would Jesus do? Can you imagine him climbing into the cockpit of a B-52 and dropping a load of bombs over Baghdad?" He: "Well, Jesus would surely want to protect the American people." I said, "Really? What about the Iraqis?" "Well -- well -- them too." Once you start talking about this in a religious frame, it's troubling. *G*

Can we say "God" in public?

Every week brings at least one forwarded email complaining that schools cannot use the Pledge of Allegiance because it includes "One nation under God." Often it is an adult-written piece allegedly from a sixth grade boy, wishing he could pray in school. Such nonsense is manufactured.

The Pledge is in every school, and few persons object to a student praying. What we should object to is school-sponsored prayer. This Grandpa is so grateful that no teacher can force religion on his grand daughters. If you are a Mormon, or a Buddhist, or a Muslim, or a Baptist -- and on -- teaching a child how to pray your way is the most effective proselytizing there is. Teaching prayer sneaks in on a person. In prayer, you can persuasively convey that God is a God of love, or of punishment, or of control, or who takes away their grandmothers, or who selects which scouts shall live.

That is not a teacher's job. A high school coach in New Jersey insisted that his prayers with the team were harmless. (Prayer is harmless?! That is another problem.) He convinced a judge that he was not teaching religion. However, on appeal a three-judge court was unanimous in saying, "(These actions) would lead a reasonable observer to conclude that he was endorsing religion."

One appeal judge was troubled by the student reaction to the issue. Two Jewish cheerleaders, he said, were "taunted, bullied and booed." Blogs about them were hostile: "First they crucify Jesus (and now the coach) .... Jews gotta learn to stop ruining everything cool."

Another blog spoke of Damn Jews and Hitler's reaction to Jews. The judge continued: "Given the nature of these venomous comments, counsel cannot seriously suggest that the evidence be ignored (merely because parents and students who protest the prayer were afraid to do so in court)." The statement points to a favorite tool of opinionated Christians: intimidation. Hate speech and ridicule will shut persons up, but it will not convert them. 8-D

We had some fun with a phrase in a statute that relates to "nonprofit organizations created for exclusively religious purposes." "Exclusively" is a technical legal term, is in all church applications for tax-exempt status, and means you cannot apply for a group that is 2/3 church and 1/3 business. Authorities check on operations every year, to see if it is a 100% church.

Senator Chambers, to have fun and to tweak religious noses, sought to amend by adding two words so it would read "created and operated for exclusively religious purposes." A Catholic asked if a parochial school is exclusively religious. (smile) Someone else, a pancake feed. Someone else, Bingo. The answer to all, in the law, is clearly "Yes" if it is done for the benefit of the church. No profit making allowed. Even lawyers on the floor were surprised and confused, so Chambers had reason to poke fun. 8-3

The Ten Commandments

The Omaha World-Herald published the three versions of the Ten Commandments -- Jewish, Catholic/Lutheran, and Protestant. Actually reading the versions is very helpful in the legal debate. People generally assume that the commandments are not sectarian, just universal wisdom. There has been a considerable re-chiseling of Moses' stone tablets. Most of the public displays are the Catholic version, not Jewish.

The differences are sectarian. The prohibition against "worship graven images" was not inserted for over 2500 years after Moses. The reformers thought Catholic statues were not proper, so tweaked the commandments. Far more significant is "Thou shalt not murder" in the original Hebrew version, which was changed by Protestants, Lutherans and Catholics to "Thou shalt not kill." In the Hebrew, "murder" is of a member of one's own tribe and "kill" is a member of a foreign tribe. There is a real difference and "kill" is a rewrite.

Humor. So the Hebrews can kill their enemy without breaking a commandment. But Christians cannot kill their enemies without considerable manipulating of other scripture.

The most serious twisting of the commandments is the authority given the Ten. Some Christians say "On this hangs all the law and the prophets" -- and our constitution. Not by a long shot. Jesus said the law and the prophets are summarized in two "laws" and neither is among the Ten. Our constitution clearly has a strong religious base, but the Ten Commandments is not the base. The real offense in this is to the Jews, for whom the Ten is a small section of their laws. We dismiss much of their [and our!] scripture in order to elevate the Ten.

Would we be willing to quote the *Koran* on our courthouse lawns, or are we limited to "our own" scripture? 5-3

The Muslim faith

The Muslim/Christian conflict is escalated by extremist partisans. Some will say it is a conflict of good and evil. Is it? Evil will always be present and is not created by religions. Muslim and Christian both fight evil.

Further, our conflict with Muslims is not historic. We had centuries of extended cooperation. Nor is conflict inherent in either faith. We point at terrorist Jihad as representative of the Muslim faith. Not. Jihad is allowed only to those who have been attacked. No women, children or religious leaders may be killed. The Jihad killing we have witnessed breaks Islamic law. The conflict is about land.

The conservative Muslim follows the tradition of Mohammed. Right? Which includes death to all infidels. Right? Wrong. To get there, you have to substitute present emotions for tradition. The prophet gave three alternatives for handling infidels, including second-class citizenship in an Islamic state. The fervent supporter of

Jihad who claims to be conserving traditional values by killing innocent children is avoiding serious study of Islamic scripture.

Gallup did a major project on "The Muslim/West Fact Initiative." The work is extensive, and part of the findings was that conflicts are more from perceptions of policy than from clash of values. The value conflict is not inevitable. "Leaders make better decisions when they know the values of the people."

Gallup found what was most admired in the west by Muslims: technology, liberty, freedom. About 7% of Muslims were anti-American. None gave a religious reason. Not one quoted the *Koran.* The 7% express moral objection to terrorism. Killing innocent civilians is prohibited. The Muslims' negative attitude to American policy was 85%. To our people, 40%.

Whereas 50% of Americans think scripture is a source for legislation, only 9% consider it the only source. We believe scripture has authority for social justice and control of a tyrant. Both faiths said that relations would improve if all of us would control extremists.

Premier Ebrahim Rasool (Muslim-South Africa), points out that Christian and Islamic fundamentalists speak the same thoughts:

> *The religious (trialogues) that we require are not simply among Christians, Muslims, Hindus, Jews, Jains, Sikhs, etc. The conversations we need are conversations of mindsets across all religions, because extremism -- fundamentalist in Christianity, in Islam, In Judaism, in Hinduism, or any other religion -- speaks far more of a common language than progressive and well-meaning people across all of those religions. Extremists have their own conversations: they slug it out on the battlefields of Iraq, in Afghanistan, in Pakistan, or where the case may be. They speak that language to each other because they are essentially the same -- even if they raise a Christian flag here, a Jewish flag there, and a Muslim flag there.*
>
> *They have their own conversations. They retreat into the churches, the mosques, the synagogues and the temples, hiding from the world, unable to deal with this world.*
>
> *And those of us who believe that religion remains essential to the world, that its values would be the savior of the world, that*

its behavior is going to be critical to temper the excesses of globalization and give the common poor people something to hold on to both in this world and the hereafter -- we have to fashion a conversation that crosses the formal lines of division among Muslims, Christians, Hindus and Jews. Unless we find one another the world will be condemned.

The key to it is, I believe, in what the Koran teaches (when it says) God says "I have blown of My spirit into you." In the same vein, (First John tells Christians) "Who lives in love, lives in God, and God in him .... God has given us of God's spirit."

Then we begin to get the answer. We can only go forward if we recognize that each one of us carries a part of the Spirit of God in us -- that when we speak to one another, we don't speak to the Muslim dress that one wears and clerical clothes that Catholics wear .... whatever. We aren't speaking to their clothes: we are speaking to the divine in each one of them. Even as we differ formally, the common ground is that each one of us carries the Spirit of God within us and is worthy of respect, is worthy of love, and is worthy, at the very least, of tolerance." (Underlines added*)* I

Paul Harvey cut through the theological fog of our religious tensions: "Each religion is unique for a reason. Each has a unique style so that people can find the best path for themselves." Here are a few other parts.

"An Open Letter From God"

My dear children -- and believe me that is all of you. .... I want to let you know about some of the things that started ticking me off. First of all, your religious rivalries are driving me up a wall. Enough already.

Let's get one thing straight. These are your religions, not mine. I am the whole enchilada. I am beyond them all. Every one of your religions claims ... that it's my favorite one. And each claims its Bible was written personally by me and that all of the other Bibles are manmade. O me. How do I ever put a stop to such complicated nonsense?

All right, listen up now. I am your father and mother and I don't play favorites among my children. Also, I hate to break it to you, but I don't write. ....I have always been more of a doer... So all of your books, including those Bibles, were written by men and women. They were inspired men and women. They were remarkable people. But they also made mistakes here and there. And I made sure of that so you wouldn't trust the written word rather than your own living heart...... My spirit is not an historical thing. It is alive right now, right now, as fresh as your next breath. Holy books and religious rites are sacred and powerful. But they are not more so than the least of you. .....

Which brings me to my next point of your nonsense. You act like I need you and your religions to stick up for me or win souls. For my sake, please don't do me any favors. I can stand quite well on my own, thank you. ....

And another thing, I don't get all worked up over money or politics. So stop dragging my name into your dramas. For example, I swear to me that I never threatened Oral Roberts. .... I never told Pat Robertson to run for President. And I have never ever had a conversation with Jim Baker or Jerry Falwell or Jimmy Swaggart. Of course, come Judgment Day I certainly intend to.

Now the thing is I want you to stop thinking of religion as some sort of a loyalty pledge to me. The true purpose of your religions is so you can be more aware of me. Not the other way around. Believe me, I know you already.

What you seem to forget is how mysterious I am. You look at the petty differences in your scriptures and say, well, if this is the truth then that can't be. But instead of trying to figure out my paradoxes and unfathomable nature, which by the way you never will, why not open your hearts to the simple common threads of every religion. You know what I am talking about. Play nice with each other, love and respect everyone, be kind.

.....Simple stuff now. Why do you keep making it so complicated? It's like you are always looking for an excuse to be upset. And I am very tired of your main excuse. Do you think I care whether you call me God or Yahweh or Jehovah,

Allah, Wakatonka, Brahma, Father, Mother -- even the void of Nirvana? Do you think I care which of my special children you feel closest to -- Jesus, Mary, Buddha, Krishna, Mohammed, or any of the others? You can call me and my special ones any name you choose if only you will go about my business of loving one another as I love you. How can you keep neglecting something so simple?.....

The clergy must stop creating a myth of sibling rivalry where there is none. My blessed children of earth, the world has grown too small for your pervasive religious bigotries and confusion. The whole planet is now connected by air travel, satellite dishes, telephones, FAX machines, rock concerts, diseases and mutual needs and concerns.

Get with the program. If you really want to help me celebrate the birthday of my son Jesus, then commit yourselves to figuring out how to feed your hungry and clothe your naked and protect your abused, and shelter your poor and just as important, make your own every day life a shining example of kindness and good humor. I have given you all the resources you need if only you abandon your fear of each other and begin living and loving and laughing together......

I hate to see you suffer. But I gave you free will so what can I do now other than try to influence you through reason, persuasion, and a little old fashioned guilt and manipulation.

I really am, indeed, I swear, with you always. Always.....

Your one and only,

God

Summary

Scriptural principles, including Christian, clearly guided our founders and the writers of documents of our revolution. The documents are not Christian, but Americans place high value on persons because of the Judeo-Christian view of creation and that leads to rights we feel persons have. Persons do not earn their rights. No baby can. We say rights are "God-given," without feeling the power and mystery of that thought. The legislature is a continuing expression of what rights we actually have.

Grandpa Lowen, blessed with a new baby Lauren, marveled at the miracle of birth and expressed some of his wonder in March 2003.

Lauren

New-born energy ~ aimlessly waving at the air.
  Exercising every body part ~ searching for her thumb.
    Looking into my eyes. And I hers.
God has voted that the earth go on.

Sleep ~eat ~ change ~ search ~
Sleep ~eat ~ change ~ search ~
Lauren frames a life cycle – but will her search be for life?

What will she discover in my world?
- Unending body functions, or an adventure for mind and spirit?
- Those who hate, or persons who care?
- The spiritually dead who abhor difference,
  or fresh minds who search it?
- A god who sharply judges, or the God who openly loves?
- Pain in harsh statistics, or mystery in warm relationships?

Her search of discovery begins in my eyes.

God has voted that the earth go on.
How will I vote?

["God has voted…." is a line from Carl Sandburg]

3. My Neighbor's Keeper

"Am I my brother's keeper?" Cain's answer to God in Jewish scripture (Genesis 4:9), when he was asked about the brother he had killed, is a haunting question. We duck when we are confronted with our complicity in events which injure, demean or actually kill. We cannot be responsible for it all, but does it help to refuse to claim no connection?

Highlight of the week was a young nurse who testified for one of our impaired driving bills. With her perky blonde ponytail and clear young voice she began to tell her traumatic story. Her voice started cracking half way through, but she kept going. A speeding car going through a red light hit her, the driver heavily alcohol impaired.

She lost her car, her savings, part of her health, and is still trying to pay the bill. She found out he had been arrested before, and as she healed learned he did the same thing again. Her pain and suffering put a human face on what it is like to be an innocent victim. Her outrage that we do so little to protect our citizens from our biggest killer was appropriate. Where do we really stand?

A grieving young widow wondered how she will raise her daughter without a father's help. He went to Fremont to pick up a new car and was headed home to celebrate. A woman who was driving at over twice the legal limit of alcohol impairment killed him. She also was killed.

That night on TV, the bartender said the woman was a regular customer and was drinking in her bar all afternoon. It is illegal in every state to sell or give alcohol to an intoxicated person. Nebraska is one of the last states that continue to <u>exempt</u> the bar from liability for breaking the law. <u>Imagine</u> if other businesses were exempt from liability for breaking the law and contributing to personal injury!

If the bar owner were not exempt from the huge cost of a wrongful death he would undoubtedly warn a bartender about an obvious violation with the same intoxicated person. If the server had not broken the law, we can assume that young mother would not be grieving. She is neighbor.

If they/we were in Sweden, we would not have these scenes. Citizens there have agreed, with a consensus that humbles us, that <u>every</u> neighbor should be offended when a person drives after drinking. Even modest drinking. To a person driving impaired, they have one question: "Why would you do that which is likely to injure <u>my</u> child/grandchild/wife?" It works. There is much drinking, but <u>no</u> drunk driving in Sweden. They demonstrate how to be "My neighbor's keeper."

The consensus of our citizens is far more powerful than laws, but we have so little consistency in our shared attitudes. We are upset with the needless death of a baby at some boyfriend's hands, but we only murmur a protest when impaired drivers kill 100 people a year in Nebraska, and seriously injure over 200, needlessly.

In Christian scripture, a lawyer seeks to guarantee his salvation with Jesus. What should he do? The response was to "Love God and love his neighbor as (himself)." --Luke 10:25,ff.

"Who is my neighbor?" is the lawyer's question, to which the story of the Good Samaritan is the response. A traveler gives aid to a hurting stranger from another tribe, in the ditch. He carries him to receive help and pays the bill for healing. It is the compassionate action, for a stranger.

We talk of compassion, but in eight years of the legislature this senator has not seen one compassionate vote. Senators are compassionate and there are compassionate speeches, saying we should help this injured soul. But the issue never received the required 25 votes. We vote dollars. This is the "real world."

However, there is a clear connection between compassion and dollars in the real world. Healthy citizens enhance our economic interests. Our dollars invested in a sick child have a tremendous return. When we see each other as neighbors we build community and find powerful results. It is a joy to see what we can do, through very careful planning, to provide resources to a young person who then simply blossoms.

Ex-felon as neighbor

A good example of 'my neighbor's keeper' was demonstrated. We were on voting rights for felons. The bill will allow ex-felons to register to vote two years after completing all terms of a sentence. One objection was that we should think about the victim families of those felonies. Some would like the ex-felons to continue to be punished, even if the court is through with them. 5-10

Since the Kruses are a victim family, victims of felonious behavior, Senator Kruse became personal in response. "I am part of a family which is a victim of a felony offender. There is indeed tremendous pain in the memories and in the ongoing losses to our family. However, I want that man to vote, to get back into society and take his place there.

"This is not to be nice to him. He may not vote. He could re-offend. His value has not been our value. I want him to vote and hope that this might, in some small way, help him to participate in the community, be active in his family, and turn away from a future offense."

We are in the business of restoring fallen citizens, not stomping on them. This is in our interest as well as the ex-felon's. The felony voting rights bill passed this week, 35 to 7.

We overrode the governor's veto 36-11. The governor applied no pressure, just said he would like for us to think about it one more time. However, the Republican Party sent all of the Republican senators a letter saying that the party and the governor have a negative position that they should follow. In response, the chief Republican senator led off by saying the governor is a fine man, but we are not voting on that, nor on outsiders (party) opinions. We were the ones who had debated it three times, had given the whole matter extensive thought and who knew what is right for us. "So we now have a chance to reaffirm our vote."

Only one dropped off the earlier vote. One was absent. We picked up three new ones. The media had a field day with hyped rhetoric, which perhaps is their job. We saw in the papers and heard on TV that the governor was hammered, defeated, slammed down, taught an early lesson, cut back in political clout, etc. Not. He politely pointed out his contrary opinion and we politely voted one more time, expressing our considered judgment. End of story. Not a partisan fight.

The governor felt each ex-felon should apply ten years later and be interviewed for voting rights. We were struck again with the horrible process we use. If any one of us were an ex-felon out of prison and doing well, would we go back to the nightmare of a court-like setting, to relive that trauma, to be exceedingly humble, and prepare to be humiliated? Would you be ready to find out if someone who does not know you considers you to be worthwhile? We do not go looking for punishment when we have been doing well in recovery. Half the population will not even walk in an office to register to vote. 5-10

"Nebraska in the Lead" was the editorial headline in the New York Times. Yo! We are pleased they are discovering all the news that is fit to print.

For those who did not see it, the subject was Nebraska's restoring the voting rights for felons, voting was a privilege taken away by many states during the early 1900s in order to further erode the Negro vote. The reporter took my quote from the transcript of floor debate and called it a high point. That is so laudatory one should not quibble with the way he edited the quote. But he did leave a thought stranded.

He left out my question, "If I were a felon, would I go through the humiliation of going to the pardons board to have its members judge if I am worthy to vote? I think not." The Times editorial picks up here. "I would rather keep my dignity. And I would much rather we allow (my neighbor) to keep his restored dignity and help him to move on." Dignity is the core.

It is a bit surprising in Nebraska that very few voted against this action. "It is the right thing to do" was the quiet assumption. We received emails. One said this was a Democrat move to get more voters. No felons are Republicans? What about all these white-collar ones we are collecting from financial fiascoes? Another said that this action was useless, as no felons would get out to vote. Let's have those two guys talk to each other, sharing their political foolishness, so the rest of us can get on with business. 5-C

The helpless as neighbor

What about when our neighbor is comatose, with no hope of waking, and is called "the Schaivo case"? National legislators did not know enough to be embarrassed by their blatantly political posturing.

Life is no longer measured by breathing. Medically, we consider her dead. Courts consistently declared her to be brain dead. A congressman yammers on about her missing two meals and starving. Well. She has missed all her meals for fifteen years. Tubes are not natural. In medical language, they are "extra-ordinary means" and do not have to be used in any case.

The agony of family and friends is quite another matter and we must recognize the great pain of the situation, especially with conflicting personal feelings and values. Tubes are so easy to put in and so hard to take out. When on a hospital staff as chaplain, the writer has stood with the family around the bed touching the beautiful young body of their loved one, warm and breathing. But dead. A wrenching scene.

In hospitals, we usually keep the body going so as to give the best chance to those who would receive the organs. It tears you up to witness the body motions we once thought of as "alive" and to know that body, with no mental activity, is dead. Your eye/memories fight with your ear/the words of the physician. One cannot judge anyone whose eye/memory wins that emotional tension.

Having stood with those families many times this chaplain is frankly amazed at their courage when they take each other's hands, including the hands of their beloved, unsuccessfully fight back their tears, and tell chaplain and nurse, "It is time. Can we have a prayer?"

With those experiences in mind, one is led to grind his teeth to think of non-family strangers, who are in <u>other</u> states, trying to keep the limp body on public display for political gain. Texas has a law that the tubes can be withdrawn in a vegetative case if no one is paying the bill. Who signed that? A treasurer probably wrote it.

Bottom line, for every adult: sign a living will, available at every hospital, and <u>do</u> <u>talk</u> about your decision with loved ones. They are the ones who will be standing around your bed, next to the chaplain, depending on the evidence of <u>your</u> support for <u>their</u> decisions.

(Late note: decisions after loss of consciousness are not new to health care debates. For years, hospitals have asked persons on admittance to share their "Advance Directive" for care if the patient can not respond.)

The Schaivo case generated much passion, some of it nearly out of control. We had a senator shouting into the mike that it may be time to put in a law that no one can remove a feeding tube.

Plus we had a caller, also shouting, that if we even <u>think</u> of trying to keep a tube in her loved one she will come after us with an army, ruining political futures. The quiet response to both was that our present law has a clear line and works very well, and that if we make it more difficult to remove a feeding tube physicians will be much more hesitant to put one in. They are already hesitant.

However, the caller could not hear because of her passion.

The next week, a writer to the Public Pulse put it much better, in few words. She said we turn to <u>artificial</u> life to avoid thinking about <u>natural</u> death. Well done. 5-13

<u>*Children as neighbors*</u>

We Nebraskans are <u>so new</u> at "crisis" services that we simply do not know yet how to do them well. Who gives help to a family whose toddler has a disability? The state? A for-profit group? A nonprofit agency? Medicaid and disability services were unimagined 40 years ago. They were not accepted by the public 20 years ago. They are now accepted -- even demanded -- by the public, but who regulates and who pays? When and how do we avoid an entitlement status? This is hard work. We will make mistakes. This is new.

Most important, what is the best way to provide basic needs for our nearly 8,000 wards of the state? Good people are working at it, but find different answers. If we add the 4,000 plus in prison, most of whom are addicts for whom we cannot afford treatment, in one paragraph you have the scariest part of future tax increases. Trying to find effective options has become a full time job for many of us. 2-8

The center piece of one new approach is "Project Harmony," an Omaha operation that has desks for every agency (government or nonprofit!) in one building. It has an attractive Triage Center, where police bring the traumatized child for evaluation and recommendation. Fact-finding interviews are limited to one with each child, on tape, by a professional. All agencies which want an interview are given the tape, saving the child endless additional trauma from a bunch of inquiring adults. The medical exam is on site.

States from across the nation are sending teams to find out how Project Harmony got past the blocks of agencies which are often in tension with each other. Visitors are especially impressed with the collaboration of police, caseworkers, courts, foster care, childcare protection agencies, medics, and care giving groups. On a tough case we may have 20 persons in a conference room, outlining the preferred options for this child. It is revolutionary.

Many citizens do not know young children can experience, while innocently watching TV, their door being knocked down, with uniformed officers storming into their lives and shouting, and with guns pointed at anyone who moves. The kids are put in the back seat of a police cruiser, sometimes with a small sack of clothing. In the old days (four years ago) the police could drive around for three hours trying to find a place that would take the children. Terrifying.

Referrals come from school (no parent at home), grandparent (reporting abuse), neighbor (parents appear to be addicted), police (meth lab and no food in refrig), officer of the court (the household story does not add up), and on.

Nebraska has made the system more human and far more accountable. We have plans for seven more centers. Children are becoming our neighbors. 6-6

Low-income neighbors

We have several examples of those being cut off of medical care, all single mothers. One quit her job (due to child care costs), went from work to welfare, goes to school half-heartedly and has no stated goals except to keep qualifying for payments. She is an expense. Another has a job, is eager to improve her situation and is worried that if she becomes ill the whole plan will collapse. She is an asset and her medical care is an investment.

Both will be cut off this week. How can you provide for the investment and not the expense, when in rules and regs both these mothers look the same? Another troubling point: they both will continue to receive medical care through emergency rooms, so compassion is not the question. We will pay, through taxes or our health insurance costs, for this parent to go to an emergency room and rack up $500 plus in inappropriate care, to treat a deep chest cough which frightens her. Federal law requires a hospital to treat any person who walks in and the county will pay for the "free" care. It is our worst plan for appropriate medical care.

Another point: neither will receive preventive health care of any kind, which is generally considered an investment. If the diagnosis is depression, the hospital will bill the county, which is required by federal law to pay the bills for mental health.

If we had covered this under Medicaid, we pay 40% of a reduced fee and the feds pay 60%. Now we will be paying 100% through the county, but the shift will cut state expense, making folks think senators are good planners. Not. We are actually adding cost.

One more, if you are still following this sad trail. The first mother above is a drug addict. We will not pay for her treatment ($5,000?), but we will pay for her care in prison ($30,000 per year), which she cannot avoid without help, and for her kids in foster care, and for our loss of income from a person who is not being emotionally prepared for employment -- at least a $50,000 difference, per year.

It is drug addiction that is increasing the corrections cost, which is the fastest growing pressure on taxes -- even beyond Medicaid and health insurance premiums.

Could the public start talking about drug addiction and its huge future costs? We could change some attitudes and make a real investment to reduce taxes, which we would all appreciate. 2-B

Poverty holds all nations back, including ours. A Zambian nurse stated: "More productive" means not only sufficient food but also additional <u>time</u> to produce that which makes life more productive and whole. Governments and citizens could do so much more. From the U.S., we give for the poor, sick and disabled in developing countries 22 cents of $100 of our income. That is from all sources, public and private. We are the lowest-paying developed country in the world. Planners say we should get to 70 cents. Well. In the last four years we have increased military budgets by $1.70. We have handed out $3.30 in new tax cuts, mostly for the wealthy. So, 22 cents?

More than half the people of the world live on less than $2 a day. That hurts our economic development in the real world. 6-1

It is so difficult to keep perspective on our challenges. We are horrified at the loss of life in a tsunami, as we should be. But we lose that many persons <u>every month</u> to the AIDS epidemic, without losing much sleep. The world will give billions to repair the first, again as we well should, but only a small fraction of that to cure the second, which will happen again next month and each month after.

<u>Clean water for our neighbors</u>

LB 32 would allow cities, counties and NRDs to assess a fee on each property, to pay for its impervious runoff. The operative word here is "impervious." The fee would be on the impervious area, which is basically roof and driveway/parking. Exhaust deposits and other nasty chemicals which rinse off in a rain must be filtered out some way.

This is a federal EPA mandate, to clean up our rivers. One should be able to eat the fish taken out of the Missouri. At present, you better not. . The feds did <u>not</u> create this obligation. Obviously, one of the prime duties of government is to ensure clean air, clean water, safe food and pure drugs. None of us can do this on our own

The problem with collecting fees on impervious surfaces is the built-in unfairness. A modest size church would have twice the roof and parking surface of a bank. Our new 40 story First National bank has much less roof than many churches or schools and would pay one-third the fee. Ouch. 3-9

Having spent many days of my youth loading and operating a horse-drawn manure spreader, this senator was taken by the new language, "runoff of nutrients." Today's larger feeder operators must have plans and permits, in triplicate, which include the precise analysis of nutrients. Cities are lagging behind.

Prisoners as neighbors

Community corrections and drug treatment are two key strategies to take the pressure off our prisons. Both will save mega-dollars down the road, but obviously new money is hard to find. So we are proposing an additional tax on alcohol, including one and a half cent on a can of beer, to pay for added treatment. Alcohol abuse costs taxpayers in Nebraska at least $300 million a year. The added tax would be $9 m., to a total alcohol tax of $30 m. That's right, one-tenth of our cost would be paid by the heaviest subsidized industry in our state. We take away from our schools to pay the deficit. 3-13

Surreal. The issue: are you for gun violence or against it? It is a strange question, producing a split vote. The sponsor had removed all reference to gun ownership, the issue that petrifies many senators. Yet we are talking about creating more prisoners.

The NRA declared itself neutral on the bill. Still, in fear of their reputation, some senators had to be called to the floor to get 25 votes, so we can boldly declare the bill: that we want to <u>study</u> what contributes to gun violence in Nebraska.

We even had one senator who said he could not vote for it because the NRA had at one time opposed study (before it was rewritten). We have never heard such a statement on the floor, openly pledging allegiance to a lobby. Unthinking allegiance, evidently.

Gun ownership is not the question. It will be here forever. Ours was a gun-toting family, but many of us are outraged by the NRA defense of steel jacket bullets, good only for killing cops. Rabbits are fairly safe. Assault-type weapons are endlessly available to those we are preparing to send to prison. The guns are everywhere, thanks to the NRA. Now in Oklahoma officials are considering arming the students. Let's see, 1,000 young people with guns and hormones. What could possibly go wrong here? Frankly, the gun owners we know are solid stable citizens. But we also have nuts. And hormones. And impulsive anger. And abuse in the home, where the guns are. What we are missing is sane discussion.

Worker as my neighbor

"There's class warfare, all right, but it's my class, the rich class, that's making war and we're winning." --Warren Buffett

One piece of the "American Dream" is to be freed from class barriers. Upward mobility means no class conflict. Instead we think everyone is middle class (ask them!) and have a sense of entitlement to a coming classless society, with beautiful homes, big or fast cars, productive and satisfying jobs, classy clothing and upwardly mobile children. Actually, most workers are frozen in place.

Reality: the gaps in class are widening. The lower class is about 4.5% of the national population, and the upper class is 3%. Is the remaining 90+% middle class? Not. We have added the working class, which is losing ground in wages, is not finding security, and yet is generating most of the wealth. About 60% overall are working class, with workers who do not have much control over the pace or content of work. Those who work with their hands are the bottom rung in our country. (Michael Zweig) Is hand labor not dignified?

Workers are lower and middle economically, but they usually do not change positions by hard work. Henry Ford provided an exception. Ford believed his workers should enjoy what they built and that they would be more productive with that hope. So, to the consternation of the capitalists of his day, Ford paid them enough that they could buy a new car and join the middle class. Old Henry made a lot of capitalist money by believing in his workers.

We are ignoring a massive working class, giving perks to management, taking benefits away from workers, and giving entitlements to the poor. We are becoming an unhealthy society, directly opposed to the Biblical sense of justice, and will feel the pain of our illness if we do not pay attention to the symptoms.

One reader wrote: "I really believe that there is a planned program for eventually doing away with the middle class. The kings, dukes and counts want the rest of us to become serfs again. Adolph Hitler came to power by turning the populace against one another." A lot of that is going on right now! If we do not respect all workers in our society we are setting ourselves up for an unhealthy future.

Example: schools systems across the nation are debating funding for education of low-income students. "Sharecroppers do not need much education." If that, in any way, is the assumption of decision makers, we can save "tax dollars" by not educating the poor. Leaders, not workers, plan the future roles of workers, but we all pay the price when human resources are not developed.

Raising the minimum wage will break our economic back? Now we are into passion that makes some goofy. Red-faced persons have told me Omaha cannot afford to pay more than $5.15 per hour. Starting wage at Burger King is $7 per hour. Who are we talking about? Business response: minimum wage sets all the other wages.

My staff hoot. They have been on the employment 'ladder,' and received no raise when the minimum went up. If a union contract is that foolish, change the contract. The real tragedy of this one is that paying people less than they are worth does hurt the economy and does raise taxes. We know of employers who have told low-pay workers their health plan is to go to the state for medical care.

Minimum Wage is the silliest debate this senator has witnessed. A few business folk (not all!) act like the end of the world comes immediately after raising minimum wage. My life is pro-business, through and through. We must have healthy entrepreneurs and steady old timers to prosper as a state. However, in the mind of some, all my votes for business are wiped out by one vote favoring a higher minimum wage – which reduces taxes.

Our proposal exempts kids and small businesses. No major business is paying as low as minimum wage. We have a few families with two parents working full time, who still need welfare to pay their basic bills. That is demeaning, as well as bad for your taxes. But there is near panic when we talk about correcting a tax problem at the same time as we encourage fulltime workers.

Our anti-worker attitudes have deep roots. Following are quotes, coming during the life of Nebraska.

"The Irish are nothing but imported beggars, animals, a mongrel mass of ignorance and crime and superstition, as utterly unfit for society's duties as they are for the common courtesies and decencies of civilized life." Jersey City Standard, 1859

"(Members of) the African race ... even when free, are everywhere a degraded class." Roger Taney, Chief Justice of the U. S. Supreme Court, 1857

"Immigration to this country is increasing and ... is making its greatest relative increase from races most alien to the body of the American people and from the lowest and most illiterate classes among those races." Henry Cabot Lodge, Congress, 1891

Worker humor. In the Nebraska Incentive Bill, business people commend 'quality jobs,' but when asked for a 'living wage' standard in Omaha they went into cardiac arrest. 1-15

The union people say a "one man" train crew is unthinkable. Why are we filling the air with dust on this matter? A one-woman crew would work, since women can multi-task. 2-5

Mentally ill as my neighbor

Background: Nebraska adopted a safe haven law in the winter session (2008) to become the 50th state to remove the criminal aspect of abandoning a baby if the child is left at a hospital.

Thus, we provide a "Safe Haven" instead of possibly a dumpster for an unwanted baby. We intentionally set no age, but said "child," which in Nebraska means up to 14 years old. Our Health and Human Services (HHS) Department chose to define the upper limit as 17 years of age. Not one infant has been left at a hospital under this new law, but 36 children have been deposited, generally by parents who are at their wits end on mental health problems.

A special session was called, but not because we have a child problem more serious than other states. Children have regularly been brought for treatment, year after year. This law provided an open back door and was used because the front doors of our states do not work well. Either way, the child and parent could get in to receive assistance. However, the media had a field day, examining each child, parent and grandparent in a way that hangs them out to dry.

So we had to shut off the media show and the top-story rating for families in horrible trauma.

Nebraska, through Boys Town, has provided a place to leave troubled children of any age, without fanfare, for over 80 years. We are proud of that kind of caring.

Through it all, the public is becoming informed on how difficult it is to deal with mental illness and the legislature and governor are willing to respond. Access to treatment is a nation wide problem. It is a money problem. We cannot afford the cost, though if we did offer proper treatment we would more than get the money back in the future taxes from the recovered person. Frustrating.

An Omaha father of a grown son who is bipolar shared the awful feelings and barriers his family experienced in seeking treatment for their son. Law in almost every state sets the bar for receiving treatment to require that (he) present "harm to himself or others."

The parents (professionals) were asked if the son threatened their lives. No? Then no treatment. He may be violent, putting fright into friends and neighbors. He can threaten with a knife or a bat. Does not count. No treatment. Whoever is in charge of that person has to pay the bills.

One exception: Commit a crime. Steal and find a drug to relieve the pain. We are tacitly encouraging that personal plan of action. He will have to do that and will readily plead guilty.

So, the writer asked the father what we will do -- we being the state. He said it sounds like we will send his son to prison. Interesting. Our state departments compete for money. The HHS department that refuses medical treatment to him has a budget cap initiated by the governor and eventually set by the legislature. The message is to keep the cost down. So we will not pay for the man's meds.

However, Corrections must receive this man if sentenced to prison, and we will pay for the meds there. We have to provide health care in prison, by federal law.

So, we will pay the bill? Yes. Guaranteed! However, then the ex-prisoner will be damaged goods in the work place and therefore in paying taxes to the state. This young man will think less of himself and employers will think less of him. His loss of pay will cost us all of his life. The rest of us have to make up his lost taxes, as well as pay the $30,000 a year for imprisonment. Investment in people is a good business principle in the real world!

Bottom line: mental illness costs real money. Ignoring it, or refusing preventive treatment, makes it more expensive. This is especially true of children. A mildly depressed child can have a highly productive life -- if good early preventive care provides a meds program for a stable life. Only if the public understands the crisis can the legislature do the right thing. For better or worse, we represent the people. 8-H

The Beatrice Home problems of care help the public know of pain, if not to understand it. When the stories came, the outrage in our legislative debate could be felt in the whole building. We went past our adjournment time by two hours as senators of both parties expressed their shock and intense frustration. The typical statement was that these citizens cannot help themselves, are totally in our care. We are failing to provide that care and our need to cut budget is not an acceptable excuse on the floor.

The statements are remarkable. Forty years ago we would not have any consensus like this. We would have blamed the families or the communities or the churches for not taking care of their own. This is a new announcement of an agreement we have never had. Now we say the care for a person can be beyond the capabilities of the family and when that happens we as a state are responsible for adequate care. Even people of faith have not said that to one another.

8-11

Elderly as my neighbor

Social Security is not a personal insurance policy. S. S. is not simply paying into a personal account, or investing in our future as we watch the rate of return. We are also paying "insurance" for our friends and neighbors. We are saying they will not be desperate in old age, with no means of support. We actually are insuring ourselves against folks coming to each of our doors for donations so our neighbor, good old Mrs. Jones, will not starve or freeze.

Do remember, government is mostly by committee and is not designed to be efficient. You may remember hearing about the woman, a few years ago, who was not considered competent, being a woman, to sign for a home loan. So her husband went ahead as the sole signer, but they would not accept his signature until they verified that his wife had full time employment. 5-16

Teens as my neighbor

This senator groaned as he witnessed waffling by lawmakers on a serious issue of public policy. For twenty-five years we have had a strict prohibition against minors drinking alcohol. There are no "if's" in the statute: "No person shall sell, give away, dispose of, exchange, or deliver, or permit the sale, gift or procuring of any alcoholic liquors, to or for any minor or to any person who is mentally incompetent." (Section 53-180)

Alcohol causes permanent brain damage in teens. The focus of my bill is on kegger parties, conducted by adults for teens. Keggers are blatant criminal acts which violate the law, cause serious damage to the health of our youth and create a huge financial cost in our society. The adult act is intentional, not accidental. The bill seeks to support the principle set forth in law with four small ways to plug gaps in enforcement. (The liability of adults passed.) 7-20

The victim and offender as my neighbor

A promising alternative that has great potential for bringing our country's incarceration statistics down is tested and available. While reducing crime and jail time, it would help to build community, could solidify public consensus on crime and would change discipline in schools -- all while taking both victims and offenders more seriously.

Restorative Justice

Could we focus on the victim of crime more than the offender? "Restorative Justice" (RJ) is a practical way of looking at wrong doing. Who has a need? What went wrong? Who can help?

Several states and nations have adopted RJ systems. Nebraska is not there yet, mostly because we have not been led to think out of the box. We do have "Diversion" to avoid court action for first time offenders, which has been very helpful in redirecting young lives and in reducing prison costs. RJ is different. A few nonprofit agencies apply the principles but the legal system does not and we have no supporting legislation.

Dr. Howard Zehr, the international guru on how to do it, reported in Nebraska symposiums that New Zealand has turned the criminal justice system there on its head, with results that reach into every community and the school systems. A young offender goes first to the RJ office. If that does not work, then the case goes to the court system.

So what is this? "Restorative" is simply an adjective. True justice is by definition restorative. What grabs one's attention immediately is the RJ system puts the focus on the victim. Our system almost ignores victims in its focus on the offender. (We even talk offenders into thinking "not guilty," which fills our prisons with persons who do not feel guilty.) If teen offenders vandalize cars and homes in a four block area (actual case), offenders and victims and community members join in an extended RJ problem-solving discussion, to agree on how to make that right for the victims, or to do what is possible.

Dr. Zehr: "Restorative justice is a response to crime that focuses on restoring the losses suffered by victims, holding offenders accountable for the harm they have caused, and building peace within communities."

Burglary and assault are the easier cases to describe. The process varies, but may lead to a serious discussion in which all are equal. The offender(s), the victim(s), the police, the school, and community members are placed in a circle. Only the one with the 'talking stick' may speak and the stick moves on to the next in line, as many times as needed. Offenders hear from victims about how it feels to be vandalized -- fears of leaving the house, bills unpaid, sudden desire to move, children kept inside instead of enjoying their yards. Whatever the fear or pain or loss, say it. The offenders describe what they did and how that felt. Parents, police, neighbors -- do the same.

Instead of imagining 'closure' in a system where the court eventually puts these two 'punks' away, victims meet the real teens, see they are not ten feet tall monsters, and are helped to "get rid of the boogeyman in the head." They are freed to leave the house every day and see the world in perspective. It may take months or years, but the offenders begin to clean up and to fix and pay for the damages, as determined by the victims and the neighbors, until realistic resolution is achieved. If no resolution, the incident goes to court. Obviously, life lost in murder will not be resolved, but RJ principles could apply to victims.

This pastor was struck by the remarkable change in community which was documented. A community that does not do problem solving, but waits for the city to take action, remains weak. Problem solving builds strength. A community that has gone through this long, challenging process is more in focus and ready for members to be there for each other. It can be transformative.

Another powerful emotion that is ignored in classic criminal justice is addressed here: shame and humiliation. The shame of appearing weak is devastating to a young person: "weak" as a 'real man' would not be; "weak" and helpless as a few women are taught to be even as they resent it. We have the shame of a teen labeled as a felon -- forever.

We have the humiliation of family members who fear having the teen go with them to church, where no one has wrestled with their problem. RJ replaces shame and humiliation with maturing responses to mistakes and impulsive behavior.

School discipline is also changed, big time. Our school discipline is based on the court system, with the principal as judge and jury. It could be a circle of those affected.

We live in a very punitive culture. Tit for tat. Serve your time. Restorative concepts are counter culture and so will take a while for public acceptance. We will find it has many values we have ignored. Citizens who were in a circle experience have said, reflecting on it, "Oh, that is what my parents did in our family." Minority persons who recall a tribal culture recognize this as the ancient way of elders' wisdom. Restorative.

We have come a l-o-n-g way

Being blessed with a curiosity about history, the author knows how we got here. Even wrote a book about it. (A) We built Nebraska on the prairie, where those in crisis were sent back to where they came from. We gave them food for the journey. In the next phase, good people of town, mostly through churches, collected food and clothing for the desperate among us. Families used up all their savings and assets in the search for healing and care for Grandma or Grandson.

That soon became too much for volunteers to carry, and some people had no family, so churches lobbied the County Board to establish Poor Farms, where nearly helpless folks could have a roof, a well for water, heat in the winter, and a garden. Next, we agreed that seriously ill persons cannot be left to die in their homes, so churches established hospitals where any person may enter. To this day, the county pays the expenses of desperately ill persons who have no money. That began in the first 40 years of Nebraska.

During the last 40 years, we have agreed that every child should be educated, should have health care, and should not be abused but be in a safe home. We will protect abused persons of any age. We will provide nursing home care for the elderly who do not have sufficient resources. A developmentally disabled baby belongs to all of us, not just to those two parents and their family. We have agreed to all that, in the last 40 years. It is very expensive when done even in the most efficient manner, with platoons of volunteers. Over 200 church and synagogue-sponsored agencies in Omaha alone provide the needed services at a greatly discounted rate.

We have also agreed that young people with the smarts and attitude should be educated past high school and that we will help them. But now we have shifted gears, from basic human needs to economic development. We have to enlist every trained adult we can to develop a career in Nebraska -- if we are to have a healthy future. It is still $$$.

Our progress in good programs is encouraging, but it is a near miracle that this week we also took huge strides in economic development, through tax incentives. For the first time we developed some incentives without a company (like ConAgra) in mind. We had rural and urban interests at the table, with the governor and every stripe of political thought also at the table. It comes to about $65 million a year. In Nebraska. Where we squeeze nickels. Cheers. We have one million taxpayers, so that is $65 each. 5-21

Democracy is more than a two-way street. We act like it is one-way. We live in a country that tells other countries what to think, listens less and apparently is too lazy to consider the basics of complex issues. We accomplish more in Nebraska, but we also have too much of the condescending attitude. We can do better. 6-1

President Theodore Roosevelt: "This country will not be a permanently good place for any of us to live in unless it is a reasonably good place for all of us to live in."

We have this image from Andrew Miller, playwright who recently died:

> *"I think my role writing plays was to be a drop of acid, mixed in the waters of life, washing a bit more rust from the edges of the social order."*

Yes. Hopefully, someone will say that of me some day. Then others will be heard to say, "Hey, that is what I have been doing too!"

Life is not so simple -- But dignity can be profound

Stella, a brilliant mathematics student from Hong Kong, lived with our family while she worked on her Master's at UNL. The request to give her housing came from her teacher at a Lutheran College, which covered college costs.

She had been cruelly ridiculed and abused by her father, for being a girl. He moved out Stella, her two sisters, a retarded brother ("equivalent of a girl") and their mother, and moved in another wife who would "give him" sons. Law required him to support both families.

One day Stella and a friend were walking on the street when they met one of her teachers from the nearby Lutheran grade school she attended. He said, "Good morning, Stella."

She whirled around and confronted him: "Why did you call me 'Stella'?"

"I said 'Stella' because that is your name."

"Why did you call me by name on the street, outside of school?"

He knew her family. "I call you 'Stella' because I am a Christian. You are a person of value and you have a name."

Stella was stunned. She told us often of this life-changing moment. Could a worthless girl have value? She decided to learn more about these Christians, and became a believer. The church sent a gifted graduate to the United States.

While Stella lived with us, Ruth was Chair of the Nebraska Women's Commission, under (!) a governor who did not support equality for wives in the work force and who opposed funds to study issues such as domestic abuse and equal rights in inheritance. Be assured, you cannot imagine Ruth's frustration as she stood between the governor and Stella, both of whom assumed husbands should be the power person in the home.

Stella brought home a boy friend who said a husband's duty is to control his wife and family. Ruth persistently and quietly shared her vision with Stella that here, in Nebraska, the day would come when equal respect for women would be in law, in homes, and on the streets. Do religion and politics mix? For Ruth, yes. It was a question of dignity, a faith value.

Post Script. Ruth's vision was validated both in the state and with Stella. Domestic abuse is now taken very seriously and a wife can inherit the farm. Stella later wrote Ruth that on her wedding day she remembered Ruth's passion for her dignity and potential, and walked out of the church, not married, determined to be her own person.

Stella is our neighbor.

A Bonus !

I GO POGO

The author proudly shares his debt to Pogo, who was the most effective voice to save us from the radical fringe in the 50s.

Walt Kelly used his Pogo comic strip to tackle the abuse of reason by far out groups in the 50s and 60s. His community of swamp critters was created to mirror the U. S. public. Through the characters he could identify and dissect the foolishness which took charge of our public life at that time. His insight continues to teach, for his characters continue to have life as you observe their world.

Pogo (possum) is the common sense character, smart but never stuffy or arrogant. Simple J. Malarkey (bobcat) is Joseph McCarthy, always with a gun and ready to shoot first, even shooting some of his own. Mole is Nixon, helping to investigate who is "submersive."

The Deacon, who speaks in Old English script, announces what God wants, what is righteous, what good people should be doing. Cowbirds and other investigators join in looking for "comsymps" (McCarthy's language for communist sympathizers) and for anyone who might seem suspicious. Naturally, that line of thought eventually leads to everyone, which is the devastating message of the swamp community. (They, by the way, know that we are looking in on them through a window and assume that we would join them if we could.)

In the real world, McCarthy stopped the media and most national leaders cold, through fear that he would charge them with being subversive. Actors' careers were ruined. He taught members not to trust pastors, and the public not to trust politicians, teachers, colleges and the humanities. Citizens, solid or shallow, were "tried" in public hearings for invented crimes, never in court.

In the end, McCarthy was exposed as a fraud by persons he was investigating and he died two years later (April, 1957) from excessive drinking. The public figures who finally got enough traction to stop him: Bishop Oxnam (and his book, "I Protest"), Generals in the Army hearing who roared their protest at being considered comsymps, and Senator Margaret Chase Smith (R-Maine), who drew up a "Statement of Conscience" in which she denounced "political exploitation of fear, bigotry, ignorance and intolerance." The media and congress did not get it at first, or were afraid to say so. "Pogo" was protested by some papers and moved to the editorial pages by others, but usually was printed by relieved editors who saw the truth being spoken in language the public could understand.

The Okefenokee Swamp (actual place) had hundreds of characters. Albert Alligator is Pogo's hapless friend and protector. Ma'm'selle Hepzibah (a sexy looking skunk- Kelly's wife) is the temptress who loves Pogo and Howland Owl thinks of himself as wise.

We begin with the Jack Acid Society. McCarthy and Nixon had joined with the John Birch society to blacklist and investigate anyone open to diversity of thought. Kelly mimicked them with the Jack Ash Society, which morphed into the Jack Acids, who were investigating anyone suspicious in Okefenokee.

We hope it is not too much of a break from religion and politics to view the whole matter from a common sense perspective. Very common. Welcome to Okefenokee, USA. (U)

83. The Black List is created by John Birch, religious, black-hat Deacon, with the help of Richard Nixon as Mole.

84. Hitting on persons certified suspicious will protect us from moderates' value systems.

85. Suspects are to be targeted first, rather than known communists, who are dull press.

86. Who is suspicious? Anyone I do not know. I do not know everything about you.

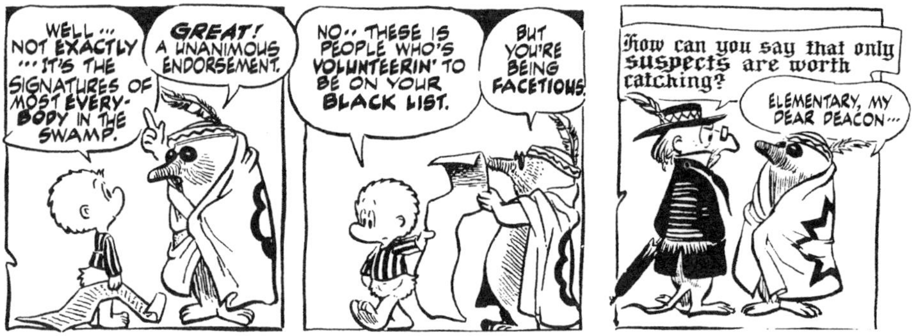

87. It becomes a chancey world when we trash the ideas of our adversaries.

88. McCarthy uses the John Birch Black List and then forcibly takes over the operation.

89. Hearings are preferred to trial. Trial by public hearings effectively intimidates, and destroys careers.

90. Can we still have flowers, the arts and serious debate in our lives?

4. Conservative or Liberal?

Politics is simply defined as the way decisions are made in a community. If you talk about an issue or community question with your neighbor, you are a politician.

Government does, again in simple terms, what you cannot do for yourself. Roads. Fire. Law enforcement. Clean water. Clean air. Pure food and medication. Education for the children in your community. Adam Smith, a pioneer political theorist, had three roles for government and they are all in that list.

Then we come to political terms like "Compassionate Conservative." Is the opposite "Uncaring Liberal"? The words are so abused we need definition.

<u>Pioneers and other innovators</u>

In the Nebraska territory, over 150 years ago two church women in Omaha City saw that children in poor families, which were most of the new families in the small village, were plainly hungry in the winter. Sometimes the family arrived too late in summer to plant a crop, or the crop failed. With a light harvest, they were limited to hunting for wildlife and berries in the long winters. Most new families did not have adequate clothing for the harsh weather.

The women's plan? It had to protect dignity. They knew schools were modest. So they decided it would offend no one to invite students to their homes after school, each day, "for education." With food -- enough it could be supper. Result: better education, building a sense of community, and every child in town would have one good meal a day, every day, without embarrassment. They recruited women from the churches to provide food, hand-me-down coats, and friendship for lonely, fearful children.

Were they conservative? Yes. They were conserving the slim population, and teaching conservative thinking. It was plain survival. They made do with what they had. They valued education, which is conservative investment.

Were they liberal? Yes. The basic definition is to be generous, as in a 'liberal' helping. They gave everything they had. They had little money, but they produced gardens and crops. Most of all they had themselves and their volunteer time. They wanted each child to develop into all she/he could be. They were liberal.

They were something else. They were practical. In their direct and caring way they are a model of how we do legislation in Nebraska. We look to see what is possible, to protect ourselves and to care for our people. We do not want to borrow any money to do that and we will stretch every resource as far as we can go with it.

We will do what is practical to help any person to be healthy, educated and safe. We are a generous people if the idea makes sense. For most people of faith, our intentions and actions fit what they expect.

The first social service program in the new territory provided burial if you died without funds. Typically, a perpetual drunk was the one found dead in the middle of the street. Was this service compassionate or liberal? Yes, compassion for a lost life. Yes, liberal, by giving more than a person deserved. Both are trumped by practical. Dead bodies in the street create all kinds of problems. Politically, we are always about improving the community.

The next major service to persons without resources was the Poor Farm. Yes, it was conservative, for it cared for people by depending on their own gardens and labor. Yes, it was liberal, for a few had not "earned" it. Many had earned help through years of work and taxes in the community. However, basically we see practical. By buying a farm with a big old house the county could provide a roof, warmth in the winter, water from a well, food from large gardens, and a base from which to find seasonal employment in the community. Poor Farms were innovative in that day, and very practical. Were they a right? Possibly. Political decisions determine rights -- which are evaluated in another chapter.

This senator's Republican grandfather, elected in a conservative county, insisted (in a tense fight) that it was in the public interest to treat the poor with dignity, providing a roof, food, work and education, through relocating the Poor Farm to soil which would provide for productive gardens. "You would not put your cattle on that sandy farm, because they would die." Now some would call that liberal. It was compassionate and progressive, but mostly it was practical. Provide good soil for gardens. S

Was the New Deal to express compassion for desperate people, or to save capitalism? We have been told both. We still do not know and continue in a national debate on it. Sadly, we are given re-writes of history in the debate, so it is difficult to learn what we should.

In our day, consider those 200 and more Omaha folks who are working on Building Bright Futures, which is a plan to greatly improve education for all our children. They are liberals and conservatives without any thought of a divide, and would walk away from such a stupid question. None related to that project are seeking control. All are longing for growth among our youth, including a high level of self-motivation.

"Conservative" and "Liberal" mean what?

Since these terms are overworked, let us focus for a bit on the use and abuse of "conservative" and "liberal." One has become a term of virtue, usually good. In colonial days "conservative" was a term used in anger and ridicule, describing those with stubborn loyalty to the king. It was a swear word. "Liberal" is now a swear word, almost never used except to ridicule. This is abuse of words.

Conservative - adj. - 1. Favoring traditional views and values; tending to oppose change. 3. Moderate ... (as) 'a conservative estimate' 7. Tending to conserve .... (as) "the conservative use of natural resources."

Liberal - adj. - 1a. Not limited to or by established traditional, orthodox, or authoritarian attitudes, views, dogmas; free from bigotry. 1b. Favoring proposals for reform, open to new ideas for progress, tolerant of the ideas and behavior of others. 4. .... based on the traditional arts and sciences (of a college curriculum, as) "a liberal education." (Definitions are from the American Heritage dictionary.)

The conservative may be seeking change. The liberal may want stronger recognition of traditional values. To be effective, each had better listen to and evaluate the other's views. When we quit using the words as clubs we have better communication. At present in the legislature, the two words are nearly useless. In the parties, they raise money.

George Washington was about as traditional as they come. However, he conducted a revolution. The conservative in his day was the Tory, supporting the king and the elite ruling class.

The new constitution was radical, declaring all (men) to be equal, blocking the church from government, promising a vote for 'ordinary' men and instituting a democracy in which renters could vote -- all a change from tradition, and therefore exceptionally liberal.

Lincoln's major thrust was to conserve the union. The huge change for which he is remembered is the Emancipation Proclamation, which as he stated plainly to an abolitionist, was not done to free the slaves (change) but to create enough chaos in the south (change) that the union could be preserved (tradition).

Slavery was promoted by many Christians as conservative, both in religion (with scripture) and in economics (to maintain, property, to prevent bankruptcy and to improve the economy). For the strict conservative mind, scripture does indeed support slavery. Those willing to change to the liberal principle of "all men are created equal" found textual support for personal dignity and worth.

A recent president spoke often of spreading democracy in the Mideast, specifically in Iraq. It is apparent he considered this to be conservative. O my. The best word for it would be neo-liberal. It was a radical concept when placed in our constitution. Much about democracy was experimental. He and frankly many of our leaders assume a liberal thought: that the desire for democracy is implanted in every person and is simply looking for a means of expression. Really? That is an unrecognized idea in most world politics and does not connect with the traditions of many religions and nations. It is liberal theory at best and stokes a war with nationalist conservatives at worst.

Claude Canaday, a Nebraska farmer, presented President Truman and his Secretary Marshall with practical ideas for what became The Marshall Plan, by which Germany recovered economic strength. Was Claude liberal or conservative? He would smile at the question.

Good legislation is not by labels

In a recent legislature, we passed four bills which raise the points of our intent as state senators.

Bill #1. We increased the use of folic acid for young mothers who were drinking steadily. These women produce Fetal Alcohol Syndrome (FAS) babies, whose defects will cost the state at least $600,000 each (average) over their lifetimes. This reduces defects. Assuming that we have only five new FAS babies each year, that is a liability of $3 million per year, which is $60 million over the next 20 years. Bonded indebtedness. Which buys nothing. To avoid great expense, we are spending some money. Is that a conservative or a liberal action? It is quite practical.

A hero's award should be given the judge who had before him a young woman who had delivered two FAS babies. When her defense attorney protested that she was pregnant again and should therefore avoid jail, the judge ordered her to nine months in jail. He said he would figure out why later. Then he looked at her and said something like: "Congratulations. You will have a baby who is well and healthy, who will become a child and an adult you can be proud of. Plan for that." A liberal who intends to conserve?

Bill #2 put up more money for school breakfasts. That seems liberal, but it is proven to raise test scores, which we need for a prosperous state, so conservatives voted for it.

Bill #3 added money to early childhood development. That sounds liberal, but the program will improve graduation rates, which is economic development. It won the support of nearly everyone.

Bill #4 was to support research on autism. We will place $1 million a year of state money into the research at the med center for many years to come, as a match with private funders. The research project provides the highest-level treatment in the nation to 60 students a year. If this helps only one in four to live a normal life, we have 15 persons who will not need the $2 million that is the conservative estimate of lifetime costs. That is a 30 to 1 pay back. Would conservatives or liberals like that best? We all do, and persons of faith are most grateful for the people who are making this happen.

Those illustrations are a good way to help readers understand that increase to budgets, which every one of these bills did, can be the best strategy to save future taxes, big time. It is essential to have good people working the plan, but when we do we are doing ourselves a favor by buying into it. Above all, we are being practical.

In the legislature we are always desperate for money. There is never enough to cover legitimate needs. If we do not vote on the long-range cost, we are not being wise. To illustrate, take a third grade girl from Omaha. She was mildly depressed, in a single-mom family. The husband left. The Mother was wise, but extremely poor. She worked full time but there was no way she could provide health care for herself and her three children. She was in tears when a pastor found her in the 90s. Medicaid provided the girl's physical exam and her meds. She is now a teacher and community volunteer. What would our bill be if she had gone the drug route to ease her pain?

The sad part of this is that the state is not very good at long range planning. Agencies, schools and nonprofits do long range planning well because they have to in order to survive. But the state budget planners are always looking at this year and the balance sheet.

Even if $1 million will pay back $5 million in three years we are not likely to do it, because the press and the public will be pointing to the $1 m. cost. Practical business judgments would say otherwise. Conservative and liberal labels work in campaigns but not in the real world of state legislation and of business. Forcing a (false) conservative label, instead of analyzing future costs, can raise future taxes.

Currently, we mix images on health care reform, which will go for years. The president calls for reduced costs, saying our present growth is not sustainable. For this he is labeled liberal. The opposition is doing all possible to protect present profits. One senator received a million dollars in campaign funds from those profits. For this he is called conservative.

Any fair definition of 'liberal' would include being generous, being supportive of openness, looking for options. Any fair definition of 'conservative' would include maintaining tradition, building on a base and caution on a new proposal. Looking at the parties, the record of Democrats shows they ended child labor, fought for clean air and water and brought us Social Security and Medicare in a highly efficient manner -- but also bog us down with bureaucracy in other government programs and often give us studies with no results.

The record for Republicans shows they gave us Lincoln, broke the Cold War, support entrepreneurs and are getting into conserving the environment -- but also put barriers on personal choice, on development, and on scientific research. Both parties add greatly to bureaucracy yet both support entrepreneurs in major ways.

"Tradition" and "Progress" as defining ideas.

Better terms for useful dialog are 'traditional' and 'progressive.' We all have traditions that we respect. Every one of us wants our community to progress. Without tradition we are unstable. Without progress we will become extinct. The world, our technology and the economy move on. Each view needs the other.

Thomas Jefferson was the president in a tradition vs. progressive crisis. The Federalists wanted to continue rule by the elite, with the federal government acting like a king and with voting limited to the wealthy. Hamilton championed the Federalists and control by bankers. Jefferson won in 1800 by lifting his equality words in the Declaration of Independence and by emphasizing the role of every citizen in creating change. (Do note, this was <u>not</u> a two-party system and campaign as we know it today.)

Thomas Jefferson was ridiculed by conservatives as the "pied piper of equality and democracy (who rejects current restrictions on voting)." Randolph, a fierce critic: "Sir, my only objection is that these principles, pushed to their extreme consequences -- that all men are born free and equal -- I can never assent to, for the best of reason, because it is not true.... "

Jefferson rejected arguments against the "extravagance of liberty" (great phrase!) and for the importance of obedience to a 'king.'

> *It is important to note that in the earliest days of the brand-new experiment in republican government that the United States was attempting, Alexander Hamilton was pushing the idea that a powerful, centralized government should be in service to wealthy bankers and businesspeople.*
>
> *Hamilton was not arguing for the free market, as conservatives today do, because the times were so fundamentally different. He was contending instead that the federal government should use all of its powers to promote economic development, and his way of doing that was to cut deals with wealthy financiers and businesspeople to get them excited about the new nation....*
>
> *In Jefferson's and Paine's experience, despotic kings and men allied with big-money capitalists such as Hamilton were the ones arguing for more government power."* J

There is humor here. Jefferson was so opposed to federal power he thought the Louisiana Purchase (an expensive stimulus package!) was not strictly constitutional. However, he wanted it so badly that he convinced congress to come together on the vote, to authorize a large expenditure in order to buy a new future for his common man.

The success of the Revolutionary War was a near miracle. It required the leadership of Washington and Jefferson, and the intervention of foreign powers. It would not have even happened without the catalyst of Thomas Paine's Common Sense. Published in the winter of 1776, the leaflet brought together the outrage and the measured language for the Declaration that summer. Referring to the British government: "How a race of men came into the world so exalted above the rest and distinguished like some new species, is worth inquiring into." A classy call to arms. I-18 f.

The use of 'tradition' depends on the interpretation. Shall we take tradition of 200 years ago or 100 years ago ... or 50 years ago? In interstate commerce, President Eisenhower touted the interstate highway as a conservative way to enhance economic development -- which is progressive. President Jefferson, who wrote our early paragraphs on interstate commerce and who refused to allow it to trump states rights, would be appalled. A cargo boat on a canal could be stopped at state lines for evaluation, taxation, or refusal. Federal interstate commerce, Jefferson felt, was conservatism (rule by a king) at its worst. Well. That debate gives us new tradition.

Jefferson called for a new government, ruled by the people. He wrote 'the consent of the governed' in clear terms and 200 years later we are still seeking to live it. We are not there yet. We have resisted voting by the poor for all of those years. Recent immigrants who become full citizens have always been resented for voting. Voting by all is radical change. However, in Nebraska 200 years later, persons of faith legislate by those Jefferson/Paine principles. Amazing.

Alternate political language

Columnist David Brooks provided other words -- an imaginative change of language for the political debate:

> *If American politics would start with a clean slate today, the main argument wouldn't be between liberalism and conservatism, words that have become labels without coherent philosophies ... The main fight would pit populist nationalism vs. progressive globalism ... The populist nationalist party would be liberal on economics, conservative on values and realist on foreign policy. [It would bring together many kinds of divergent thinkers.]*

He suggested they would stand up to the big-money interests who value their own profits more than their own countrymen... we are tired of both the corporate elites and the cultural elites.

> *The progressive globalists would be market-oriented on economics, liberal on values and multilateral interventionists in foreign affairs. Like Tony Blair was. We need to reform education and improve skills so that more people succeed. We need to reform entitlements so the economy can remain flexible and not buried by debt. We have to work together to address global warming, oil dependence and protectionist barriers .... We have to confront Islamic extremism .... manage the movement of peoples without shutting off the flow .... open up trade, not shut it down.*
>
> *Politics is become less about left vs. right and more about open vs. closed.* *K*

Most evil actions come from people who do not think about the harm they are doing. Martin Marty, a native Nebraskan who is now a leading academic for national churches, says the real division among us is mean vs. non-mean, without labels. We do not become evil on purpose. It is too chaotic. Labels disrupt thinking. Communities prosper with caring people who oppose anything mean. The mean spirit pushes us all down and holds back progress.

A good illustration of the mean is the trashing of the administration by the party out of power. Honest dissent is a service. However, most of what we get is creative twisting, hoping to find a label that will eventually stick and hurt. It lacks integrity and dignity. Worse, it disrupts community. We should be looking for what we can support but instead we are asked to distrust the ideas of other citizens and to reject open dialog. Thinking only one way is a definition of naïve.

Tightwads

A small but noisy group of earnest citizens claim that the simple definition of fiscal conservatives is those legislators who are willing to cut all budgets. Let tightwads control. Not.

This senator is a certified tightwad. My father and grandfather were fiscally conservative office holders. Neither was stingy, but both were very creative tightwads. My Dad negotiated his price on

Sears best bike, which two of us could ride tandem to school. The second (used) bike came four years later.

My standard cap on lunch is $2. Admittedly, that was a bit extravagant when it was set in the 70s. Drinks are overpriced, so never buy one, of any kind. Tap water is free (and better) so we boycott bottled water. We creatively save electricity.

Negotiated so good a price for my only new car that the dealer offered $1,500 in cash not to take delivery. Put 80,000 miles on one car over a ten year period, and sold it for more than the cost. Fun.

So, know all about tightwads! Most do not qualify as fiscal conservatives. Why?

A fis-con has clear standards:

- can distinguish between an expense and an investment
- will pay a fair price for a guaranteed-quality product
- would rather repair a roof than repair water damage
- works continuously to spot expenses that have no production
- gets a special kick out of honestly cutting a budget

Too many emails use slam terms (socialist, big spender) instead of reason in discussing the budget. A bit of humor. A recent email warned us to be on guard against a sinister plan to imbed a socialist chip in all our brains. The Texas woman did not tell us how one would have a lobotomy (her word) without knowing about it. However, her stress does stir the imagination. How did "God votes" chips get implanted in so many brains? Where is this socialist?

We have to work hard to find a true socialist, which she fears. (One national columnist says he can find only two in the country.) But socialism is all about us. It means doing something as a community. We protect the senior who has no resources with Medicare and provide an income floor for such a person with Social Security. These are not insurance or investment plans. They are to protect the desperate through the resources of the community. An insurance exec insisted all insurance is socialist, as we pay for someone else's loss.

Medicaid does it for those who are younger. You can send your message by FedEx or the Post Office will deliver it for 44 cents, to the most remote rancher in the sandhills. Socialism at its worst.

Celebrate the hope that we are free to think. We are indeed a robust collection of thinkers, who can be led astray in an election year but who are, in the end, a wily crowd of decision makers. 8-1

Applying labels

When this fellow was a boy, one political party wanted frugal government with a lot of individual freedom and initiative, and the other party wanted to rescue families in Depression crisis through government programs. Our family went with frugal!

Now it has nearly flipped, but is mostly confused. The frugal party spends our grandchildren's money for subsidies to rich corporations and the other party calls for more individual initiative from stabilized families.

However, both have a mix of all that and are willing to go into debt. We have a mix of politics and interests on the legislative floor, but 90% of us know that every child must have an excellent education and be safe with health care. There is no do-gooder thought to this. It is economic necessity, an investment -- or we are in trouble.

Rush Limbaugh is predictable and shallow, but fun. So listen a bit to fun that is dangerous. To an older caller who in a quiet and humble way asked that he consider other points of view in order to find the truth, Rush said, "I am the truth. Why would I be taking this time if I did not have the truth?"

At no time did he add a qualifier like "what I consider to be the truth." In answer to the man's question (before he cut him off as way out of line), Rush defined liberals as interested only (!) in controlling you and conservatives as the ones who want you to grow. Well.

Senator Schimek googled her name and discovered she is a wild Jewish liberal. She has a bill that would require home schools to have minimal accountability through testing (as we do with all other schools). We have a few home schools in which children are seldom taught. The parents file their status every year on time, so they can legally keep their kids out of school, but that is about it.

Since the legislature is responsible for every child, not just those who are indeed well educated in home schools, it seems reasonable to have requirements. "Conservatives" object and call her Jewish.

Web blogs point out, at length, that this is a Jewish move and that is what is wrong with America. Quotes:

> *(The home schoolers) should have drug the Bitch out by the hair and took turns Jap slappin' the Bitch for a few hours."* (No, we do not know what that is, but you can bet the dude carries a concealed weapon.)
>
> *The only thing worse than Jews is Niggers, who are Jews with tans. If you're not mad as hell you are not paying attention.*

The senator did not know she was Jewish until reading this. They have proof positive. She and Herb named their sons Samuel and Saul. She is a kike or a kikealike. Since the writers declare they and the home schoolers are the only true whites, how would you like to meet them some night on a poorly lit street? Obviously blogs do not an issue make, but a few nuts can ruin dialog.

So, google Lowen Kruse? O my. Over 180 hits. Two pages of them are articles about his trying to stop teenagers from having wine in communion. He did not do that, but what the heck. Maybe he is Jewish. Obviously there has to be a reason he would try to stop teenagers from receiving communion -- but why ask him?

These characters give conservative a bad name. They should have met a really classy conservative, William Buckley.

> *His tone and level of civilized discourse set him in great relief to the shrill type of commentary we often hear today. .... He felt deeply hurt .... if something he wrote or said hurt someone personally. .... He believed that if government would just leave man alone, the human spirit would triumph. .... Buckley was hardly a saint .... His idea of a compromise was to deny both uneducated whites and blacks the vote. .... Conservatism has lost something. In the conservatism spawned by talk radio and TV, the haters and know-nothings are back, ranting about immigrants and liberals."* *L*

Sigh. We miss your thoughtful, strident ways, Mr. Buckley.

Using labels as club or mud

Trash talk hurts. We get a lot of it.

A condensed quote by Tom DeLay, 2003: "We are trying to change the tones in the state capitals -- and turn them toward bitter nastiness and partisanship." Is he doing health care reform?

There is a lot of that going around. The following examples of distortion in the rhetoric of campaigns come from the '08 elections.

Obama will ban talk radio. (Who manufactured that one, do you suppose?)

McCain is such a hothead he cannot be trusted with decisions.

Obama was a community organizer, so mixed with ne'er do wells and cannot be trusted with national decisions. (Ignore that the man graduated summa cum laude from Harvard law school, was a professor of constitutional law for eight years, etc.)

Obama lacks family values. (Amazing. A 16 year marriage, with two children, in a Protestant church, wife drops out of a very lucrative legal option to be with the kids, Dad is there for them, urges other fathers to be there -- but not an "American family?")

(Fill in name) associates with Keating, Ayers, lobbyists, crooked politicians.

An elitist. Used by both parties. (Also said of Kennedy. Translation: he talks in fluent fashion.)

Obama's shadow: he believes in Biblical social justice. (We all know that will not work.)

McCain's shadow: he continuously changes who he is. (Others do not change? We put a priority on getting them to change.)

(Fill in name) is taking away our God-given rights. (Like guns! Or marriage? Hello. God gives no rights. God gives life, but no right to keep it.)

"I am a maverick." (Particularly humorous. By definition, a maverick is a calf that has not been branded. Law says the calf is owned by whoever feeds it. Hmmm. Which will change if the calf wanders from herd to herd. Once branded a calf is not a maverick. To be fair, they have redefined the word to mean independent of the original brand. But then the calf is owned by those who feed. That is a fun image in a lobbyist world. A maverick supposedly has withdrawn from the herd, from tradition -- so is a liberal?)

Poor little persecuted black boy is trying to make it in the real world. (Who started that? Minority children do not know a real world? Persecuting persons disqualifies them for a job?)

He is a Marxist. (The term is used by persons who show no evidence of understanding what a Marxist is. In the 50s, we called anyone we did not like a communist.)

He is a Socialist. (The accusation is thrown at anyone who wants to work as a community on an issue. Being a Socialist party member is quite another value and system.)

"Spread the wealth" is the same as Socialist "redistribute the wealth." Not even close. ("Spread the wealth" is the battle cry to maintain a Middle Class. "Redistribute" is a code word to remove a middle class. It sounds sinister, and it is, so that is why it is used. If you want to be Biblical, the command is to redistribute all possessions every so many years. If you want to be accurate, today the wealthy <u>receive</u> from redistribution, in recent years increasing income three times faster than the poor. The middle class <u>loses</u> income position, while doing most of the production.)

McCain's pastor openly favors destroying Islam.

Obama's pastor (or fill in name) is anti-American.

(Name) receives out-of-state funds. (Said of a local candidate and not true. This was in a robo call from a group that <u>does</u> receive funds from out of state. Hello?)

Robert Nelson, following Obama's election, summarized much of the above:

> *....to listen to only one line of thought, especially the one that makes you most comfortable about who, what and where you are -- usually by sucking up to you while tearing down others -- is un-American to me.....*
>
> *To deny the results of our democratic process seems absolutely un-American to me."* *T*

Amen. This has gone from silly to sinister, especially in encouraging racial fears. Can we move on? Can we get back to the real world? Most important, can we get on with being a true democracy, with <u>open</u> <u>exchange</u> of ideas, and with the shared goal to improve our communities? 8-G

"Why are your papers in order?"
East Germany humor during Russian control

Legislative practice

The conservative and liberal labels do not work because they are not used honestly. When a label becomes a swear word it is not likely to carry much truth. Political parties love to use labels and in the time of campaign the air is filled with puffery, grand promises and slandering images. Parties have the task of selecting candidates, of checking their worthiness for public service, and of helping them to present themselves to the public. It is an important job and they usually do it well. However, they create and promote labels to influence swing voters. That hurts us all.

Persons of faith want leaders with informed common sense. We should show high respect and give great appreciation for elected leaders who listen to all the voices and give us plain messages about what we must do now to deal with the future. Many do it well.

Thankfully, our legislature is nonpartisan. In campaigns, candidates may have promised to cut taxes or to help everybody, but the legislature is the real world. Neither promise will be kept, because neither is possible. We are free to be compassionate or non-mean, but only if it is practical.

There is a world of meaning in this for the person of faith. This senator pays a lot of taxes (gladly, even if it is difficult), but pays many times more in charity. Without the work of nonprofit groups, the state budget would be in a shambles. Nonprofit providers do what the state wants to see happen but cannot do. They do it with less money and with creativity and vision. The miracle of volunteers and commitment is beyond words, and is especially practical.

The debate on concealed carry is an interesting example of a conservative value. It is actually a very liberal interpretation of our constitution which allowed for use of individual weapons to defend the country. General Washington needed those guns. Now we make something else of it and act like his army concealed their weapons. We bend the constitution to argue for opinions of interest groups.

Public education was basic in almost every state constitution. A letter to the editor labels the public school as a "socialist enclave." Both are weasel words. Social Security is seen as a help for seniors to "pursue happiness." Talking without end about whether it is conservative or liberal is useless venting. S. S. is progressive and is accepted by both parties. The question for all of us is how to make it work in future years.

Claiming the stock market as a conservative value in that strategy is a strange use of the word -- especially in a climate when an exec of a major stock company is paid $230 million for being fired. Some would dare to call that payment liberal. Others call it irrational conservative business polity. It is not health giving.

Recognizing rights of homosexuals is a liberal value, as it would be a change. Consigning them to hell in the name of religion is a liberal interpretation of scripture, which has no reference to homosexuals. Yet we call it conservative.

In legislative budgets, a tax cut is an expense. When one is elected one's language changes because the job changes. State funds become our bank account. We are elected stewards of the reserves.

We were about to use $9 million of our reserve on a tax cut and this senator complained pointedly to those close by. One said, "It is only 9 million, Lowen. Not a big deal." Words of a true conservative. We are elected to be stewards. Another responded to my jibes with "My people really want this." That is not management.

The double talk is common, understandable and humorous. Reagan was a strong president and an obvious example of a public symbol for anti-tax talk. Well, this citizen gave Reagan a good listen until he figured out his grand kids could not afford him. Reagan perfected the art of talking meanly about taxes while increasing the bills for the above services and passing the costs on as debt. His 'anti-tax' rhetoric included: "I believe that a country as great as the United States can afford anything it wants." We like that. Reagan was a great president because he drew citizens together in a tough time. However, if a family uses his words they are dysfunctional. 6-1

The role of religion in political decisions

This pastor never brought the church to the floor of debate and never felt the need to vote for the church. The bishop or the church did not once tell this senator how to vote, though we engaged in invigorating discussions. Strong dialog helps us think through complex issues. Moral training affects decisions, but it is part of who we are. Every person has a morality and bishops should respect that.

It also helps that the public is generally religious and surprisingly caring in tragic situations. It helps that we consider ourselves a democracy, where all have the chance to vote. The tired community organizer in a recent film told a mean-spirited cynic: "This is a democracy. The poor vote."

The finest public role for religion is to help build community, in all that it means.

Street sign in Rochester, N. Y.

God created us for community. We are born into family. We long for relationship, but it takes leadership to overcome the barriers. Christian, Muslim and Jew are peacemakers -- in a family, in a congregation, in the world. The Golden Rule is basic teaching in all five major world religions.

As we saw, Wilberforce, with the Christians and Jews, brought an end to slavery in England thirty years before we did in the U.S.

Religious liberty is more than the freedom to believe. It is also the freedom to let believe, even to listen at times. Religious liberty has to assert the great spirituality of all human beings while persuading them of better ways to make decisions, and to worship God.

From Rasool, a Muslim political leader:

> *The first victim of globalization, the first victim of the onslaught of science, the first victim of the onslaught of technology is often tradition, culture, and religious belief -- not because they are mutually exclusive but because they shake the foundations that we hold so easily; they force us to go back and find the relevance we need to present to the world. In the words of J. K. Galbraith, the Canadian-born American economist: 'The more uncertain people are, the more dogmatic they become.' This is because they retreat into the few essential truths that they can hold on to, and they become dogmatic about those few essential truths because everything else has changed.*
>
> *....... (Changes include: family structure, place of women, MTV, HIV/AIDS, our desired control of future generations.) ....unless we reinvent ourselves, we will not be able to speak either to women or to the young.... truly, the more uncertain we become, the more dogmatic we become.* I

A website (godvotes.org) claimed to inform voters on "electing God's choice in 2008." O my. The selections are their choices, not God's, reflecting their twist of scripture, their twist of candidates' words, their twist of Mormonism, their twist of who is immoral, their twist of what pastors think, etc.

All in red, white and blue. They sway many voters through this dishonest charade. It is deception at its worst, in God's name.

On the schools, much of the distracting heat along the way came from rhetoric. We have had quite enough shouting that others do not care about children. Or do not want multicultural education. Or are disinterested in quality education. Or that OPS teachers do not do a good job. Or that low-income schools are being shorted in funds. That is not only baloney, it contains flat out lies. Some of it was scripted by attorneys, in preparation for lawsuits. We have stacks of it on our desks, have listened to it read into our proceedings (for use in lawsuits), and have heard it on TV. 6-15

We know that if we do not provide education for children of immigrants it will cost us real dollars down the road. Not to deal with drug addiction today costs us dearly in the future. When we pay those big future budgets is it because we are conservative now or liberal later? Neither. We are foolish, rejecting the practical.

Both Hitler and Saddam would claim to be conservative, mandating tradition (and bigotry) in an authoritarian manner. When you kill people in order to change ideas, which label are you?

Let us quit using the terms as weapons. This senator considers himself a fiscal conservative, but will promote new ways of handling old problems. He will not call himself "liberal" at that time, as the term has been robbed of dignity. All of us speak of being open and of seeking worthwhile progress. 7-1

Then there is the "faith-based" plan of the president. Since we have had these programs for many years it is hard to think of them as new. All that is new is that now churches will be allowed to use government funds to gain members

Holy Name Housing, as a good example of what faith-based used to be and can still be, gives a clue it is religious by its name. It has done a wonderful community work for nearly 30 years. A corporation spun off from the church, its books are separate so a clean audit is done every year. The workers are faith based and giving tremendous advantages to developing communities. 1-11

5. The Unicameral Legislature

<u>Our democracy is representative</u>

A legislative guru, Dr. Alan Rosenthal of Rutgers University, described the brief course he was presenting to government teachers gathered at the capitol. He said we should shout it out: representative government works well in the United States.

In spite of all our gripes, our system is representative. We have a process for continuous and intense evaluation of laws. We have a fluid and vigorous exchange of ideas as we develop public policy. Plus, the process is not predictable lockstep -- results vary in the same body, on different days and in different years. The system is alive. Truly representative democracy is flowing, rather than rigid. 4-2

On representative government, he added:

People do not know the issues in most cases. One thing they all know. They would not want to be mistreated or abused in the way they might want others to be mistreated or abused. If they belong to an unpopular religion, they wouldn't want their rights to be disregarded and crushed down because people say their religion is violent, hateful -- ought to be stamped out."

The Unicameral has distinctive procedures that are in contrast to other states. We are nonpartisan. A senator does not need permission from anyone to file a bill. Every bill gets a public hearing, where the committee chair invites those supporting, opposed and neutral to speak. If a senator is curious as to how the public would respond to an idea that is not ready for prime time, drop in a bill and watch the ripples.

Since we have only one body to vote, we vote three times to move the bill on. The first two rounds are open to extended debate. Opening statements by the sponsors are limited to ten minutes. Other speeches have a five-minute limit and may include asking permission to question another senator.

In response to my weekly journal, readers have shown the liveliest response to the local color, the daily routine, the private exchanges of senators and staffs, and the human touch that holds it all together. This chapter will collect a variety of these tidbits recorded in "Krusing the Capitol".

Nebraska has excellent legislators. We have variety, like the state, and represent all kinds of folks, some of whom are 'hard working' and some are a bit nuts. We are all of that. The open debate is fair. Most are able to listen and dialog. 3-1

There is a true collegial feel on the floor. Though speeches, on camera, included some outrageous putdowns this was not the case as we dealt privately with each other on matters of strong disagreement. Public outrageous statements and bizarre untruths are a painful price we must pay for free speech. A wide-open debating society is an unusual experience. You can actually say what you think. However, expect a candid response. 1-23

A big lesson learned in the legislature: there comes a time to take a deep breath, ignore the shouting, and do what you consider to be the right thing. Then, give a pat on the head to anyone still hyperventilating. 8-12

On balance, public attitude has more weight than law. We are more likely to mow our lawn and improve the looks of our house because of the neighbors than because of law. We can change the feel of a neighborhood by getting two or three owners to fix up. Others will follow. The legislature is a taillight, not a headlight, with rare exceptions. We must wait for the public to support a law before passing it. Leadership comes in helping to educate the public on what laws would be beneficial.

The legislature is a jolly fellowship in many ways and we have good fun. Today in our private committee one bald fellow was chastised for playing with his hair when his hand was up late in a series of quick votes. Was he voting? When his hand came up again, the chair asked if he needed to go to the restroom. He said yes, ten minutes ago he did. "Well, then it is too late. We have to move on."

A lot of Catholics in the body. The joke this week: the new priest asked the old priest how he did in his first time in the confessional. "All right, but you could do with a few more 'Tsk, tsk' and a few less 'WOW !' " 1-13

Defending "States Rights"

A recent quote: "Federalism is fast becoming extinct." You do not hear the word much except in erudite political philosophy. Way back in 1800, John Adams and Alexander Hamilton were Federalists who believed in a strong central government, run by elite land owners -- the ones who could be trusted to know what they are doing. In fierce and sometimes intemperate opposition, Thomas Jefferson insisted on states rights. As previously noted he did not believe the feds should be allowed to do anything except defense without permission from the states.

Over the decades came strange ideas like interstate commerce, which eventually included an interstate highway system. Or pure food acts. Or regulation of investments, airlines, internet, broadband, or weights and measures. State rights have been slowly eroded by federal regulations. Make your own list.

It is a process to be expected. We grumble a lot about it in state government, but we are losing. The humorous current note is that states rights have been considered a conservative battle cry but corporate business and Republicans are taking them down. Corporate business does not want to relate to 50 governors, 50 legislatures, and 50 sets of lobbyists. The insurance lobby is asking for federal regs.

Businesses, understandably, want unified regulations. We know the erosion cannot be stopped. But all of us chuckle as a Republican leads the charge to remove state regs and a stalwart Democrat takes to the floor and cries out, "Who is going to protect the consumer? What is going to happen to the little guy? How are our rights going to be protected when the regulations go outside of the state?" 5-4

Lack of strategic planning

Thirty years ago, the writer was one of several who spent full time training the leaders of our churches to use "Management by Objectives." There are many congregations in our state which are still alive because they took that planning seriously. If you know and believe as a group where you will be ten years from now you will figure out the best first step this year, to effectively begin going that direction.

"Strategic Planning" is the current buzzword for it and successful businesses use it all the time. They establish a goal for the future, to which intermediate objectives will bring them. They know what to drop now, what to start next year, where to invest, where to sell off. However, in Nebraska state finances we are mostly trying to figure out how to balance the budget this year, without investment and without a dream of a better future. We actually voted against doing long range planning. Groan.

Some agencies have strategic planning. Our Department of Education shows plans and uses phrases that demonstrate they have a strategic plan. Most larger school districts, which are an extension of the legislature, know what is ahead.

Our huffing and puffing on water resources is evidence that we are trying to get folks together on a strategic plan. It also shows how difficult it is.

For several years, our Appropriations Committee asked that Corrections put in a strong drug treatment/mental health program for prison inmates. Most state prisoners have mental illness. At least half have serious mental illness. We "store" offenders for two years, on average, at $30,000 a year, with little treatment. The foolish reason was it could cost up to $5,000 to offer treatment. After their release, due to the illness, we soon put some of them in residential treatment, for over $100,000 a year. But we save $$$ this year!

We begged Corrections for a change, to get treatment going earlier, at a lower cost, and thus reduce future taxes. A side benefit would be to treat the mentally ill with more respect. A new warden and good support has brought forth a strategic plan. Wow. Families of addicts in this generation and taxpayers of the next generation will call you blessed. We achieved the planning only by pleading. 7-14

Partisanship

The writer has been an active member of both parties and truly appreciates them. If you are an independent you do not have the benefit of committed kibitzers. Parties provide a forum for comparing ideas and informed people to debate them.

However, the lockstep doctrinaire mindset of some leaders, in both parties, is a real detriment to good legislation -- and therefore to providing the best for our citizens. We understand that old-style leadership wants everyone in line, but that is not how it works anymore. Senators were told how they were supposed to respond to redistricting, a horribly partisan exercise, and to the governor's vetoes. It did not go over well with most.

The governor has a right to speak his mind, and we have deep respect for his ideas. But when his staff tries to force everyone to obey, it turns off staunch members of his own party and he will pay the price in the future.

In north Omaha, Independents will be the swing voters in future elections, as they will be in most state elections. More and more, voters look at the person. A party endorsement will be as much negative weight as help. People perceive that the religious right has taken over the Republican Party, and that the Democrats will be reactive to that. Both attitudes are a turnoff to the public and reduce the credibility of the candidates.

Both parties claim to be for the little guy. A few candidates are, but do not believe it, unless the little guy can afford a lobbyist.

Reactions to partisanship come through loud and clear in the legislature. Most who register R or D are thinking the same way as an independent. Part of it comes from the seismic shift in party stands. When this fellow was a Republican we stood for fiscal caution, no debt, and freedom of individuals. Now the national Republican position is nearly the opposite on each. The same story happens on each side, as parties are dynamic and do change. The "general" public is confused by the changing party statements and is frankly dismayed when a good candidate turns out to be a party creature.

Ugly political ads are aimed at only 5% of the voters. In this new tech world is there not a way for the rest of us to get on with our lives without seeing the demeaning insults? At least half of attack ads are baloney. You can see it coming when the victim is pictured in really bad light, with a face not even a Mother could love. Twitching eyes and despair are written across the forehead. Baloney is small bits, ground to disguise the source, and repackaged with other bits of unknown origin.

The most annoying ads are the ones where you know it is false. Three colleagues campaigned for other offices this year and were trashed by ads. One Republican, two Democrats, each of whom we have come to know as exceptionally well qualified, experienced and committed. We have no question about their integrity even when the going gets tough.

Each has been trashed for 'raising taxes,' as one example. The correct language would be 'voting tax shift.' We have worked to protect property taxes, which then forces other taxes up. The total budgets have been held level. These con artists tout a "raise" from one part and ignore the other. It is plain dishonest to select your statistics while ignoring the truth. Scaring folks with carefully selected bits is unfair to baloney. 4-Oct

Worse, following a national election we are victims of endless creative trashing by the party that lost. They are disingenuous in spinning any good action into the beginning of the end. It is dishonest, self-serving, and the best evidence the public has to distrust all government.

Remember what the Clintons were called in a national campaign when they came to office? “Serial killers” led the list. The same two guys are now dreaming up similar charges against the Obamas, leading off with foreign birth. Republican leaders say it is nonsense, but there is enough anti-government feelings to fuel attacks on any president.

Making far more sense than partisan posturing, an email from "A Taxpayer" came with this message: “I pay taxes in order to provide necessary services and I would rather pay more taxes than not have necessary services." When we emphasize necessary services, many quiet folks feel that way. 2-A

Airing tensions

Bad blood and past hurts can boil between a few of the lead senators. At the worst, we were seconds away from a bloody nose or two. Shades of the Territorial Legislature! There are back room fights that should stay there.

Many times we watch a senator speak eight to ten times on a hopeless cause, without any real resentment on the floor. We have an open debating society, which brings out humor as well as outrageous statements.

We have genuine respect even in very sharp differences. This week one senator pleaded: "I laid awake last night, trying to think of some way to get you, my colleagues, to understand what a terrible mistake this is." Since this was his fifth time to object, we irreverent types in the back row said to each other we laid awake last night trying to figure out how to get him to sit down. 1-21

Corrections has had large cost increases in the last fifteen years. So the legislature decided to close a minimum-security facility, with the assurance that those who would actually be released were good inmates, have served real time, are in for nonviolent crimes and can be safely released.

Well, the governor and team acted like it was the end of civilization. Called the plan absurd and said the legislature voted to put 500 criminals on the street. That is an out and out fabrication.

It got worse. Our Appropriations Committee was accused by the governor of breaking arms and stifling debate "in order to force the body to do what senators did not want to do." Not even close to what happened. The kind word for all of this is "incomprehensible." This citizen never knocks his governor or president. He is my governor, my president. This kind of statement simply does not make sense. He must have had an overload of dill pickles. 3-19

Chambers plays one of his games

The interesting reaction this week from inside the capitol is related to Senator Chamber's bill to prohibit hunting, fishing and trapping. He became quite animated in opening the hearing on the bill, motioning to each side as he exclaimed "<u>stop</u> that fishing, <u>bar</u> that hunter .... <u>protect</u> all our fish, birds and animals .... " Big smiles. Free child fun.

It is all a ploy of course. He wants us to vote unanimously against this bill, to prove that there is absolutely <u>no point</u> to a proposed constitutional amendment to protect fishing, hunting and trapping. Most agree. There is no point to it. Hunting will <u>never</u> be prohibited in Nebraska. The amendment would add clutter to the constitution, diluting the noble purpose of such a document. However, a few of the public are so noisy we will do it to get rid of a nuisance: irrational fears that unknown "liberals" are out to take away our freedom.

The most interesting part is the emails we receive. Several have asked us to oppose his bill. The easy answer would be to agree and sign off. However, this senator responded that a vote against the Chambers bill will prove his point, that their constitutional amendment is not necessary. If advocates really want the hunting amendment they should try to get at least a third of us to vote for the prohibition, so there is a threat to hunters -- and they could raise a pile of money to 'protect' their members from a phantom.

In my childhood home we could hunt, to provide food for our household just as our ancestors did. We now have a wild turkey hen residing under our deck, close to food (bird seed) and water. Why not shoot it? Why are there laws standing between us and food? The natural flow of increasing population creates restrictions, giving rise to the fear that the wild unfettered west may be taken away. Sorry folks. Get over it. Omaha was a frontier town for only 20 years.

Surprise People

Every job has plenty of deadening routine, including the job of pastor. So this pastor greatly enjoyed the energy of a couple in love, young or old, yearning to be married. Naiveté helped. The world sings for them and the music can be felt. No mountain is too high, no river so raging, that they could be blocked from guaranteed happiness. Loved it. You hope that your assistance in the planning will not reduce the glow from their joy-filled idealism.

We have a few idealists to brighten our days at the capitol and they do inspire. Most advocates of interesting bills know some mountains are very high. Removing the death penalty is one example where hopeful persons face the odds. Senator Chambers has introduced at least twenty bills on the subject.

After all these years, and with countless defeats, old timers still come with energy and young timers have the enthusiasm to stir the pulse for one more look at very emotional issues. The star witness at a death penalty hearing, for example, was a man from Oklahoma who spent 19 years on death row before the court reversed his verdict on new evidence and declared him innocent.

We cannot imagine what that would be like. We do not have comparable experiences of arbitrary life and death by which to learn. How would he define "patience"? Or "justice"? What thoughts has he had about trust or human error? After 22 years in prison, he has been virtually blocked from normal enjoyment of marriage and children. He is a surprise and his challenge is a gift to our thoughts and feelings.

8-4

We have a parade of fascinating, challenging individuals, often little known. What a privilege it is to meet them in that tall-steepled office building.

Campaign Baloney

Persons of faith want to depend on integrity in officials. Here are ten candidate lines you should not trust:

10. "I am more pro-America (than my opponent)."

'Twas the leading line of Duke Cunningham, who was willing to sell out "American" interests if he got paid enough. After saying, "John Kerry will depreciate our intelligence services in a time of war" he sold intelligence to one of the companies that bribed him. How many lives did that cost?

9. "The only reason he says this is to be politically correct."

Not. Being 'politically correct' is the politically incorrect thing to do nowadays. The phrase is used as swear words, divorced from original meaning. If being over the top p.c. is the argument, for example, against a women's rights issue, it is probably the only (pathetic) argument the candidate has. Sadly, using the label has proven to be an easy vote getter.

8. "Family values are threatened by my opponent."

(Many ways of saying that.) Baloney. Find one leader who opposes family values, does not want a moral society, does not care about holding families together, or does not see a connection between personal values and the way our country goes.

7. "My opponent is against the best interests of our country."

False on the face of it, but it was the opening line of one Richard Nixon when he first ran for public office in California. He won, even though there were many who noted from that line he was tipping his hand on his lack of integrity.

6. Whispering sweet words like --

"I will work for the Blue Skies Act." That was the name of the act to clean up our air. The act actually lowered air quality standards.

5. "The senators/congress/legislators are too spineless to do the right thing." Spine is seldom the problem. When you can't get the legislature to do what you want, that line sounds bold, making you a true leader. My favorite: we are accused by letter writers of being too spineless to oppose wasteful spending. That would take spine?

4. "Limiting funds is limiting free speech."

There is not much free about 'free' speech that was bought for a million bucks. Public complaints about out of control campaigns are one of the remaining clear expressions of free speech. We are in a hopeless mess.

3. (Pick one from each list):

Equal rights/Equal access/Nondiscrimination -- **favors** -- Hispanics/Africans/ women/gays/elderly/low income persons.

2. "My opponent lacks integrity."

Said in several different ways, the assertion is usually said by those who lack integrity themselves. Takes one to know one? No. You do not have to be a criminal to recognize crime. Rather, we project our anxieties, fears and sins on others.

Integrity is too valuable to misuse. My integrity is essential to what I have going for me -- in home, family, community, and legislature. Lose your integrity and you are so diminished as to lack punch when you really do care.

1 1/2. "This is a Christian country."

The person saying that is either naive - which is unlikely for a candidate - or "pulling the eagle's tail" as my debate coach would say. She graded down anytime a student used a line like "I love America." Easy to say. No real meaning in a political context. Or "tax-paying parent – who is not? "Hard-working" is another fluff word, as is "Christian" in political talk.

Which kind of Christian we are talking about? Christians range from those who want Palestinians killed so that Israel is triumphant so that the end of the world can come -- to those who think God does not love you if you are not born again -- to those who seek to live out Jesus' most-used instruction to his followers: care for the poor. These can be mutually exclusive, as when you have an unsaved Palestinian who is poor.

We do not live in a Christian nation. Never have. Pilgrims tried that and folks soon looked for escape. We find no evidence that Jesus would have killed off the Indians or supported slavery or helped dictators overthrow elected leaders in eleven countries in the last thirty years. Right wing groups even sell books trying to document the "Christian" fabrication. In a new book, Newt Gingrich is "outraged" that Christian teachings and churches do not receive more governmental favor. Aside from his faith stance, he does not document any reason why Christians should be favored.

1. (Drum roll) "I will cut taxes."

On the face of it, not true, as no one person can do that. No one. Carving a bit off rates while increasing the budget in anticipation of increased receipts is not an honest tax cut.

Public costs go up. Most state and local budgets have very little fat. Some have none. The Feds have fat, but really do not want to give it up. Our larger state departments, such as corrections, health care and education, are under funded and cannot be realistically reduced. The rates may change, but the total bill for all taxes and fees will go up. Guaranteed. The actual basic cost is going up.

This line is to be distinguished from carefully honed language, as "I will look for ways to cut expenses and gain new efficiencies." Every elected official should do that all the time, so the words can be honest. If we do not fight to hold down taxes we will be swamped.

There is the ten. You are welcome.

Absolutes sound reassuring

Be wary of absolutes, such as 'every person with health care' or 'no child left behind.' They can be a helpful challenge goal but are never a believable promise. "No Child Left Behind" began in the 90s as a worthy goal - what we should obviously strive for. That is a legitimate use. Also legitimate is rhetoric that challenges us, such as: every American should be respected, have access to health care or receive a quality education. It is the promise to fully reach that goal soon which is suspect.

Absolutes come in many forms. A dangerous one, in public discussion, was the absolutist call to arms to get tough on crime, throw away the key, etc. Absolutist hype has never worked for long and cannot. In this case, it fills jails, takes money away from prevention, makes the public more angry, skews serious dialog, and causes a loss of respect for the law.

Our national prison population is the highest in the world! Our system is flawed. When we question absolutes we can talk about the solution, gain more insights and develop a more informed public consensus -- which has more effect on crime than any other factor.

Following are political pronouncements which carry warning flags, flying high.

As, "Flip-flop" politicians are what are wrong with our country. At the same time we place value on politicians who will listen -- and change to our views. So which is it?

Or, people who favor a smoking ban are against my freedom and therefore un-American. The problem is that secondhand smoke is deadly and costs us tons of money. Then we have the small matter that it is the duty of American government to provide clean air and water.

Or, the minority who oppose the war oppose democracy, in which the majority is right. We know better than that. Democracies can become harsh dictatorships for the minority. Iran is the closest to being a democracy in that region. Can we live with that and will we fight for that democracy? The disruptions come from politics and passion. Hopefully, we can someday sort this out and give honest support to those who care about freedom.

Or, leaders who say people have a role in global warming should be driven into the wilderness. They want us to ignore clear evidence of warming (from any source), which leaves all of us on an earth where life conditions are deteriorating. Such talk avoids thinking.

Or, "Give people what they want.... to do as they please.. Reject restrictive laws." Sounds good but then private choice preempts the public common good. Even the Lone Ranger cared about community.

Or, a person driving drunk is expressing free will and does little harm. We have, for example, "He causes less harm than an undocumented worker, who puts a load on society." This is particularly offensive, since the drunk is costing us big time and the worker is actually paying more in taxes than he receives. Among issues that we can do something about, abuse of alcohol and other drugs is the heaviest cost hit on our society.

Or, supply and demand set (gasoline) prices. To believe that, we would have to believe that those running the companies are stupid. Not likely. Prices vary as much as 25 cents between villages and 20 cents in a day. Gas prices go up and down even while the cost of production remains stable and no one is running out of gas. Prices are set by profit plans and driven by stockholders who want what the market will stand.

Or, consumption is our greatest power in our economic base. The people have great power -- much more than their capacity to eat. We have more power if we carefully examine what attitudes we slowly assume without question.

Or, fiscal conservatives have fiscal responsibility. Or, the opposite for liberals. Neither is to be believed. Clear-eyed fiscal responsibility comes from well-informed planners with experience. 7-D

Or, the world is going to pot and those who do not think so are the enemy. This simplistic view gives evidence of a very limited sense of history, ignoring:

• the basic values expressed in most governments,

• the higher quality of life created by diverse cultures, and

• the dramatic changes in rights of women and minorities in the history of many developed countries, including our own in the last 200 years.

We have miles to go, but we have come a long way.

<u>Our majestic capitol building</u>

The Omaha World-Herald asked the author to research and describe the capitol -- a welcome assignment. The following contains part of what we learned from that.

Nebraska has a rare gift: our magnificent capitol building. The combination of bold design and superb artistry was unique in the 1920s, and today shares an elite place in national architecture. It is handmade, from stone to cabinets.

Several fortuitous conditions came together for it to happen.

If attempted 20 years earlier, there would not have been the technology and equipment to construct the tower. Twenty years later, too few stone hand craftsmen were available.

If Thomas Kimball, nationally known Omaha architect, had not managed the bidding eminent architects would not have responded. The winner, Bertram Goodhue of Philadelphia, trusted Kimball and submitted his dream building.

Without Kimball's reputation we would have a copy of the national capitol, as other states were building. Local politics used local talent. That process blocks bold plans.

The tower required steel, a newly designed product, in place of the usual cast iron. Without Dakota sandstone bedrock the tower could not be supported.

If Goodhue had not contracted with four exceptional thematic consultants/artists, the stunning progression of art would not be.

The "Roaring Twenties" allowed the legislature to be brave. The body authorized $5 million in 1919, but when they saw how grand their capitol could be they doubled to ten. Today no state could afford to build it. (The current 10-year renovation is $57 million.)

A national-level natural history scientist was amazed when he saw the mosaic evolution ribbon entwined on the floor of the rotunda. The World-Herald reported earlier that a current expert wondered who got the early sea creatures right 75 years ago, when few knew. The answer: Dr. Barbour, a researcher right here at UN, knew and shared his drawings with Hildreth Meiere, the New York lead artist for the new capitol.

One of my favorite stories to tell fourth graders who come through is how Meiere and her recruits ground and fitted the thousands of pieces of white Italian and black Belgian marble in a warehouse in New York City, transferred them to large sheets of brown paper, then slid them onto railroad flat beds. The artists came to Lincoln to unload the precious cargo from the tracks, which came right up to the edge of the rotunda. (A gap in the west wing allowed rail cars to bring in the heavy stones.) We are gifted by artists and workers long gone. Mosaics in recent years had to equal or surpass a high standard.

Professor Barbour included little known and long extinct sea creatures in the sequence of God's creation. The endless ribbon goes on to the woolly mammoth, which was probably hunted by Native Americans. So the art story touches us. All of this surrounds massive circles, 11 feet and 15 feet across, and panels nearly 20 feet long. The theme is creation of water, fire, earth and air, surrounded by Mother

Earth in the gifts of crops, children, Garden of Eden, mountains and rivers.

Surrounding all of this, including fresco reliefs of the outside, are "interwoven themes of history, law, religion and human accomplishment," as the W-H put it. Included are labor, virtue and the "noble life." In the north hall are more recent colored mosaics of a blizzard, plowing, tree planting, railroad and building of the capitol, all in rich detail. We are skimming past winged angels, Moses, the history of settlement that surrounds the top of the chamber in gold relief on mahogany, and the chamber's random-colored pillars to represent a pluralistic people. (The designers were very aware of our diverse cultures through the early fights between nationalistic groups.)

Art in the capitol

What a prize location we have in our chamber. The senators sit directly beneath the beautiful gold-leaf fresco of Lewis and Clark. Thirty feet above our heads is a mahogany wall, six feet high, setting off the large ceiling. Lewis and Clark have fifteen running feet of the stimulating artistry.

On the large beam supporting the ceiling over my head is my logo. Imagine, my own personal logo, in gold. This is the familiar old lion emblem, from European roots, walking on rear legs with fierce talons stretching from its paws, and a split tail, with a knot tying the split ends. My name, Lowen, means lion, so this mascot is a really old Lowen. He has been in a few frays, had his tail split, but does not quit. Just ties a knot in his tail and keeps going.

The artistry in the capitol is truly exceptional. Quite a few Greek artist nude figures are in the floor mosaics, which often draw stares from fourth grade boys. Girls are not as surprised. Adults note that diets were not in vogue as a Greek priority. The capitol presents all ages with a bit more understanding of the cultures of the world.

When this writer was younger he did not think that much about the tremendous value of the arts in our lives. If any of us had been raised in an unpainted cement block room, with no pictures or windows, with no music -- add other possible arts deficits -- each would be a very different person. We would have figured out how to grub out food and clothing, but caring about the community would be thin indeed. It would not be a happy scene. Art changes who we are.

6. Taxes

Purpose of taxes

"Gracious God, thank you for taxes and for a community willing to band together to mutually provide services to our people."

Taxes are a blessing, good for us. Taxes are a welcome help in our lives. There. You have a politician saying what some claim no politician will openly admit. Granted, this fellow is a geezer who will never run again and is not counting votes.

However, this geezer is passionately interested in the public good. Put simply, people of faith should be grateful for the ways to buy what we need.

Some basic needs are hard to buy where our family lives. We live in a North Omaha community of 50,000 people -- larger than Grand Island -- with no hardware store, no clothing store, only one "dinner" restaurant, no movie house, no office supply, no computer support, no auto dealer, and on.

Now let's think about what we can buy. With taxes. Roads and streets. Police and fire protection. Good schools, from kindergarten through graduate degrees, including training in the trades. Clean air, and good water to drink. Sanitation, sewer and indoor plumbing. Tested measure at the gas pump and the meat counter. Trusted ingredients on cereal boxes. Traffic lights to protect us.

Regulations that provide attractive parks and prohibit unattractive businesses. Control of banks and businesses so they cannot do whatever possible to take our money. Planes with licensed pilots and a universal worldwide code of airport safety. Delivery of our mail, around the world, with international protocol.

Wow! Look what we can buy, right here in River City.

Plus, consider the list of state responsibilities: University system, state colleges, community colleges, K-12 local education, special education subsidy, state patrol, court system (including parole and probation), prisons, health, human services, Medicaid/SCHIP for low income children, Medicaid for seniors in nursing homes, aid to low income students to get them on an education track, public assistance, mental health supplement, Medicaid for disabilities, property tax aid to low income seniors, aid to cities, aid to counties, aid to Educational Service Units, a governor and constitutional offices, a legislature and 45 agencies.

Do we want regulated giant corporations? Regulated local liquor stores? The neighborhood kids to have an education? A system that will train and keep some students in Nebraska? A strategy for a flu epidemic? Drug and crime watchdogs? Speed limits? It's all taxes. We are grateful for public servants (interesting word!) who carefully manage our public money. 6-8

Someone grumping about taxes pointed out that we do not set the fees for the above and we do not know what some of our tax bills will be. Quite true. It is also true that we do not set the fees at the gas station or grocery store. We do not know what our next electric bill will be. Certainly, we can look at the price before we buy, but as these are necessities and we will pay the bill whether we think it is fair or not. We can change life style and buy less gas, but we can also change life style in order to pay less taxes.

Do taxing authorities need watching? Yes. Accountability is in short supply, especially on the federal level. That is a separate question. We want the services but we must be ever watchful of the manner in which they are provided.

In summary, the anti-tax rhetoric of a few is tiresome, dull, and plainly off-point. They luxuriate in soaring words of self-praise about being better than "taxers" but have not one specific 'entitlement' they are willing to let go. Pay your bill, fellow.

Taxes are our business

An important lesson for all: we tax ourselves. Senator Tyson had a reputation of being the most conservative voter on the floor. He liked that. He had a rich round loud baritone way of voting "NO!" that always brought a chuckle.

The Northeast Community College, in his town of Norfolk, was in a desperate way. When we set up state aid, with a cap on budget growth, the college was at a low point. They grew fast, but had to cut or limit good programs, even vital ones, to be able to survive. So they wanted three years to catch up by using a higher local tax, then go back to the same levy cap as everyone else. Makes sense, and some of us voted for it. But it got nowhere.

Senator Tyson pleaded with the body for these citizens' right to tax themselves. It is a several county unit and all senators from that area joined in.

Listen carefully to his words. "This is a great need." "We are only taxing ourselves." "Education and economic development will be seriously crippled if we do not act." "Our businesses and people are ready to act." 3-16

Every one of those statements applies to almost every tax issue on the floor. We are only taxing Nebraska. Not Iowa. The need is great. Economic development will be hurt if we do not act. Yes. Yes. Yes.

A pain in the head is the tax "relief" mentality. "Relief" is a spin word, created by an interest group. They influence earnest souls to assume taxes are like a headache, and one must find relief. The challenge of paying taxes gives appeal to such language. However, when we think that way too long we screw up the process, miss some real opportunities and actually raise taxes.

So let's think about "tax assets." We all manage assets and if we listen to those with experience we can do that very well. We can avoid poor long-range choices and get creative.

Tax assets include funding for schools, roads, police, fire, courts and prisons, and health services. We do not want relief from any of those. We do want creative, efficient, community-planned management. 5-20

The community keeps changing/adding to "rights."

We now agree to "rights" to services which we did not accept earlier. A very conservative senator, speaking on services at the Beatrice home for disabled disadvantaged persons, recently said on the floor "When persons are helpless they are our responsibility." None questioned it. Why? The community agrees it is a "right."

Really? How did that happen? It did not used to be that way! A helpless person was the responsibility of family, friends and neighbors. We have shifted cost from the neighborhood to the total community. It is quite understandable and even commendable, but we raised our taxes when we changed our thinking.

Some even call the new policy "God-given rights." As we will see in the chapter on rights, there is no such thing. The only rights you have are what a government body agrees to. A baby born in Darfur has no right to services. The above senator's statement represents a lot of tax money. We have changed our collective mind and now we agree to pay, to declare a 'new' right.

That is one example of dozens of "rights" the community decided and expects the legislature to fund. This may or may not be the best way, but the decision is made. The people have decided it is the best way, so the task left is how to do it well and efficiently.

Thirty years ago, if a child was born mentally retarded we told the parents, "You have a problem." Now we say, "We have a problem." Free instruction for children was always in the Nebraska constitution, but we ignored it. We are still new at it and frankly are trying to figure out what that means and how to do it efficiently.

Special education was $150 million in a recent year. Since we have 1 million taxpayers in Nebraska, that is best understood as $150 per taxpayer -- a goodly sum. That figure does not include Medicaid payments for the health of many of these children/adults, over 7,000 of whom are wards of the state. They are our children and we have all the bills. We are not able to cut a single dollar from special needs costs for the coming year.

That is why taxes go up. Tax watchers are a helpful lot, generally, but they would rather cut back agencies than the real spenders. If we took an unreal 20% cut across the board on all state agencies (except corrections and human services where cuts are only delays) and include a 20% cut for the governor, attorney general, etc., plus the legislature -- nearly all the functions of state government -- we would cripple ourselves and cut only a total of 1 cent of every dollar. The high cost is not there. 7-7

The community also wants services that help us work together to be more efficient. Examples follow.

Which government funds help the neighbor in difficulty? Housing is one that pays. Douglas County helps 1,400 families a month to avoid homelessness. What if we did not do that?

Government policies greatly impact movement of people, employability, and opportunities. Quality preschool costs half as much as job training, is ten times more effective. Older worker programs for ex-offenders save us money. Reach out to employers. We add 2,000 ex-offenders per year and 60% of employers reject them. So: retrain, certify quality, expunge record (for public access) after so many years. Get them back to productive life.

The times they are a'changin'

Public attitudes are changing. My generation wanted a job with a stable employer. Now over 22% of our work force are working as free agents. Would older folks rather be free or safe? Give us safe. Would we who are older rather work by the hour or by contract? By the hour is safe. However, the movement is to contract.

Some people like being employees. At least that is the rumor. Not baby boomers. They liked globalization. Carl Camden, University of Illinois center for HR management: "Globalization is a new word, but it not a new concept. It began 60,000 years ago when the first migrants walked out of Africa and still maintained old ties. Only .03% of the U. S. workforce lost jobs in 'offshore' in 2004 and 05."

In the last decade immigrants helped start one in four new businesses in the U. S.

Plus, your job will not exist in its current form several years from now. ATMs replace bank clerks. Globalization has had a small impact on the social contract. Technology, on the other hand, has permanently eroded the semi-fixed nature of work that enabled the old social contract to function. And finally, the rise of the free agent workforce and their new perspective on work challenges the fundamental desirability of the old contract.

Add to these shifts the coming tsunami of tax problems: roads and health care. Other parts of the world are competing vigorously in transportation. We invest only .3%. China is preparing to go to 35 times that. We are status quo on essentials like roads, which receive little increase in funds as they compete with all other interests.

The task of taxing

Taxing is exceedingly hard work. We have a most intriguing competition of self-centered interests -- of gaining benefits and preventing pains. The bottom-line question is how to be fair. Special interests trump fair.

As an example of competition, on one bill, with all other options apparently closed, the stage was set for the fun part: how do we broaden the sales tax base? Nebraska now receives $1 billion in sales tax and there is another billion available. We need only 1/20th of that, so you can see it is easy for anyone to say, "It surely does not have to be me."

What should we tax?

- Repair: a combine, or a lawn mower, or a car?
- Install: a furnace, or a roof vent, or a camper top?
- Professional service: a lawyer, or an accountant, or a dentist?
- Construction: remodel or new, corporate or personal?

A lawyer noted that taxing lawyer services would bring in too much money, so that is not feasible. (Smile) One by one, more serious comments sought to protect each interest.

A senator held up items on the floor and illustrated our inconsistencies. Tax a sheet of paper? Yes. Which is made into a newspaper? No. Made into a book? Yes. Into a monthly magazine? No. Into a magazine-type journal? Yes. 2-11

A quiet in-joke going around the floor: "Let's adopt the governor's budget and go home early." We know his budget would not work for all, but those it favors contact us to essentially do that. It is tempting. The budget is the legislature's. It is our job by the constitution. The recommendation from the governor always needs more exposure to the broader group, for a test by the people. A letter to the editor says our "tax more" senators just do not get it. All they have to do is pass the governor budget. O my. It would be fun to avoid our work.

My wife took two 20-year-old garments to her tailor friend in Lincoln. So, this husband went to pick them up. The tailor said there would be no tax on Ruth's jacket, but there would be a sales tax on my trousers. Naturally, this created more than the usual interest in an apparent sexist abuse of males that might be uncovered.

She said Ruth's jacket was a repair, trying to get it back to a previous condition. The zipper did not work well. For my trousers, she said, she had to "manufacture an expansion" on the waist and manufacturing is taxable. To my amazed "But, but..." she replied by pulling a tax code from under the counter and flipping the pages in my face. "It's in there. I had to talk with someone about it."

Well, one recently trained in tax law had a response: "My trousers were being returned to their original condition because they originally fit me." Sadly, she is not a lawyer, and simply follows instructions. Can you imagine? Not only does one have to carefully manage expansion of assets, but also he has to pay taxes on it. Is nothing sacred? 2-10

A reader objected to my calling our present tax cut an "expense." He said it is simply returning a taxpayer's money, which rightfully belongs to that payer. That is an interesting point, and one often stated in the political season. Not accurate. It is not your money after you paid the bill, either to the government or to a car dealer. We are elected to manage the funds, which have never covered all the legitimate bills. We have to find funds to pay for a tax cut. 6-13

One speaker urged that we cut school districts and universities by 25%. "How?" He did not have a clue. "Just do it. Be bold." That is unthinking, not bold. Another thought teachers' salaries could go down or that class size should go up across the board. "Just do it." Sorry, in the real world our salaries are low and class size is studied.

Tax increases reduce economic production, which reduces taxes, so increase is to be avoided. By far the greatest future cost, larger than all of the above, will come from future costs of present drug and alcohol addiction -- especially when we send addicts to prison with no treatment there, to learn crime from professionals. We are headed to huge costs in crime, corrections, lost production, family breakup costs to Medicaid, and on. That is the painful crunch we have. We take money away from economic growth to pay for drugs and alcohol.

A big personal disappointment came from within the business community. Business people generally support economic development and items critical for us. Development has helped our businesses, helped North Omaha and helped the state. But this week they would not step up to the plate at the governor's request, for a short-term loan from 'their' fund when we have a huge budget problem. They said they could not stand pain, but that state employees and low income people could. So we will have to add over $20 million more to tax increases.

The governor's plan was to delay a portion of the payments on tax incentives, extending the payback period from 8 to 10 years. Man, such a howl. O.K., then come up with another plan. Their answer? Raise sales taxes. Do not spread them to lawyers services, just raise them one half cent.

The plan was quite beside the point. They would not respond to a clearly pro-business governor who was desperately trying to avoid tax increase. That is extremely disappointing. They are better people than that. 2-10

Good news. The problem areas of our state finances are few in number. They are:

- more prisoners every year
- more elderly in nursing care each year (5% annual increase)
- local school costs keep rising, and we are still low in salaries
- Medicaid for children is rising fast
- health insurance rates are killing every budget

The bad news: those items account for 56% of the budget. We are trying every way we know to reduce all of the items (except the number of elderly!), but they will still go up and of course cancel out a major share of the cuts we can find in the other 44%. In a nutshell, that is the budget dilemma. 3-7

Note: in 2002, Nebraska was in a very difficult budget crunch. The major threats to our economy? Drought and grasshoppers. The state was in a similar financial crisis, in the 1870s. The same two reasons dominated the drag on the economy. What happened to all our high tech advances?

Tax shift

Total taxes will not come down, for reasons that will be obvious. We are talking the entire base. "Taxes" here includes all state and local taxes, fees, health insurance, and licenses. When we cut one group's taxes, someone else's will go up. High private rates in nursing home fees are partly because you are subsidizing below-cost government payments to nursing homes. It is a tax shift. Health care premiums also subsidize the government's failure to pay its bills.

We are paying for all health care, one way or another, and our bill is the highest in the world. We are 38th in quality of care, so that is not where the money is going. It is a dysfunctional system, in which we give excellent care to some and pay for the uninsured in very expensive ways. Silent tax shifts cost $$$.

In Nebraska, we deliberately give relief to property taxes, to give local governments room to do what is needed. Nearly one billion of our state budget (38%) goes to property tax relief. Property taxes would be (on average) 50% higher if we did not shift. One can see the recent effect of that in a comparison of the proportions of totals in 1994 and 2005. This includes all Nebraska tax for state and local governments (does not include fees, which of course are also taxes).

Income taxes	26% and 32%	(1994 and 2005)
Sales taxes	28% and 29%	(")
Property taxes	46% and 39%	(")

So we have evened it up a bit. Is that good? No one cheers.

President Bush pushed through "Leave No Child Behind" (NCLB) legislation, with long-range effects. Since it is clear that education is economic development we generally support his initiative. Put another way, leaving children behind in my district is costing the state big time. However, the price tag of NCLB is steep.

Two teachers in large "core academic" classrooms (one to be a paraprofessional) was one startling requirement. Who pays for that? State or local? (Feds promise to kick in about 18% more than now, but that clearly is not likely and will not pay the bill.) More tax shift.

Prioritizing is a tough job, since the items are so diverse. All items are necessary, in one way or another. For example, the state constitution requires free education to all resident persons between 5 and 21 years of age. That includes aliens, low income, retarded, and developmentally disabled.

When we reject persons for Medicaid, where does the cost go? To the counties. County board members are very frustrated when they get these persons, because first, most counties do not know what to do with them, and second, they pay 100% of the cost while Nebraska pays only 40% if federal Medicaid pays the bill.

Health care is a strange area. We come close to having universal health care. Those out of it are males and some women, 40 to 65 years old. All over 65 years old are covered. Mothers and children get covered, if low income. Mental health is covered, by federal law, as a county obligation. Disabled persons are usually covered with Medicaid. Any soul, by federal law, can go to an emergency room free, which as noted above is a drain on local taxes.

If we put everyone on Medicare we would save a ton of money, but we would have to increase payments to providers, as they currently subsidize Medicare.

Shall we tax 'sin'? The proposed $50 million from cigarettes (@50 cents a pack) should be a slam-dunk. That is not because it is fair, but because we are desperate. The state cost of cigarette use is very high, <u>and</u> it will reduce the number of teenagers who get hooked on the habit. A few of us hope to push for $20 million from alcohol, to help cover the over $200 million deficit we have from alcohol abuse – a good chunk of public funds. Do not hold your breath.

Levy caps are thought to hold down property taxes. Not usually. We would be better off trusting local control, which is a powerful force for local responsibility on levies. We found several examples where taxes will come down if caps are removed. Several jurisdictions levy the cap when they do not need it. The local people do not argue, since the cap sounds conservative, but the levy is more than needed so funds are stored for the future while board members think up ways to use them.

Worse yet, some schools are deferring maintenance until the building starts to crumble so they can go for a renovation bond, which is easy to get. That costs more taxes in the long haul. Plus, a few small districts are really in trouble, as there is a freeholder provision by which large landowners can prevent a levy override vote. People find loopholes.

Senator Warner instituted the caps in a clever move to even property taxes (raising some) and said it should be removed in two years. That was in 1996. 3-8

We had a recent tax shift but the media finds more public interest in the increases than in the reductions. They talked about "Increasing taxes" and "more spending." Not one reported cutting taxes more than we raised taxes, which is what we did. For the two-year budget we are reducing property taxes, through school aid, by $200 million. We raised taxes by $117 million, to pay for the property tax cut. We cut state programs by $215 million in addition to that to pay for the rest of the cut and revenue loss.

That is a tax increase? Talk radio was going berserk with their skewed 'facts.' The public talk is downright dishonest. We shifted the tax base, with less property tax and more sales and income tax. That is desirable. But where is that reported? How will the public understand the facts when the talk is spun negative?

We must admit that countless farmers, business people, lobbyists and educators have stepped up to the plate with us, openly said it is the right thing to do, and thanked us individually for taking the heat. My staff reported over 50 phone calls on one day, plus nearly that many emails which they gave me. Mostly citizen support. Five of the total opposed what we were doing, but it was obvious from their phrasing they did not know this was a shifting of the base, not an increase.

It is sad when these false statements scare people. One person was worried about how she could pay for the extra tax. The average household decrease is $100. It is cruel and totally unnecessary for this poor soul to worry. She probably listens to the radio. Sigh.

The World-Herald editorial says the senators are acting cravenly, are ineffective and undisciplined -- can't do the job and knuckle under to special interests. That is plainly not true. The tax shift was essential budget management.

Those campaigning for office want something to talk about, so we voted out a package that cuts every taxpayer by $1.75 per week for the next three years. Please be sure to put that into the economy or we will not reap the immense ripple benefits. (Later note: the "benefits" were not detectable.)

You are waiting breathlessly to hear how we did this. Keep breathing. We cut $250 million over the next three years. We will get $120 m. of that by adding to the property tax. (Isn't this fun?) We hope that the economy does better than expected (don't forget the cycle from the tax cut) and give us $130 million in <u>more</u> taxes. Well. If there is a problem, take it out of our savings account (from <u>taxes</u>).

My cynicism shows because this is ridiculous. In fairness, the package had an excellent spread -- even increased Homestead Exemption limits, to help the elderly avoid those property taxes.

A friend asked his work shift, on break at a manufacturing plant, how the state should solve its problem. Unanimous: raise income tax. He found it amazing. It would apply to them. They understood that if a business chooses not to cut services it has to raise the rates.

Unfortunately, those who pay the most income tax have lobbyists and the poor do not. So we lowered income tax and shifted the cost to sales tax, which is paid more by the poor. Every faith group would object, but to no avail. 3-3

Have you noted that we Nebraskans collect (state and local) taxes at the rate of $3,077 per capita but we spend at the rate of $7,231 per capita? What a deal. Getting that second figure takes tedious wizardry, since no state has a single treasury and all those governmental units do not report what the Feds give them. That is partly why projection/guessing is used on more recent years and why you can find different tax rankings for Nebraska. Some are plainly dishonest, but they give quotes to folks who want that result. 6-11

<u>When cutting taxes is not a cut</u>

In view of all of the planning above, it is maddening to have a local board cut necessary services in order to appear to save a few dollars. A small example: every adult in Nebraska pays $400 per year to fund the problems of teens getting alcohol. Each adult pays $200 a year for drunk driving costs. That adds up to over $1,000 per year for a couple. Cuts to local services will increase that $1,000 in the future, while not helping now. Yet we praise those who cut.

From last year's state cuts, a caseworker reports she has cut off aid to the family of a disabled child, to assist in care. The mother will have to quit her job (reduces state income) and put the other children on Medicaid (adds to costs).

In another case where work-to-welfare benefits were removed, the single mother has to quit her job and go back on welfare in order to care for her children. It is particularly painful because this mother was excited about working and has been studying to improve herself, but does not yet qualify for a salary that would pay for her childcare. We did not allow enough time for her to get a certificate, so we lose.

We are already seeing an increase in emergency room care -- doubled at some hospitals. That is a very expensive way to deal with an infection but the poor have no choice. Instead of the state paying 40% of a physician visit (perhaps $30), the county must pay 100% of an emergency room visit ($500?). If a county does not pay it, the cost pushes onto private-pay bed rates, increasing health insurance costs.

A few leaders wanted to cut taxes by eliminating the med intern program. The interns provide the medical staff for our low-income clinics, some pediatric care and a good amount of Medicaid care. It would cost several million to replace them. Plus, counties are required by federal law to serve certain children. Their added costs, which go on property taxes, would be well over $3M. 2-A

Mix in with that a real shocker. We have all heard that cutting taxes boosts the economy. We are told that every day. How many times have you been told that increasing government spending boosts the economy, by the same rate? Research shows very similar effects. The key effective factor is the dollars in the economy, and research shows only 26 cents of a tax cut dollar goes to the economy. So (the Feds) do not cut taxes by 10 billion. Improve the infrastructure by 10 billion and you have long-term benefit plus an economic boost. Fiscal conservatism at work. 5-D

Future budgets are far more scary than the present year. If we do not make serious changes we will be in huge trouble within ten years. Put another way, our present increases are due in large part to not making changes 5-10 years ago.

Those saying "Cut, Cut, Cut" -- like a chicken trying to cackle -- think they are in opposition to those of us who overrode the governor. Not really. Most of us feel more strongly than they that changes must be made. Real changes. Our difference is they want to do it for now, by not paying our bills (as we see it), and a goodly core of us in the Legislature want to make long-term changes in systems as well as tax structure. It simply must happen or taxes will go up after we are out of office. Whatever our politics, we stand together on it. 3-22

Universities and colleges will cover some of their loss by increased tuition, but we may lose our museum research, for example, which is the heart of Morrill Hall. Artifacts that are gone will not be back, and millions in research grants could be lost as well. We will lose students, who are very quick to detect changes in quality.

When adding money cuts future taxes

We heard back this week from our medical research institutions on how they used the $10 million we gave them last year from the tobacco settlement $$$. Wow!

The four research systems are the Med Center in Omaha, Creighton University, UNL, and Boys Town Research Hospital. With the year only part over, they have obtained well over the ten million in outside grants, and have recruited and employed 73 persons, including about a dozen top researchers who have been "stolen" from labs in other states. Strategic planning works. 3-6

About 3 out of 4 women in prison have mental illness. For youth in both state and local, 2 of 3 under 24 have mental illness. Further correlation shows 3 of 4 with mental illness are drug- dependant.

Untreated mental illness exacts a high cost on our society. Incarcerating a mentally ill person increases the problem. Jail was never intended to be our public psychiatric service, but we seem to be in a mode of wanting to avenge their behavior. The mentally ill are more likely to be arrested, will receive stiffer sentences and are less likely to receive treatment for their illness when we jail them. If we treated them while they are with us, we would find it a good investment. Plus, one wonders if we train our guards on the best ways to interact with the mentally ill.

The Fetal Alcohol Syndrom request referenced earilier was for $500,000. We reduced it to 20% of request because we do not have the money. No business would make that foolish cut! 6-9

There is another startling fact that affects our budgets big time. A comprehensive study of underage drinking in Nebraska shows that our cost for this activity is $435,000,000 per year. Can you think of anything we could do with that money???? Should we invest in prevention? 1-17

The dilemma of the week: we had over twenty citizens come to our hearings to state where we are missing the mark in prevention, in education, in caring for the desperate. Most of them had excellent ideas and centered on money in order to get our attention. They had their evidence, track record, and future plans well in hand. One group would, with $1 million, return $3 million in savings three years from now, and keep that up.

On the high end of investment, one group will return ten for one. They will provide dental care, with inexpensive coating for teeth of first graders, which will save millions in health care. They will recruit and train more volunteers from the community to care for mentally ill in their homes rather than in institutions.

They will help prevent grade schoolers from drifting into drug use, which is one of our biggest gaps in public policy (and for which we have few programs). They will start drug treatment in prisons, where about 55% have serious mental illness. This program would be near the beginning of the offender's sentence, which would help successful ones to qualify for parole and get back to our communities and to jobs. Now we are talking real world!

Citizens brought similar solid plans by which we could save millions in guaranteed future tax costs. But we do not have the front-end money. We are not talking about programs by starry-eyed idealists. These are proven programs in other states, done by our neighbors with a good track record. However, we are told the public generally is saying, "We do not want that. We would rather have an income tax cut." That is spin. Only a few wealthy want it. The rest know they will benefit from what comes to the state economy. 7-9

For example, the new tech campus at UNO is going great guns. They are successful in recruiting students away from Cal Tech, Stanford, and MIT. By providing exceptional staff and equipment, this new enterprise is rated by some as the best high tech campus in the nation. We do not want to fool with that.

Basic strategic planning will save tens of millions. Lack of a strategic plan is why taxes have increased on such huge problems as drug and alcohol abuse, and child abuse. They will go up in the future. There is no way to cut loose from paying those bills if we do not prevent them. 7-14

Our grumpiest vote this year was to pay for operation of our new prison at Tecumseh. It was a terrible mistake, in our current judgment, but well supported in the 90s by both senators and people. Law and order. Lock 'em up and throw away ye old keye. Well, that kind of thinking will cost us $20 million plus in operations every year from now through the end of our lives.

Why your taxes will go up

Our taxes have been going up. They will continue to do so when you count all the costs. We are not talking about levies or rates, as they can vary or seem stable. Ignore tax shift, in which one tax goes down and another goes up.

When we talk taxes, any politician who promises to reduce taxes overall is a liar or a fool. The bottom line, the total we actually pay in local and state taxes, fees, licenses in all forms, for roads, schools and universities, prisons, agencies, disabled, health services, and public assistance -- is guaranteed to go up. Take a deep breath and let's have some final plain thought about taxes.

The state is the focus of the book, so this will ignore federal tax. There are four items which have caused the major tax increases of the past ten years. None are operating funds, where some persons naturally assume there was expansion in good times. Not true. Our increase in basic state governing was about 2 1/2% per year, below the inflation rate. Our total increase in budget was nearly 6% per year.

No one has come up with a way to cap a single one of these four budget busters. Public attitude is a major part of the reason each is so costly. Together, we could clearly reduce these costs. However, stubborn refusal to change or strong feelings about each of these four items prevent major legislative change.

1. Drug and alcohol abuse is the major reason public costs go up.

As a society we have yet to say, "We don't do drugs." That change would make a huge difference in costs.

A meth lab is discovered. Police put in overtime to track it, do surveillance. That's just the beginning of cost. We lodge the offenders in prison for $30,000 per year. We lose the income and sales tax which a productive citizen pays.

It gets worse. Over half of drug users have a mental health problem. A child with mild depression, untreated, will usually "self-medicate" – which is finding and using a drug to stop the pain. Then this youth gets hooked, drops out of school, goes to Kearney for $40,000 a year, and yes, pays no taxes as a productive citizen.

We have taken many actions to cut those costs. If the depressed child is low income, we provide medical care through Medicaid and save a ton of money down the road. If the adult offender is "only" an addict, which half of them are, we can provide treatment for $5,000, through diversion, in place of $60,000 for two years in the pen.

2. Education is labor-intensive and is complicated.

The major increase in state budget during the 90s was in Special Education. A little secret 40 years ago was that retarded children are citizens, guaranteed instruction in our state constitution. It took us until 1990 to accept that "every person" includes the disabled and the mentally ill. The good news is we did a major fix in the 90s. Special Ed is very expensive, and we are still learning, but the major increase has been taken.

What is left is teachers' salaries. We rank 44th in the nation. Yes, we can and will do efficiencies, but does anyone claim we will be cutting staff compensation, which takes up to 85% of a school's budget?"

The public piece on education is parental involvement. Twenty students in a class is a challenge, but if two of them are troublemakers, whose parents excuse them and avoid teacher contact, that class production is cut way down. The two take more effort than the twenty, which forces smaller class size and drives cost up.

3. We have more elderly in Medicaid care.

The annual increase in the number in nursing homes has averaged 5%. Can Nebraska reduce the elderly population? "Thin the herd?" There is no plan to do so! (The lie that federal plans will do that is just that: a shameless lie.) Does anyone think we can cut rates by 5% every year? That shifts cost to the private pay residents in homes, who are already carrying too much of the state load. Nationally, we have cut Medicaid cost increases from 13% per year two years ago to 4% this coming year. But we cannot hold it to that in the future.

The public simply has to get over the thought that nursing home care is an assumed right. Most citizens should get long term care insurance or prepare in other ways. We could give a tax deduction for premiums and save the state part of the money.

4. Corrections – prisons/courts -- are part of #1, but there is more.

The number of Nebraskans under some part of offender supervision is 1 in 44. No nation in the world is that high. The cost is huge. In one year, while we were cutting everything in sight, corrections went up 12%! We are chopping children off medical help and sending the money to prisons. It is total frustration.

The public can help by being more supportive of parole efforts. We are not thinking about releasing violent offenders, or dangerous persons. That reaction is ridiculous. We are talking about offenders who will be released in six months. Release them early and give them parole supervision. Don't dump nonviolent prisoners on the street as they jam out (come to the end of their sentence), with no place to go. We win two ways: save real dollars by reducing prison time and give each offender a counselor to help make the transition. Persons of faith have major investment in these issues.

Ex-offenders are not welcomed in the community, which adds greatly to corrections expense. It means they eventually go to old friends and are back in prison. We find that 85% of their children are headed for prison. Look at what we are doing here. We are banishing from the basic community anyone who goes to prison, for whatever reason. Like an ancient tribe, we assign them to a group of outcasts.

The corrective? Before they are released the community can make a friend, plan for support in transition, locate an employer who will hire a good recommend, and let the family members know they have encouragement for their part. If every church in Omaha, for example made a friend of one prisoner a year, we would save lives, enhance families, and do taxes a great favor. We have employers very open to this, but they are not going to advertise it as then the prejudiced public will hesitate to patronize them. We have twenty organizations in Omaha, for example, that know what to do and how to do it. However, the public must become involved.

Strategic planning works. Serious minded planners can effect tremendous savings over the present way of doing things. We are working hard on long-range solutions. The road will not be easy, but costs must be reduced.

7. Senator Chambers

Senator Chambers -- gifted and complex

Senator Ernie Chambers is a legend in the unicameral and in Nebraska. His gifted mind and fluent speech dominated floor discussion for his 38 years of service. This chapter will quote many examples from the writer's perspective, recorded in his journal from the final eight years of that career.

Front and foremost, Senator Chambers earned and deserved the respect of his colleagues and of thoughtful citizens. Most of us felt his attentive friendship off the floor and appreciated his perspective on complex issues. He was genuinely the "champion of the underdog" as his byline proclaimed. With his trademark T-shirt uniform, he traveled the state to meet with persons who had been sidelined by society. His biting commentary on Black issues often was a necessary reminder to those of European ancestry of the legacy of slavery and its continuing effects.

Second, Senator Chambers was trained in law, knows Nebraska law inside out, and truly appreciates well-crafted legislation. He studied every bill, which is an impossibility within normal working hours or in the first years of service. It takes years of study to skim bills for the nuggets. He worked full time, year around, on behalf of all citizens, and confronted the remnants of slavery that we still accept.

Additionally, he was trained in using the rules of the legislature by an old master, Senator Terry Carpenter, who was brilliant and manipulative. Their mutual admiration was quick and strong. The writer married a Scottsbluff woman, so could tease her family about "Terrible Terry." During one election period, the exchange with Dad Bob was as follows. "Are you going to send Terrible Terry back to abuse the rest of us for four more years?" "Oh yes." (Bob, not a supporter, was deadpan in his replies.) "Why?" "It is over 400 miles from Scottsbluff to Lincoln. You have to kick dust pretty high in the air to be seen in Lincoln. He does that, so we will send him back to you."

There is even more distance between cultures. A Black senator has to kick dust pretty high in the air to be seen in Lincoln and across Nebraska. Senator Chambers did that full time. Ernie is a good man, but he does not trust authorities or the police or prosecutors one inch. Those of us who live in Black neighborhoods understand that, as almost any law that is written to control white folk can be used to pile on to black folk. Ernie told us about that, daily.

Third, we must also state that Senator Chambers, on the floor and in his newspaper column, sometimes was outrageous and shameful in his rhetoric. He called himself the "King Cobra," ready to deliver the final death strike.

The Catholic Church was a special target, but "the Whites" and "All of you" in the legislature shared the spotlight as targets of his vindictive slander. Most of his hate-filled statements were not true, deliberately so. They hurt others, and hurt himself, greatly crippling his effectiveness. He could stop most any bill but he could not get his own bills going without the threat of blackballing several others. Terribly sad, but true. Senator Chambers could have been an even more exceptional leader, as he was equipped for greatness.

Senator Chambers was a product of the Civil Rights struggles of the 60s, when he was a leading spokesman for the new Black Pride movement and for action in Omaha. His election following that decade of tension, riots and political ploys was testimony to his worthy representation of "his people's" anger about continuing prejudice based in slavery.

Continued slavery was expressed in demeaning treatment at work and in the community, and embarrassing trickles of public help that demonstrated an assumption by white power that Negroes were fools. It was an awful time and he lived it. Chambers has never moved past resentment for past hateful actions, and he should not move past pointed barbs about the continuing smug condescension for Black persons by several leaders.

The sad disappointment on the floor was that he showed little personal change during his career. His rhetoric in the 70s is phrase by phrase identical with his words years later. This writer's frustration is not the result of studied insight. It rises when, in the same week, we hear Senator Chambers repeat word for word his fiery rhetoric from when he was an angry young man in the Black Panther sixties, and then feel the contrast as we join the circle of the African-American Achievement Council where Black leaders, with equivalent passion, speak to our current situation.

The two worlds are on a continuum but are now a different time and audience, with new images in speech. My black neighbors are not fools, but Ernie's rhetoric allows shallow, intellectually lazy European-ancestry leaders to continue to make prejudiced assumptions. 7-17

Senator Chambers has a well-developed philosophy of public service. In the Omaha Star, the Omaha Black newspaper, he stated how he felt about being elected to office.

> *A public office does not exist for the benefit of the one who occupies it. It is a public trust that carries obligations and responsibilities to the public.*
>
> *The office holder serves his or her constituency. But people need to understand that 'to serve' does not mean to serve as a slave -- that whatever people tell you to do, you must run out and do it. I'm not a puppet. I'm not an echo. And I'm not afraid.*

In running for the Legislature, I made my beliefs clear and told people they were commissioning me to use my intelligence, to inform myself on the issues, to gain knowledge of the system, then to exercise my best judgment. It is not my role to reflect ignorance on these matters." 4-8

We become quite frustrated with those who make strong statements on behalf of God. In a poem, Brother Chambers took on persons who know they are right and who do not want further input, with religion as their protection against thinking. His words are a bit of therapy.

In the realm of "**Saith the Lord**,"
Room should not exist,
For the well- or evil-meaning
God's intent to twist.

One may argue, "God meant that;"
Another, "God meant this."
If God meant not either one,
God's true thought both did miss.

Thus, when one spouts what "God meant,"
It's pretty clear, confusion'll
Demonstrate he's all mixed-up,
Fanatical and delusional. 5-1

Our constitution is to be protected

Senator Chambers is offended anytime we trifle with the constitution and he is correct in that. He resists a vote for change, and has filed over 30 amendments this week to stop an attempt to mess with the constitution. Since there is nothing of substance to amend in this proposal to guarantee (forever) the right to hunt in Nebraska, Chambers uses his ample imagination to have some fun. Here are a few of his amendments. To keep it simple, the words in parenthesis begin each resolution and the phrase is his proposed amendment.

(Resolved, that we guarantee the right of....)

...trapping trappers.

...hunting for a way to defend and protect the Constitution of Nebraska from frivolous amendments that would clutter, demean and trivialize it.

...hunting for the wreckage of Amelia Earhart's airplane.

...hunting, running, jumping and sweating

...hunting, creating, recreating, conversating and procreating

...trapping moonbeams and daydreams

...hunting an end to religious strife and intolerance

...hunting for Noah's Ark

...hunting for the link between Noah's Ark, Joan of Arc and Archimedes

...fishing for the secret, if there be a secret, behind the enigmatic smirk of the Mona Lisa

...hunting for weapons of modest destruction

...hunting and supporting Big Red Football

...fishing for compliments

...hunting for and trapping liberal Nebraska Republicans

...hunting for world peace

...hunting, laughing, crying, sneezing... farming... scrounging, dancing (53 in all)

...hunting and sitting on the front porch on a warm summer evening, drinking a glass of cold lemonade, dreamily watching the silvery moon rise to begin its journey across a darkening velvet sky powdered with stardust.

Hey! Do <u>any</u> of that, before it is prohibited. 5-9

<u>Affront to Chamber's aide</u>

Senator Chambers has an aide who is a black woman, has been here for many years, and is fairly well known. But a staff member near the legislative chamber did not recognize her. One of the lobbyists saw it all and reported what happened.

She approached this clerk, asking for a form. The person appeared not to understand and asked her what she wanted. She asked again, but did not get the form. Another aide came up, as she stood there, and asked for the same form and was handed it. Chamber's aide asked her what words she used to be successful. It was the identical question she had asked.

She was upset, told Senator Chambers, and he came on the floor, steaming, to ask for personal privilege. Old timers around said they have never seen him so angry. He said white men may not stand up for their women, but in the Black world every man feels it is his duty to defend any one of their women. This was his aide and so he had a double responsibility to stand with her when she was a target of offense. He was very plain about it, as one might imagine, and said as he was signing off that if any persons resented his message or style that he would be pleased to step into the hall with them and to translate it into communication they would not misunderstand.

Even in quiet senator talk, no one found fault with these comments. All were amazed at the insensitivity of the incident. Subtle racism is like that. 1-8

There is more to the story. The "offending" staff person is an older man who said he simply could not hear what she was asking in the noisy rotunda. Quite possible, but the mix of cultures adds to problems of hearing. The clerk, his boss, said he was considering an outside investigator for the matter. Chambers was unimpressed with those responses and gave several examples of the slights which Blacks experience as they try to go about normal routines. 1-9

Not even the student press would report the Chambers incident. However, the following week Chambers began a pattern of filing an amendment on each bill, speaking about the incident, and then withdrawing the amendment. By the time he had done that six times the press had a story and did go back to cover the original incident. Only then could we move on.

Fun with Ernie Chambers

The legislature was tied up in amendments on a bill, replacing sections. One amendment was so complex no one knew for sure what it did. Chambers wondered on mike if "Parson Kruse" could sort this thing out for us. The 'parson' responded that he was too busy writing a song about it. (Chambers writes a poem for us most days.) He has a lot of free child and lit up with joy, asking to have it sung.

So the 'parson' began to sing: "The foot bone connected to the head bone (pay attention, that was no mistake) and the head bone connected to the thigh bone....." It was a fair satire on the disconnected amendment. Chambers loved it and said he would come up with a name for that back corner of the room. Some time ago he christened a front corner the "Culture Corner." We hoped our corner's name would have something to do with virtue, but others asked for a curmudgeon title. 1-12

Chambers asked the body if he could go with Parson Kruse to his church on Sunday, April 1st. Said he wanted to go to the front, confess all of his sins and claim to be washed clean by Jesus. Then when the congregation all shouted "Hallelujah" he would shout back "April Fool!"

The Parson responded he would be pleased to have Chambers go with him to 'his' church, but this particular congregation would not know what to do with someone who confessed all their sins, so were not likely to give him his straight line for 'Hallelujah.'

Chambers greatly enjoys these free-child moments, but something serious is also going on here. The exchange documents his rigid caricature of the church. He feels all Christians are hunting scalps for Jesus. Most congregations do not include public confession, nor do they focus on a public emotional conversion experience of 'being saved' (as his pastor/father did). Congregations are putting their major energy into serving the community, as their expression of being faithful followers of Jesus while indeed nourishing the spiritual growth of their members.

The Speaker, in making announcements upon adjournment, mistakenly said that at the Omaha televideo site "Senator Chambers will lead the Omaha Chamber of Commerce team." (The Chamber is his mortal enemy.) Brother Ernie was speechless. For one minute.

1-18

Chambers tried to sideline a Kruse bill on final reading. It involved funding for local transportation of the elderly and handicapped and Chambers assumed it would help those nasty Roads people get more money. When Kruse stated that was not the case Ernie withdrew his blocking motion.

With a flourish. He stated on the floor that Senator Kruse had drawn and quartered him and he had to give up and withdraw. Chuckles all over the place, because he had not retreated from anything for a long time. Kruse's seatmates turned to him in mock amazement. "Lowen, how did you do that?!" Response: "Ernie is subject to the secret prayer of a truly righteous man." 4-13

Joke of the week: Sen. Chambers, warming up to the attack on anyone opposing his bill: "I am going to say what I think, even if the governor does not like it." Really? News flash! 7-6

New word: pleonastic, which is using more words than necessary. You can be sure this senator will be using 'pleonastic' on the floor. Dare we create a new religion: Pleonasticism? And assign it to Senator Chambers, to fill his proclaimed gap in personal religion? 6-5

A typical rant on (Roman) Catholics

It was hard to find civility on the floor this week. (2002) Chambers went on a tear, trashing Catholics, schools, FBI, and lots more -- and the governor's people used plain blackmail to prevent veto override. Aside from that ugliness we made some progress.

Most of us do not say much about Senator Chamber's rants, because many times his cause is right and the Lord knows Black citizens have much to be angry about. But this week he was out of control. Old timers say they have never seen anything like it.

We prize a free forum and are strongly committed to that -- free for every one of us. Any of us can make outrageous statements or talk about a peeve that is far afield of the subject at hand. But the rudeness hurts us all. We are committed to not being a censor, but how do we walk the fine line? The public will not understand that we have no answers, in a free and open forum, for someone out of control.

Senator Chambers threatened to extend the session to Christmas ("not to New Years, just Christmas") to discuss (discuss? -- we will not being saying a word) Afghanistan and the Catholic Church. They are connected in some sinister way. 1-20

He chewed up quite a bit of time one day on the Catholics, who he said were behind the move to prevent cuts in scholarship aid. Two of the 18 schools whose students could get help from the fund are Catholic.

Discussion on the issue in the Appropriations Committee centered on the thought that we were raising tuition and that expenses for college are going up, so we ought to at least keep the same funding for the neediest of the students. There was no talk about Catholic schools. The vote was unanimous.

Chambers asserted that the four Catholics on committee pushed it through at the instruction of the Vatican and they are just pawns of the church. Well. Five of us clearly were not pawns of the Vatican and we voted for it. We heard a lot more about how bad the church is, how anti-black, anti-poor, anti-education, and in general how repressive of members and the public at large. We have heard it all by the hour.

This time Senator Nancy Thompson stood to make a quiet and powerful speech, about how she had not been able to get jobs because she was Catholic, and was discriminated against in other ways, but that she had never been so abused for being a Catholic as by Chambers and it was time to say so. That was the first response to all his statements during these months. We handle him with silence.

Well, Nancy broke the dam. Foley spoke next. He is the one person on the floor assumed to be put there by the Catholic Church and he was raging mad. Called Chambers a bigot and said Catholic-bashing was the new form of bigotry. Engel followed in a more temperate way, but was very pointed in noting despicable behavior and attitudes directed toward (Roman) Catholics.

It was getting to be a Catholic parade and Parson Kruse feared that the Protestants would appear to be giving silent approval to Catholic-bashing. So he spoke, saying he had not ever expected to represent churches on the floor, but now was the time. Silence by Protestants ought not to be considered quiet approval of these shameful remarks, by anyone.

Chambers had told how Sacred Heart would not allow black kids in their school in the 50s, so the Protestant Parson then updated some of the values of past Catholic witness and work, which is considerable, and brought it back to the present, in which we have absolutely no evidence to support the unwarranted Chambers attack.

The national Catholic league issued a statement calling Chambers a bigot and asked him to resign. The local Diocese did not respond and said on the side they did not expect him to pay much attention to anything that they said. The rest of us stated it was time to move on.

Chambers stopped the filibuster when the floor agreed to a compromise on the figures. Without one vote to spare. This senator's vote was not there. There is little percentage in giving in to bullies. Ernie was apologetic later in the hall. So we will move on. As an aside, it is puzzling that we should even consider balancing the budget on the backs of needy students -- who we desperately need in the work force. 1-B

Other unwarranted insults

Chambers handled one of us in such an insulting way you will not see it in the paper. A senator wrote about him in a newsletter, in a negative but fair way. He punished her by not letting her bill be considered. That is unworthy of him and of the legislature. As noted, we value the open debating society we have. We have agreed that anyone can say what he or she pleases, and he has made use of that more times than we can count. "Open" is for all. He will hear about it and will feel the sting. 2-12

One freshman was startled when he tried to get a bill sent back one step so he could amend it to kill it. We really went around on it and Senator Chambers insulted him a couple of times. It involved whether state troopers should inspect school buses. (We said "No.") The new senator heard from a retired trooper, an expert who said they found serious problems on their inspections, in spite of two other inspections.

Chambers lampooned this so-called expert, wondering why the Pope and President and several others were not calling on him if he is so smart. The freshman responded to the bait, which other senators have learned not to do, and plainly said he did not think we had to belittle public servants in order to do our business. Chambers replied our new man was too thin skinned to appreciate humor. 1-4

Senator Chambers punished us one day, with lengthy harangues on Catholics and Israel, because, he said, we would not pass his bill to ban employment discrimination on gay persons. Small problem. He would not let us vote on it the night before, when we were running out of time. We had the votes to pass his bill. But he refuses to limit debate and, by the rules, he is the only one who could request that we stop talking and vote on it. Strange logic. We refused to go back when the needed votes returned.

Chambers had an amendment to remove some obsolete language, left over from the six-day war in the 40s, which authorized Nebraska banks to buy stocks in the "new" Israel government. It was obviously no longer necessary and several of us supported his motion. Nearly everyone would have. However, most did not vote for it because he was using it to do a tirade about anyone who supports Israel. Which includes "<u>your</u> President" in case you wondered. Well, too much yammering and it did not pass. So we were punished some more for our sins against him.

It would help if senators agreed to his reasonable proposals, but Ernie puts out enough smoke that a few lose track of the point and cannot be sure of how to help him. 2-14

We generally avoid comments about Senator Chamber's egregious attacks on persons, churches, and institutions. However, this week's tirade was particularly shameful. The man went out of his way to insult, one by one, name by name, key leaders in the Omaha community whose loyalty to and generosity for public endeavors is unquestioned: Walter Scott, Warren Buffett, David Sokol, Richard Holland, Charles Durham, Susie Buffett. The attack had no merit and no truth, was denigrating and cleverly demeaning -- to them and to all of us who are grateful for their leadership.

Ernie threw in one of our finest senators, an educator who has given his career, his energy and wisdom, to provide heartfelt caring for every kid in our schools. Are these the finest and most generous persons in our community? No. They would say there are many more. These corporate leaders have set an example of community support for which the author is profoundly grateful. We have a <u>remarkable,</u> exceptional city. Omaha has made amazing changes because of their leadership.

Their offense is they oppose his bill. Well. The diatribe had nothing to do with our quest for a workable solution and clearly diminishes his authority in the field. Enough on this one. To comment is to advertise it, but to be silent is worse.

"Controlling" Senator Chambers

Time for a little more fun. Senator Chambers has 19 bills in this (limited) special session -- more to come. One declares that being Senator Chambers is a class one felony. (Penalty is death.) That is because, as he points out at length in the bill, he is so brilliant and the governor is so annoyed.

The governor very foolishly said he wanted to handle lethal injection in a special session "So we could control Chambers." O my. That is throwing red meat to a hungry wolf. Chambers loves it and is determined to prove that he cannot be controlled. We already knew that. Our money in this personal duel is on Chambers. But why drag us into a personal feud and waste our precious days?

Chamber's strategy is to overload the system, which is easy to do in special session, with only one general subject. It is much more difficult to do in general session, where we sideline what we do not like and go on with something else.

For example, every bill must have a hearing. Therefore, he will file 20 bills, with sometimes only two words difference between them. Plus, on the floor you can eat up the clock by hopeless motions on pulling each of those bills which are killed by committee. He, by rules, can speak for 20 minutes on each motion. Plus, on the floor you can try to amend any bill with one of the killed bills, with the straight-faced assertion that it had a hearing. Or you can "gut" a bill and try to slip something else in. The methods for wasting time and making everyone anxious as the clock ticks down are endless.

Senator Chambers stalled enough other bills at the end of the regular session that leaders had to pull the lethal injection (death penalty) bill for the year. He hates that bill and he could permanently delay it by taking extended time on other priorities.

He started on Tuesday by dividing a comparatively simple amendment into 15 parts, then filing several amendments on Part #1, and drolly announcing that "We will be taking a leisurely stroll through this very complicated bill." Two full days later he said he was ready to wrap up Part #1 and would prepare amendments for Part #2 for the next day. Very few people can pull this off and fill all the time with comments about grammatical errors in the text. But he can and he does, running out the clock. 4-9

<u>*Clash of two large-antler bucks*</u>

The reader probably has a stubborn friend. Or two. We senators have two exceedingly stubborn friends on the floor. Senator Foley brings a fetus to every bill he can, whether it fits or not. Senator Chambers objects, whether it matters or not. Thereby we chew up a great amount of time, with no production.

The fetal issue is important but it is not the real point of debate. Also, it is not as important as some other agenda, especially when the two men are deadlocked and are simply wasting time waiting for the other to collapse. Their competitive ways prevent action on some "real life" issues. We will not complete our work on preventing child abuse, slowing down the death and mayhem from alcohol impaired drivers and getting critical support for troubled kids. All are about persons, all are life, and all would prevent harm. But all are delayed for another year.

Both men are a little bit right and a lot wrong, with no interest in listening to each other or to be in dialog. It is exceedingly frustrating, and a lesson to all of us.

Foley says life begins with conception, which in recent years we grumpily concede is an acceptable basic premise. But that is not his point. He in effect diminishes the birth day by angling to build a case to also make the fetus a "person," a complicated legal term. Most of us think the birth day is a big deal. Life becomes independent at birth. Eventually, quite independent! The census counts a newly born baby.

Chambers says being a person begins at birth and Foley has conjured up an extremely complex plan to make a fetus a person. Law has literally hundreds of references to "person" with assumptions of personal decisions, rights, and responsibilities. Few could apply to a fetus. Chambers correctly asserts that the "fetus as a person" campaign carries great mischief.

So, Foley attaches fetus language every chance he gets and Chambers enjoys a field day in challenging it. Neither wins any points or converts any minds. However, time is abused and some critical work on life issues is set aside. An example follows. 4-13

We were aghast at the response from both men on an amendment. It was all win-lose. Neither can abide the thought of the other winning. Foley was extremely foolish to throw down the gauntlet and start a victory speech on a small vote. Chambers was overreacting, as he could stop the bill later as easily as he had now, without threatening other necessary bills. A threat that was mostly smoke a month ago can become reality when we are down to the last days.

A senior senator, with choked voice, urged the men to respect the beautiful work we have done in a tough year. Our speaker's negotiation is our usual way of getting past an impasse, and though we grumble at the speaker we always back off and let the process go forward. However, these two men refused to budge.

Other senators pleaded with Foley, as we stood in the aisles during Chamber's next speech, to pull the bill or move for cloture, which would end the debate. He refused, saying that would give Chambers a token victory. We said not taking the bill back hands Chambers the victory, as the bill is dead. Pulling it away maintains dignity and gives base for life another day. "No. He must not appear to win." So we were forced to adjourn for the year, killing all the other critical bills which were being held up for action on the last day. 4-14

For six years Chambers has been trying to get a break for low-income people on auto insurance -- that they should not pay three times as much as the rest of us because of where they live. And for six years the insurance lobby has kept him tied up with studies, postponements, and continuances -- anything to prevent action.

This was his week! The major amendment passed without a negative vote and it became apparent the bill would do the same. So, for his closing, Brother Ernie went into a lengthy thank you mode, a la the Oscars, thanking everyone but his mother. He thanked those who stood by him, his staff who prepared endless re-writes (each by name), this fellow and another senator for help on the home stretch, the committee (which had been the one who turned him down so many times), the leadership, his generous colleagues.... etc., etc.

This was too much. With a few winks and gestures around the floor as he spoke, we set it up to all vote "NO." The front board lit up a bright red, like a Christmas tree. With his one green. He gasped, then grinned and we all switched. Simple, but fun. Especially for our very own Ernie. 1-13

We will close with a poem from Senator Chambers, a craftsman with words.

On the playground, in the sandbox,
  With her little hand,
Little Lilly built a castle
  From the moistened sand.
    First she scooped and then she patted,
      Formed and shaped each part.
    When the castle was complete,
      Joy engulfed her heart.
To the grown-up eyes of cynics,
  Who, in judgment stand,
Lilly's handiwork was merely
  Shapeless mounds of sand.
    Who said every miracle -- must
      Be a noble thing?
    Who said every miracle -- makes
      Each heart soar and sing?
Too it is a miracle -- how
  Life's reversals can
Transmogrify angelic Child
  Into embittered Man.
    Let the sweet Child build sand castles,
      Play at Blind Man's Buff;
    Stand aside -- for LIFE will level
      Castles, soon enough . . . . .

"Transmogrify" is the genius work here, and the reality which startles. "Miracle" is the mischief maker. Transmogrify means to transform in a bizarre or unexpected way. The embittered man was a sweet child. Was the radical change a miracle? Or was it of <u>our own making</u>? Life has many miracles. Do our votes mess with the Creator's plan for miracles of health and wholeness?

160. Intriguing insight into a lonely Nixon, without dependable friends and wanting to be included.

8. Rights and Entitlements

Rights

We have fighting words in legislative language. Among them: "Every person has the right to food/shelter/health care." "Some people treat food/shelter/health care as an entitlement."

These two words are thrown around in the press, in the legislature, on talk radio, and in grumps between neighbors. What do they really mean? Over the past year the author has asked for a definition from many groups -- including senators, immediate family, staff, a class at church, and collections of erudite friends. No clear consensus! In general, we agree it is a basic right if I want it for myself, and a nasty entitlement if you want it.

So, what is a right? It depends on who says so, who will guarantee it, who will defend it, and, if needed, who will pay for it. In all cases what counts is actually the consensus of a community -- a local, business, professional, or governmental community. A 'right' can quickly become a contest of loud voices in a community or council. Rational thought, even a bit of it, is in order.

Try the dictionary.

Right - "Something that is due to a person or governmental body by law, tradition or nature." (Nature?!)

Entitlement - "A governmental program that guarantees and provides benefits to a particular group."

Clearly, 'entitlement' has the best focus. A child in Nebraska is entitled to a free education. Simply be a child and you have it. Guaranteed. It is in the Constitution. More on that later.

And a right? The United Nations Declaration of Human Rights says every person has the right to food, clothing, shelter, medical care, security of person and education. However, we know the 'right' depends on a community to provide it. Is a denied right a right?

Our Declaration of Independence declares a God-given right to life, liberty and the pursuit of happiness.

> *We hold these truths to be self evident (!), that all (men) are created equal, that they are endowed by their creator with certain unalienable Rights, that among these are Life, Liberty, and the pursuit of Happiness -- That to secure these rights governments are instituted ...... deriving their just powers from the consent of the governed.*

We of course are not sure what those rights mean, as life is compromised for our troops at war (by governmental action), and none of us is at liberty to do as we please in an ordered community (by governmental action). The pursuit of happiness is dreamy idealism if we do not define it.

What is a 'God-given' right? Both of the above authorities assume rights are given by the simple fact of (God's) creation, of being born, of becoming a human. However, God does not enforce it, so the fact of a right is left to "the consent of the governed" -- that is, to our collective opinion. Christian, Jewish and Muslim theologies affirm that collective community opinion is formed under God, for God's created. Our opinions keep changing! God may or may not get a fair listen in the debate. Does God give rights? Perhaps. Does God provide rights? No.

There was one right in Nebraska Territory: to stake a claim to land (if you were of age). You had no claim on food, shelter, medical care or education. The first entitlement for the destitute in Omaha City was free burial. If you wanted more, you were free to leave -- if you had good shoes or a horse. Like almost all entitlements, the burial was more for the benefit of the community than it was about caring for the individual. Dead bodies, not buried, create problems.

Slowly, we have granted a long list of rights. A child has the right to medical care. Even to a lead-free environment. We pay for it! We declare that every person has the right to clean air and water, though we are having a difficult time providing it to all and the feds recently reduced the restrictions on mercury in the air.

An elderly citizen with little resources in most developed countries has the right to food, clothing, shelter and medical care. (In the U. S., this was a change of_our collective mind, to do all four, as expressed in Medicaid care for children and the elderly.) If a legislature, or a county or a city does not provide funds, where is the right?

We have now laid the base for the spirited fights. Does a fetus have a right to life? Does a pregnant teenager have the right of choice? Does a resident have the right to smoke-free air in public places? Does the citizen have the right to drinkable tap water? Does a person have the right of free speech, of choice of worship, of reading a free press, of private communication (as in emails), of owning property? In every case, this is a right only if we, the relevant community involved, say so and provide for it. Otherwise, none is an actual right.

Further, we rank these. We have declared that the right to liberty is a higher value than the right to life. For over two hundred years the United States has instructed our military personnel that liberty is our top value, more important than their lives. We tell police officers that freedom in the community may cost them lives. The author told his mother her choice to pray to die was valid. To a homeless man, we provide clean water and clean air but not the regular medical care every child may receive. We rank our rights.

As noted, nonprofit agencies provide services well beyond what the government alone can provide. However, unless the government is a true partner in providing the assurance of stability in the service, it is not a right.

Another perspective: what is the 'God-given right' of an adult dying of disease in Africa? Health care becomes a matter of the Gates Foundation, through medication, treating 40 million (!) persons in one year and saving lives. Maybe it is God-given! That depends on your view of how God moves among us and your understanding of our part, and Gate's part, in God's creation. 7-F

Entitlements

Intriguing word. It sounds like something old, from the beginning of law. Most entitlements are recent. We snarl at the word. We talk like someone else did this to us. It is fascinating to discover we join together to initiate entitlements, we do it regularly, and collectively we refuse to back up.

Certain benefits become the rights of citizens and/or residents. The Declaration of Independence promised "Life, liberty and the pursuit of happiness." We were in trouble right there. The pursuit of happiness could involve benefits, unless you are a cynic who stresses the word "pursuit" (only). 'Pursuit of happiness' was the expression of that hope that every person should be able to live a productive life. (Which is an excellent definition of happiness.)

Dr. Henry Rosemont, a constitutional scholar, provides a simple frame for our thoughts on rights. Life and liberty are "First Generation" rights. Basic and pure, even if in conflict with each other. Food, clothing, shelter, health and education are examples of "Second Generation" rights. The first generation rights mean little if left as generalities. Second generation gives specific content to life and liberty. Here comes the crunch. Granting the right to food, for example, limits the liberty of those with enough food. Entitlements chip at freedom while adding to it.

Entitlements are a fascinating part of our rights. In the first 'complete' Nebraska constitution, every person living in the state between the ages of five and twenty-one received an entitlement to "free instruction in the common schools of this state." As noted, it is the most expensive sentence in the Nebraska Constitution. The right to 'free instruction' is not limited to natives, or citizens, or rich, or smart, or those able to walk or see or hear or talk, or those who speak English, or whose parents are employed -- "every person"! Entitlement.

When the Nebraska territory was organized, residents were not entitled to aid simply because they were destitute, or to medical care, or to education, or to free burial if they died. Caring neighbors could help out with food or a shovel, but it was not an entitlement. If the family breadwinner died the survivors were told to go back to where they came from. Neighbors helped dig a grave and load the wagon.

Forty years ago we chose not to help the family with a mentally retarded child. We ignored the constitution, which requires free instruction. We considered it a family (and church) problem. Now, training of developmentally or mentally challenged children is an entitlement that no one questions -- even though it is very costly. The quaint constitutional term 'instruction' became a far broader concept than to 'teach.'

The first entitlement in local history, as noted, was free burial by the county. No questions were asked. You could be saint or sinner, an infant or a tired old derelict. The "rugged individual" who cared not what happens to anyone else and who was completely self-sufficient is a myth. Once upon a time he could try to live alone on the frontier. He had a 'right' to lay claim to some land, but that had so many restrictions and pitfalls it was not a clear title to anything. He moved when the neighbors got too close. However, he eventually died and the county guaranteed his burial.

The first good example of a more typical entitlement was shelter. As with all entitlements, residents initiated it. In Douglas County, again as reported, commissioners bought a "Poor Farm" after about ten years of avoidance of the public clamor, so that desperate or ill persons could have a roof overhead, a stove for heat, a well for water, and a garden for food.

Then the residents, and especially religious folk and physicians who found they could not provide needed health care voluntarily, said it was time for a hospital. Douglas County commissioners built a cheap shoddy one on the poor farm.

"No tax money will be used." Selling off a parcel of land was not truly conservative. The roof fell in before it was completed and the repair on the hospital was endless. However, the hospital entitlement has evolved to a law that emergency room treatment in a fine, high-tech facility cannot be denied to anyone.

Somewhere along the line we agreed that clean air is an entitlement. Free choice, which is never free except in self-serving statements, is now trumped for owners of restaurants, as it is for owners of smokestacks. Clean water. Pure foods. Dependable prescription drugs. Mail service. Phone availability. Access to legal services. Care for neglected children. They now are entitlements, each initiated by residents and a government. The public will not give up a single one of these, even as taxes to provide them go up.

It is instructive to note that the most noisy advocates against rising taxes do not ever suggest a change that would clearly reduce taxes big time: throw grandma out of the rest home. The cost for low-income elderly once was a family and county obligation. It is now 75% of Medicaid costs. Care for low-income elderly is an example of a well accepted (expensive!) entitlement.

The health care we provide for low-income children is better than is available to insured adults. Economically, children's health care is a wise use of public dollars and becomes an investment that is helpful to the economic health of the state. There are good reasons for providing guaranteed services. We are primarily protecting ourselves, not the child. However, we created a new entitlement.

Children should have transportation to public school. The elderly should not be denied drugs, or transportation to the doctor's office. Any one of us has the right to medical care in an emergency room (if there is room) and the county is to pay the bill if no one else does. Granted, much of this is for our emotional protection. We do not want to see a story in the paper that some poor soul wriggled to a lonely death on the sidewalk for lack of a prescription or in her own home for lack of a doctor to set a bleeding broken bone. Out of embarrassment as much as compassion, we agreed to an entitlement.

Age 65 gives entitlement. Otto Von Bismarck picked that age. The Prussian general was quite sure that no one in the army would live that long. It still seemed safe, frankly, in 1935 when S. S. was voted in. The elderly have created their own revolution.

Their revolution has great economic impact. Add to that the lowering of retirement age for a few public employees, a very expensive proposition. Reducing the age by 15 years adds greatly to public cost and, for the State Patrol, for example, reduces pension. It is a foolish recuirtment tool, not needed, done for political reasons.

How to pay for entitlements is an ongoing question which legislators face continuously, but that is beside the point here. We have agreed to entitlements and, as the definition of the word implies, they will be provided -- however they may be supported in public policy. We grouse, but pay. In Sweden, by contrast, paying for entitlements is not a matter of contention. The public supports the policy that those who are able to pay taxes have an obligation to pay public bills, even for persons in poverty.

A local leader recently stated that a high school grad who is bright and dedicated is 'entitled' to college or trade school training. Really? Are we headed that way?

In summary, we are always slow to say it, but we have agreed that every resident has entitlements. The force behind entitlements is public agreement, but the reasons vary from showing respect to desperate persons to protecting ourselves from future heavy costs. We have given up our "pure" freedom for the broader freedom of a safe and healthy community -- the freedom to pursue life and happiness. 6-2

Assorted "rights" arguments

What about the rights of states vs. federalism, noted elsewhere? Will states protect our rights, or simply create a weird patchwork of rights? Will congress come to agreement on those rights when the weird becomes chaotic?

Social Security established rights. It is not an annuity. Talk about the future of Social Security, by all sides, has avoided the central purpose of the Social Security Act: to protect me (us) from taking a collection to care for the destitute elderly person in our neighborhood. One excellent contribution to the discussion is from a columnist (David Shribman) who has recognized that the debate is not young vs. old, stocks vs. interest rates, or Republicans vs. Democrats. It is: "Personal freedom vs. collective responsibility." Wonderfully concise!

What about Freedom of Religion? Is that an entitlement? Dobson (Focus on the Family) and several religious right leaders urged pastors to defy the IRS and have their congregations endorse candidates. They call it religious freedom. Not. No freedom escapes its consequences. Religious freedom is about freedom to worship and to discuss public issues and is not freedom to control elections and thereby the state. 8-D

A thoughtful senator objected on the floor to requiring citizens to log in (register) at drug stores on a specific drug. He felt this is compromising our sense of freedom by quietly fitting in with public opinion. If the bill requires a log he will not vote for it, even though we are anxious about controlling the drug.

My, that brought a flood of thoughts. This pastor remembers a military officer coming to his home in the McCarthy years, to check on his sermons. The Captain was more nervous than the preacher but be assured his visit was chilling to a pastor who felt 100% loyal to his country. Later, the pastor also joined a protest of the nuclear weapons buildup, when we had enough nuclear weapons to destroy the world 20 times over. That should be enough.

The World-Herald caustically described us as unpatriotic and willing to hurt our country. That thought was not rational, but it was loud in the public. Humor: six years later the Republican Party adopted Nuclear Freeze in it national platform.

In full disclosure, this pastor also remembers his congregation in each of these situations standing in support, unflinching. So this senator voted against registering at the drugstore. No one is free. That would be chaos. However, there is a line in demanding conformance and we must continuously define it. 5-17

Smoking ban journey

"It's a free country! I have the right to smoke." Sounds rational. However, someone else can state that it is a free country and (he) has the right to breathe clean air. In fact, it is a government obligation to provide clean air and clean water. In fact, pushing to the limits, it is stealing for someone to take away the right to clean air, which is another's property. To be rational, and not just sound that way, it is not a free country. Never has been. The first pioneer could not set his spade into any place he chose. Pioneers today, in powerful 4-wheel drive vehicles, had better stop at the red light, like it or not.

A few statements are incomprehensible. You can see the face talking and hear the words, but they do not fit rational thought. We see those who promote a local option on a statewide smoking ban. Everyone agrees that smoking in a public place is a major health threat, especially to the young and the nonsmokers. We all accept that the effects of smoking, especially among the elderly, cost the state tens of millions of dollars every year. If and when we go to a ban, how does one even <u>think</u> about a local vote on a health issue?

The words we hear are "It's a free country -- everyone should be able to do as they please." Not anyplace we know. The list is long.

"The state cannot mandate how a business will operate." In health? Let's have a local vote on the temp in a meat cooler. Or the temp of water in the dish washers of restaurants. Or staff washing hands in the rest room. All are health. All a mandate. All a nuisance. All cost money. Local vote? Incomprehensible. 7-16

(2005) One senator has a 'smoking ban' proposal that limits towns and cities to be no more restrictive than the state. Upon careful reading, it is a ban on smoking bans, as it does nothing to prevent smoking. Clever title.

As a result, letters in the Lincoln Journal really lit up the place. Lincoln recently passed a ban on smoking in all restaurants and bars, by a big margin. This would void their action. Sooner or later someone is going to put this up to a vote of the whole state. When the smoke clears on that one it will be a very clear day.

The process of seeking a ban that the public accepts is an excellent lesson on the interplay between the public and senators as legislation develops.

The current bill, as presented, would ban smoking in restaurants but not in bars which do not serve cooked meals. The opposition won the first round by concocting an appearance of confusion. Who is covered? What kind of food? What about food prepared in a microwave? What if Little Leaguers are standing there? What if there is Keno? Why not make Keno exempt? Are Pickle cards a food? Endless amendments.

Hello? Anybody thinking? My staff checked with the supervising agency on how to test a bar. It takes no more than one minute. If the bar cooks and serves a hamburger, it would be smoke-free. If not, it would not be affected.

All except two of the opponents were rural. They were thinking of a small town, with only one restaurant (usually with alcohol). What on earth would this small town do, they asked petulantly, if they did not have a single restaurant in town that would be smoking? Well, hello again. The same thing Omaha would do because it also would not have a single smoking restaurant. 5-7

(2007) The smoking ban is on hold while the two sides see if they can compromise. We have enough votes to pass it, but not enough to force it to a vote. If we do not pass this bill, with all of its carefully detailed exceptions, the people will bring a petition to vote and it will take no prisoners. A public petition has to be quite simple and is not subject to negotiating discussion. It would pass, big time.

(2008) In the legislature the smoking ban is now ready to pass and is very popular with our constituents. We took off the opt-out provisions for local jurisdictions and moved the start time to June one year away, at the beginning of the warm weather. Ease into it with patio options. Everyone agrees second hand smoke kills people. The fuss is about telling someone how to run a business. It is not much of a fuss, as we set parameters for businesses in many ways. A delivery business cannot drive any speed the owners choose, even if they have a Hummer and will not get hurt. Health regulations, which this is, protect us in meat markets -- even while putting restraint on business.

This senator had fun strangling a rabbit. The debate was on the smoking ban, in response to the argument that the ban compromises freedom. Strange argument, since we will live with restrictions and breathing clean air is a basic right. So, to have a bit of fun, this guy said he was dismayed that he could not shoot a rabbit in his own yard, going into his flower garden. His Mother shot many a sinning rabbit. That rabbit has more freedom than he does. If he could catch him/her he would cheerfully strangle the rascal, but then he would have the visage of Senator Chambers glaring over his shoulder. Chambers whirled around and nodded vigorously, stating later that Senator Kruse is correct in believing that he does not have the right to shut off the breathing of a rabbit. How about in a bar?

(2009) How about for a child? Admittedly we are exhausted after all the debate, but a few senators are <u>shocked</u> that promoters of the ban are not willing to settle for <u>mostly</u> clean air. Clean air and water are government obligations. By what mind do we stop on the journey, after a major gain, as though this right is up for negotiation?

Political leaders also create confusion on clean water rights. Omaha sewer lines are polluting the river and it will cost over $1 billion to fix. We hear talk of this as an "unfunded federal mandate." We love those words. The most conservative voices join in asking for federal help. These are not federal sewers. They are ours. The feds did not create the right of clean water or arbitrarily announce it. Enforcement is their job and providing clean water is our job. We created the pollution. Fix it, folks, and pay the bill.

Concealed Carry

"Concealed Carry" of handguns is a hot issue but frankly does not make much difference. It supposedly intimidates criminals, but there is no verified supporting evidence. In fact countries without it have 80% less homicide by gun. It does stir some passions.

"Concealed Carry" is a curious piece. Our present Nebraska "ban" on concealed carry of weapons is actually very loose permission. We now say persons can carry a hand gun if they think they need one. (!) We are one of only four states with some sort of ban. The NRA has to get rid of the ban for 100% of the states, for their fund raising. So they pour $$$ and emotion in. We passed it. Now all those who are carrying are criminals unless they give us $100, take a course, get an eye exam, and get on a national gun registry. Yes, really! Plus, they cannot be a felon, unstable (?), talk back to Grandma, etc. Plus, they cannot carry in churches, schools, legislature, bars, courts, all kinds of offices --a very long list.

These are new restrictions which the NRA agreed to so they could cross off one more state. What a crock. Freedom loving Nebraskans insisted on this fiasco. It is hard to complain when the NRA shoots its own foot and makes carrying expensive.

Several police groups objected. A survey of Lincoln police showed 85% in opposition. The Black community will be harmed by it, and strongly opposes it. A few young Black guys will think this gives them a right to defend themselves when attacked by a White man. Not. Black men do not have that right in this territory, partner. This is a law for Whites.

We have sent to prison Black persons who acted purely and fearfully in self defense, and will again. The author has witnessed it with a Black friend who was everything we want a father to be: responsible, hard working, and helping raise his sons. He was sent to prison for defending himself against several white men who were intent on beating him, on a public street in the daytime, with witnesses. His only fault was he was black. Terribly sad, and wrong, but this is the real world. If you are Black you do not have the right to defend yourself against a White. 6-2

First, a withering array of statistics. Some claim concealed carry reduces crime. Others claim statistics show it increases crime. Frankly, neither side makes its case. Reliable studies (hard to find!) show very little difference. Next, the public wants it/does not want it. Both right. Rural areas want it, urban areas do not. Next, police want it/do not want it. In general, police associations oppose concealed carry, but you can find quite a few enforcement individuals to quote on the other side.

We heard this is a second amendment "right to carry" issue, with much righteous-language emotion. Clearly, carrying concealed is not a constitutional right. You are supposed to keep your rifle in the back window, as any rancher knows. We hear children are endangered. That depends on quite another factor: how the gun is stored or protected in a child environment. 6-10

Who wins? We do not know. Those who carry concealed now -- which are many -- may now do so with some inconvenience but almost never a penalty. That is greatly changed with this bill. It will now cost them. A big deal for us in these decisions is public cost, which we assumed was covered with the fees. Turns out we will have to add some tax money to pay for background checks. Also turns out that once you get clearance you basically have lifetime privilege without review.

The National Rifle Association is controlling the vote, so the decision is not really based on fact or public opinion. The clear fact is that more guns have not reduced violence in the homes or on the streets. Public opinion opposes the sale of heavy weapons whose only use is for intentional murder. The show goes on.

The NRA is using this to tout their 'wins' with their membership. Not unusual. Those of us who are opposed were able to prevent amendments to their wording, which allows for cities to opt out and ban concealed carry. Omaha and Lincoln may do this, since the danger is more urban. 6-10

What does my faith say on this one? Some of us are followers of Jesus. That is a big deal. We do not fuss with Jesus on other issues. Why should we here? We do not want to kill anybody, nor threaten to kill someone, nor threaten serious injury. That is all a handgun does. This senator does not want to live in a society which depends on threat to kill as a defense – cannot think of a single problem we have that will be helped by pointing a gun at someone. But we will point guns and fingers. We can do better. 6-1

A Patriot

The Fourth of July and the rockets red glare, coming amid a flurry of public comments about patriotism, causes this fellow to ponder the meaning of "Patriot." The comments are often a putdown of others in our society. Is this what makes us great?

The author is proud of our country and yearns for her bright future. As a young teenager in World War II, he daily feared for our survival and joined others to do anything helpful. We eagerly collected scrap metal, recycled, agreed to rationing. He later tried to get in the service. He understands "love for country." It can be without arrogance or put down.

The author has never worn a flag lapel pin and will not. Ties designed to resemble the flag are colorful but will not be worn. It would be, for me, a disrespect of the flag to wear the flag. It is a free country and some will choose to wear it.

We had a big flap in a church about flag etiquette. So we studied to know what was correct. We found more than one authority. The Navy protocol ordered that the flag of worship is the only flag to be flown above Old Glory, only during the time of worship on the ship. None disputed this guide, so we accepted that as our rule and placed the Christian flag in preference over the U. S. flag when in the sanctuary, but not elsewhere.

In our reading, we were reminded that the flag is never to touch the ground when being unrolled, is not to be destroyed except through burning, and is never to be worn as clothing. Yes.

Again, sincere people may do otherwise. But it is a bit of shock when some activists criticized one of our candidates for not wearing a flag lapel pin. What? Is that what our country stands for? Then, when he did wear one there was criticism that he must not be sincere, and that no candidate should do that. So we read that he is not a patriot. And others criticize his opponent for signs that he is not a patriot. Without question, all twenty candidates who wanted to be president are patriots. They had better be, or the public's steady abrasion during the campaigns will wear them thin.

Next, should you cover your heart for the singing of the national anthem? We had more of the same pompous judgmental pronouncements, with no evidence on what the person under examination really thinks. This senator has been gently chided in the capitol rotunda for placing his hand on his heart for the singing. More than once he has been told that gesture is reserved for the pledge of allegiance. Military personnel have orders and the rest of us have opinions. So where are we? Hopefully, every citizen has high respect for both the flag and the anthem, but for so much more. Our jewelry is not the measure. Nationalism, whether shouted or whispered, is not patriotism.

Have you marveled at the close calls of the patriots who won freedom for us in the Revolutionary War? It is simply amazing that they succeeded -- which includes sorting out the devious tangles after the war. This patriot is grateful beyond words for their passion and commitment. It was truly revolutionary. Please note, they were critics of their government/king, did not wear his colors.

The signers were a model of commitment to each other. It was their shared declaration of independence without reserve. They put on the line "our lives, our fortunes and our sacred honor." To each other. It was breathtaking. If they failed each other they would be hung together. They declared a vision beyond personal differences. The new soldiers were given a vision of opportunity and justice for the grubbiest guy in the trench.

A peculiar right -- to have religious freedom -- became the founders' gift to the world as well as to us. Freedom from oppression, and justice for all set a high standard for the new nation. We are not there yet. Does that vision still drive our patriotism?

Did they wear a lapel flag? Then and now, the persons who are on display can be genuine or they can be fake. Pastors learned long ago that those who shout "Amen!" may be the most useless when it is time to be counted. A spy will wear a lapel pin or praise the president or shout down the earnest soul calling for change.

So who is a patriot? The young adult who turns away from a good job to be in harm's way in defense of country is a patriot. The parent or spouse who, with fear, encourages that loved one is a patriot. The elderly church member who prays for the safe return of military personnel, and who openly says the country is wrong in sending them on this mission, is a patriot.

The citizen who gripes about what the government does, but does not vote, is frankly in question as a patriot. The opportunities for our grandchildren depend largely on our vision and drive -- and vote. The person who supports paying taxes for necessary services to a neighbor is a patriot. The caseworker who strategizes a full life for an abused child is a patriot. The person who carefully evaluates government policy and openly disagrees with some of it because of the direction it takes our country is a patriot.

Brief comments cannot describe all the traits we value. What are defining traits? Several are consistently there. The patriot is looking ahead and yearning for a productive future for coming generations. A patriot is willing to criticize, even strongly, when government actions do not meet that standard. Patriots commit to each other in community.

Oddly, July 4th is the day we declare to be our day of celebration. It was <u>not</u> the date of the adoption or the signing or the public announcement. No matter. We have <u>declared</u> July 4 and so it is.

Declaring makes a differenceWe also declare our vision to each other through our acts. We act to secure the future of our neighbor's grandchildren. We <u>declare</u> that diversity of views, of personal talent and of language and culture -- is not a handicap, but a gift. We <u>declare</u> that we will accept and develop those gifts. We commit to each other.

Patriots declare, "Let it be so." 8-C

176. Suspicion could include a baby. What is that young one thinking?

9. Race

Persons of faith have a strong consensus on equal treatment for races. We do not consistently live up to our stated ideals. This chapter summarizes what we say, challenges our dormant attitudes, and describes a basis by which most legislators strive to vote.

Racism

Racism -- weighing the values of a person by color of skin or other physical characteristics -- is a fact of our time, and of every time. It is to be expected.

The tendency to pre-judge is not bad by itself. Each of us assumes and assigns selected values and attitudes to persons we meet according to their appearance. Skin color, hair, height, weight, attractiveness -- and so much more -- stimulate assumptions in our minds. A fat person lacks self-discipline? A tall person is a natural leader? A cute, perky woman would be a fun friend? There is no way to avoid thoughts that connect between this stranger and the experiences with someone who was similar by appearance.

When the writer was a teenager hoping to get a date, a neighbor told him in clear terms he should not date a blonde, because they make poor mothers. The older man earnestly added: "This is not prejudice. This is fact. Look around you (and you will see what I see)." He gave an example.

There is the simple prototype of prejudice. We have all experienced it. We have all expressed it because we can tell by looking that someone is different. We see color of skin, or hair, or body size/characteristics and we pre-judge a bit of what a stranger will think or do. Prejudice is pre-judging limited data.

Racism is not that simple.

Recent research shows that 75% of the U. S. public would have some degree of preference for a president who has white skin. We know that every day President Obama's life is under continuous threat from persons who hate what his skin color represents. We call them nuts, but they can be driven to action by bloggers who would not physically attack someone, but who create flaming rhetoric. Talk shows stoke those dangerous fires, pushing subconscious buttons.

So there you have it: preference, twisted opinion, and violent hate, all driven by reactions to skin color. Reactions are formed through a complex mix of relationships with family, friends, associates, competitors, neighbors, faces on TV and stories in the news. We are not good at sorting and discarding.

It is not that simple, of course.

Attitudes toward one's self include racial association, a sense of being outcast or included, and personal value and potential for life. The writer's Mother was a Dane who married and moved into a German community. She lived there 60 years, until her death, and never felt accepted. Was she accepted or was it her?

Did she resist changing to the culture of persons who became her lifelong friends, or did they resist hers? Aside from exchanging recipes and desperate advice on a sick child, the neighbors had little or no interest in her Danish culture and heritage. Racism does that.

Mother's low-lying anger was steady and real, so the writer experienced first hand some of the feelings of a minority person. That includes the deep frustration of living in an environment you may affect a bit, but which you did not create and which you are powerless to change. The majority will smile and nod at you, but will laugh and shrug when you step away. The condescending smiles made her furious.

However, it is not that simple.

Self-attitude includes the mix within the racial or ethnic group. There are dark Blacks, light Blacks, and those who "pass." Whites hardly think about it, but persons of African ancestry are very conscious of shades of color and wonder about all the reasons for it. Some carry attitudes about it.

Jewish persons are quite conscious of their fellowship, however diverse they may be, but are happy to confuse the rest of us. Omaha confined the Blacks and Jews to basically North 24th Street for the first century of our history. However, in the 1950s Jews could "pass" since the important Jewish identifier was surname. A Jewish family would ask a friend, Swanson, to buy a house west of 42nd Street and then to quickly resell it to them. They broke the barrier. Blacks had to wait for agitation, riots, a national Housing Act, and the relocation caused by the North Freeway to gain passage into the larger community. Their barriers were not actually broken. If your skin shows color, you cannot escape some persons considering you inferior.

It is not that simple. We have what it takes to reduce racial antagonisms and provide the setting for cooperation, growth, and development -- to become a true, exciting, vibrant community. We are no longer who we were, but who will we be?

First, it requires appreciation for persons we have come to know in a close way. That takes a while, but most of us have friends who help us unknowingly break barriers. The writer lives in a Black neighborhood and frankly is often not aware of the skin color of minority friends.

President Obama has received a gift: there are times when he appears to live unconscious of race. Presumably this is a gift from Hawaii, to him and to us. That isolated set of islands contains such a pervasive mix of race that those who are raised there have a wonderful, freeing blessing. Race is not where the conflict is. Can we get over it?

Obama still has to deal with it. If he should have a teenage daughter who became pregnant, there would be hell to pay -- by <u>us</u>.

Every negative attitude toward current Black family culture would come out of the woodwork and we all would be hammered by it.

Ironic, isn't it? Black family structure has not been able to recover from what the White system of slavery caused: the selling of husbands, wives and children, and the breeding by owners. The actual ownership and control of individual bodies forced the breakdown of a powerful tribal sense of family and community which was the heritage of these African immigrants. "Welfare" added to it.

Second, we have to cultivate a genuine appreciation for each other's culture. Schools are doing good work here and the young is where it will happen.

Third, we must confront blatant racism, calmly but firmly calling to account those who hate. There is much in the mix described earlier that does no harm -- even more of it that is downright interesting and fun. Many of us owe so much of who we are to minority friends. We have been changed and we would not ever go back. But hatred? "South Pacific" had it right. We must be carefully taught to hate. Name the beast and help to expose racial enmity.

Fourth and in summary, we can receive and enjoy each other's gifts. Gifts are of music, stories, laughter, art, genius, creativity, energy, faith, and commitment.

We are into recruiting minority young adults to learn more. We go after teens who are not on a level playing field and never thought about more schooling. We go directly to them to urge them to go to a college where all who qualify are welcome. So why is that opposed?

Because there are always the likely quick conclusions of goodhearted readers, let's add to the note about our personal life in a Black neighborhood. Every family except one (a widow) is a two-parent family, every adult is working or retired, every home is well kept. It is safer here than in our former home in West Omaha, because neighbors pay attention to what is happening.

That is the setting for our story. We asked our nearest neighbor to come help move furniture. He brought along his 6 foot 2 inch, twenty-year-old son, a welcome addition! Ruth has been a family advocate in this integrated community for thirty years and she cannot change. At break time she looked into the eyes of the shy young man. "Are you employed? (No) Would you like to be? (I have tried.) I have a job for you. I have researched it and you can start Monday. It pays $8.50, which is not a lot, but it will get you a work record." He studied her face, inquiring.

"It is in West Omaha." You could see his eyes backing up. Whitey land. His Dad noted he did not have a car and would not have one until he had money to buy one. Ruth: "He does not need a car. The bus is at the end of our block. Takes one hour and fifteen minutes. Only one transfer. Tickets cost $13 per week. Do you have $13? (Dad nodded vigorously that he had $13.) They are ready for you and they need you."

Will he? He is shy and has been hassled racially. Police follow him in the street, women at the mall clutch their purses when they see him, white kids look past him. Is he prepared for that first lonely step? What would his friends say?

Racism is so frustrating because it pulls us all down. There it is, wrapped around and through the young man next door. Hesitant, even fearful. Hopeful. But if the Ruths of the world cannot get to him, we have a mess on our hands, politically and economically. Plus we have one more man who could have been our asset.

It is that simple. 8-E

Racism in Nebraska history

A columnist in the Omaha paper stirred quite a flap by forcing us to remember that J. Sterling Morton of Arbor Day fame was also a hard-core racist. That is well documented, including a short item in the writer's history of the Nebraska territory:

> *The hot spot for slave-issue friction was in the territorial legislature. J. Sterling Morton, strongly pro-slavery, and Andrew J. Hanscom, noisily antislavery, had no respect for each other's views and both were especially clever in devising political tricks. Their debate did not solve the issue!*

Nebraska was in the middle of the slave fight. Morton chose his side and pressed it. Slaves were owned in Nebraska. The slavery issue for Hanscom was human: slaves are people. For Morton it was economics: slaves are property. A, p. 31

Later, when the Irish came, attacks were by race. Irish was a race in Great Britain, and by extension, here. When descendants of slaves greatly increased migration to Omaha in 1900, the Irish felt competition as well as compassion because they were being replaced. In their home country, Irish were identified as a different race, like Blacks, and they understood that. When they migrated to United States they had to be carefully taught how to "become white" in the new country. They did that by acting like Blacks were the opposition. (Check out a 1996 book: "How the Irish Became White.")

However, Jews moved close to Blacks. From their experiences of persecution, they held views similar to the slave descendants in Omaha and established close friendships. These examples greatly oversimplify thousands of experiences, but illustrate the diverse attitudes which helped form who we are. The pattern of picking who will be on the lowest rung continues. 7-17

We have made tremendous gains against Black-White racism since the 60s, to the point we often avoid talking about it. However, racism is alive and well in Nebraska. The talk and the reactions must change or we will never get out of this swamp. We now are in an awful debate whether Omaha is first or third in the nation as worst in poverty of Black children. <u>In the nation</u>! Only half of our Black children graduate from high school.

Unemployment for Black, Hispanic and Indian young people is many times higher than for whites. Several factors are involved, including the continuing imagery of slave ancestors in young minds, contributing to lower self worth and to reduced expectations.

However, these figures are not possible without racism in attitudes, in language, in arrests, in prosecution, in hiring -- and in living. We are beginning a major initiative in education, but racist remarks and attitudes were everywhere as we discussed it. The remarks have a terrible price and the only way to do better is to openly talk with each other, to identify and confront those attitudes. A friend came out of a board meeting with his arms waving in despair, talking to the wind: "People, listen to what you are saying!"

The Irish made the effort to "become white." It took two generations. They put up with the ghettos and horrible treatment until they could do the same to the Italians. And the Polish. Then Greeks. All of them joined forces to put the Africans on the lowest rung. One thing in our future is clear. In two generations Mexicans will own homes in west Omaha and we will look for a new group to misuse. It helps if they look slightly different.

After the slaves were freed, the U. S. had major "Homeland" projects, with big money raised, to send all Africans back to where they came from. After all, they were not here legally. The Omaha Herald complained that the Republicans were trying to have freed slaves come in and thereby transform Nebraska into a Negro colony, to out vote the whites. Some politicians tried to send them all back. In Omaha (1909) citizens drove every Greek person out of town in three days, for the stated reason that we did not like their culture.

We have expressed this beforeand are doing it now with Mexicans. Our hypocrisy of pious statements and complaining about proposed changes is wearing thin. Worse, it is hurting the majority more than those we blame for the problem.

For the author's Nebraska history, he interviewed two men who were present for the 1919 lynching of William Brown in Omaha. Both reflections were hauntingly somber. Each boy's father, who objected strongly to the action, took him to be a witness. Neither man, remembering the horror, today would claim we are innocent.

We look at the 1919 picture of triumphant men, every one in a suit, white shirt, black tie and hat -- to symbolize his (assumed) important role in the community. Witnesses said all were drunk. The mayor and the Chief of Police risked their lives to stand in the way of harm to one of their citizens. William Brown had no chance, even after he was dead. The men emptied their six shooters into his charred body. They had a spooky, <u>uncontrolled</u> <u>fear</u> of his race. There were hours of animal behavior, while 10,000 people watched. We continue to object to our hanging trees, even while we quietly watch.

Those who defended our Nebraska racist attitudes made much of our freeing the slaves in Nebraska in 1861. However, the legislature did not mean it when we said they were citizens. Six years later our legislature declared that Black men could not vote. Previous to that a slave was bought and sold and shipped by freight within Nebraska with a tag around her neck. Full citizenship came very slowly. For over 100 years Blacks were limited in where they could live and work in Nebraska. They still experience limits.

Only fifty years ago, it was illegal for a Black person to walk on a sidewalk in certain neighborhoods in Omaha. Persons now living experienced that and persons now living voted that. The only permit to be there was to declare you were a "servant" in that neighborhood.

Was a servant the new slave? In the minds of living persons who did not want to be a servant, it was an extension of slavery.

Fifty years ago, a storybook in grade school told us that the raisins in pancakes are black boys who greased the pan and got covered with batter. No white boys. Is that fun? Who smiled? Fifty years ago, in Omaha, Black teachers were required to have four years college and could not work on the same school staff with white teachers, who often had only two years of college.

Forty years ago, any person living in the Kruse's present home could not get a bank home improvement loan if they had Black neighbors. Redlining was a bank effort to drive property values down and whites out. It worked and made a lot of money for white bankers. It was a clever way to undermine property values. Block improvements or sales. Wait, drive down the values, and buy them out. Today, we can point to neighborhoods where Blacks are not allowed. Anyone over 50 years old has witnessed and lived the effects of slavery, even if they were not aware of the family pain.

Our Nebraska History magazine has a remarkable academic article on ethnic history in Nebraska, by Deborah Fink, a Nebraska native. Those over fifty have lived what she describes. Blacks and Indians are not invisible. Whites are invisible, and we made that happen, she says. By the 1950s we did away with serious attention to white ethnic divisions. We defined America our way.

> *We were not even to think about the possibility that we could experience the misfortunes of others. As whites, we were rational, capable, advanced, favored by destiny, magnanimous, and superior. Our task was to live up to our heritage of greatness and to ignore the gap in the details about where we had come from, who we were as a people, and where we fit into history."* M

A few current racial comments are relevant to reality, but most are hopelessly out of date. A few Blacks make statements that are straight out of the rhetoric by angry African-American activists in the sixties. Many of us were there, as activists and protesters, and remember the rhetoric. It was powerful, and together we moved out of the sixties. In 1968, 4% of Americans accepted black and white mixed marriage. Now it is over 80%. 8-A

Racism in incidents

The previous section has events from history and the Chambers chapter recounts a racial incident in the legislature.

Most racism is subtle. A small event several years ago illustrates the insensitivity and the reality, with some humor added. Several of us, all members of a bishop's cabinet and in business suits, were on an elevator in a Grand Island hotel, breaking for lunch. Included in our group was Dr. Emmett Streeter, a prominent Black leader from Omaha. He entered the elevator first and had tucked his small frame in a back corner. Two white men, also in business suits, got on the car and continued their conversation with each other.

One of the men glanced at us, looked straight at Streeter and told him what floor he should take them to. (The elevator was self-operated.) The fun is that Streeter and Ed Murphy, his bosom Irish buddy, enjoyed making a scene of such things. They went into their act without a word. Dr. Streeter made a big fuss of elbowing his way through the crowd to the controls. He switched from his Kansas accent to "Yas, suh" etc. and tried to serve these two fellows. They faced back to the door and kept talking with each other.

The elevator was acting up, would not stop even with the floor, and once went back up. Ed nearly exploded in telling off the newly recruited operator. Red faced and using the N word he shouted that Emmett obviously would never amount to anything because he could not even operate a stupid elevator. The two men whirled around, backs to the wall, to defend themselves against an elevator full of racists, and fled the first time the door opened. The ministers broke into spontaneous laughter, noting later the two men were racists to be feared. The ministers almost missed their own floor in their enjoyment of the impromptu drama. A

This is the same Reverend Streeter who was spit in the face by a gas station attendant in central Nebraska when he asked for water for his feverish little girl on a hot day.

Most parents and teachers feel that Omaha Schools do well with minority students. However, one mother named a teacher and school in which the part time music teacher spit on her daughter in front of the class. The daughter followed the teacher to the front and said she was offended, but that she had been taught to turn the other cheek. The teacher allegedly told the student that if she turned the other cheek she would spit on it also. The teacher defended herself to the principal, who was very firm in her reprimand to the teacher, saying she was upset because she had just come from "dealing with those animals at North (High School)."

That is a troubling example of our continuing racial challenges among people who <u>should</u> know better. All of us have learned that a story told by the person with an angry point to prove is only one side.

The intimidation of Hispanic minority persons was evident at a rally in South Omaha, held to help Hispanic citizens register to vote. There was a Mariachi band and lots of smiles. Fun. Across the street from us was an organized protest, with burly types waving huge flags and calling out complaints. (In English. Hmmm.) We sent two fellows across the street to find out what the beef was. We were 'supporting illegals.' Our men said these are citizens. "Well, you cannot be sure of that -- they look Hispanic." We were taking strict documentation, as required for registering. More flag waving and shouted protest. We discovered Hispanics in the crowd who had birth certificates from Nebraska and were afraid to approach the table to register to vote. 6-8

David Kaufman, Grand Island merchant known to the author, spent a fortune to quietly enable 83 Jewish families to escape Nazi Germany and become established in America. It is ironic that the ones he brought to Nebraska were heavily restricted in where they could live in Omaha. O

The standing room crush for Obama when he visited Omaha in 2008 has a fascinating historical parallel. Mike Kelly, World-Herald columnist, reminded us that almost exactly 40 years earlier, in March of 1968, presidential candidate George Wallace packed the crowd into the same civic auditorium, but with a different message. He was in Omaha to declare the inferiority of Blacks and his intent to use segregation to maintain the United States as it was. Wallace incited the race riots which followed in Omaha. Can it be that only forty years later we get a mixed race crowd to whoop for change? Be encouraged. We have come a ways. 8-6

Metro Omaha Schools and Race

(2006) Omaha is currently in a huge bruhaha which is basically racial. We are developing school systems with a painful racial division. It is getting worse, and solutions are not effective. We have 75% of the African descent students in one district where the European descent students are becoming fewer every year.

A few leaders in neighboring districts in the two counties say "That is not our problem." The legislature, which is charged by the constitution for the education of every child, responded firmly: when any child is shorted in educational opportunity anywhere in the state, it is our problem, for every one of us. You will be involved.

Senator Chambers used the structure to pull a "Gotcha" in the word of one headline. He has tried many ways to force the white community to publicly recognize that there is segregation in housing. "Some neighborhoods are different color than others." True!

Plus, he is furious with the superintendent for enabling the neighborhood schools plan. So Chambers was successful in attaching an amendment that mandated action to divide OPS into three districts along "community of interest" lines. The senators were so angry with what they perceived to be the arrogance of OPS in dealing with other districts that they passed the motion. It did not last, because it was an artificial ploy, but it illustrated frustration in the legislature with any school that does not deliver top education.

Historic slavery is evident

A major disappointment in the legislature was our failure to pass a resolution expressing our apology for slavery. The resolution was not a big deal, except that it could provide a teachable moment for Nebraskans. So we let it go. However, the comments in the debate were deeply disturbing and are a big deal. They give clues as to why we cannot get past the continuing effects of slavery in our midst. For half of the writer's lifetime we have even had laws and rules that were an extension of slavery. He did not support those laws, but he is ready to apologize because he could be part of the solution. (This has nothing to do with the red herring of "reparations." We are not paying anyone. Money is not the handy answer.)

Senators declared we are innocent. "We were not there during slavery, never voted for it, and did not own anyone -- so there is nothing to talk about." Really? We are not slaveholders but we joined a going concern. Our state budget carries costs from a slave mentality still held by some in both races. Perhaps we do not have the precise words for apology, but whites had better find words to express how we feel about the black race, as distinguished from the India or Chinese races who fare much better in our public life.

There are two basic slavery facts: whites were in power and blacks survived. We are not past that, and both peoples have responsibility for our deficit. How can it be that 100 years after "freedom" Blacks are not fully free?

Jim Wallis: "We whites have not confessed, let alone repented of our sins. We will not think it." Our president and local Black leaders are trying hard to move us to genuine acceptance of the experiences of one another. A quiet, humble confession from all sides would help.

Slavery was one part of a stratified system, in which persons have their "place in life" assigned to them. The barriers to "moving up" are subtle but real. Our current stratified society includes layers of class installed by slavery. We are a part of that, as are black leaders who accept a system that they escaped. They avoid looking back.

Two specifics of slavery are still with us and are evidence of a stratified system. Slavery taught both races that Negroes are inferior, and forced that opinion deep into our consciousness. Second, slavery broke up African family units, greatly diminishing the role of father. The perception of inferiority, again by both blacks and whites, and the weakened black family unit are two current realities. Several leaders in both races move strongly to counteract this, but the general public is not engaged. Could a teachable moment lead to change?

School "problems" are increased by assumptions that black children will not perform as well. Those who do well are called "exceptional." Kids who silently feel they are inferior will not do their best. A college admissions counselor spoke this week of the challenge of intimidation that many black youth feel as they walk through her door. I was certainly ill at ease entering college but I did not doubt I could do it, mostly because every one around me agreed.

A distinguished innovative educator, Paulo Freire, discovered that oppressed people in Brazil were not truly aware of their plight.

(Think black youth.) He found creative ways to get past that and found that then they were powerful in changing a sense of inferiority. They were the best teachers for the next generation.

> *As the illiterate learns and is able to make such statements, his world becomes radically transformed and he is no longer willing to be a mere object responding to changes occurring around him. He is more likely to decide to take upon himself... the struggle to change the structures of society."*

Will we empower the black young adult to be free?

Mexicans and Racism

In recent years the target is Mexican immigrants, legal or illegal. We excuse our attitude because some are "illegal." Forget that they have never been arrested, charged, or in a court that said they have broken a law. Forget that living here breaks no law. Local officials are called 'cowards' for not sending police after people who are not breaking a law.

The noisy wrath of a few about 'illegals' is a sham that covers a pervasive racist attitude so effectively we fool ourselves. Our problem is the culture and values which we assume by skin color. Plus, we have federal ineptness that does not keep up with legitimate requests. In Omaha, a legal resident applied for his wife in Mexico to join him. The application was fully approved, but she cannot come for six years. Say what?

The evidence of racism is in conversations, comments and emails that are shameful in their attacks. We hear angry jabs at "12 million who snuck across the border." Well, 5 of the 12 flew here. They came from non-Latin countries, to study and work, at universities and research labs. They simply did not go home. Where is the outrage against the multitude with white skin?

The heavy racist overtones of the Hispanic tension are deeply troubling. There are death threats, assaults and of course angry rhetoric. Many persons with Latino appearance have been killed, and in retaliation, others are killed. The KKK in some parts of the south is growing as members restate the discredited White Supremacy claims. The whole challenge of Mexican and Guatemalan persons who cross the border illegally is laid on anyone who looks Latino.

These racial attacks are not new. Irish, Germans, Swedes, Polish, Mormons, Italians, Greeks, Catholics -- have been told to go back to where they came from. Indians enjoy some humor by broadening the "Go back" command to all of us. As noted, there was a major move to apply this to Africans, even though it was the majority population who had brought them. Where Blacks became the majority in the south, fear increased, and with fear came more mayhem.

Emails accuse Hispanics of being criminals, of taking jobs, of coming for welfare, of sneaking into our educational system, and on. Let's look at the facts. There is plenty of emotion to go around!

Facts that favor Hispanic immigrants

First, most Hispanics are citizens. Some have been here for generations. Senator Ray Aguilar, a Hispanic from Grand Island, is one of hundreds of Nebraskans who have been angrily told to "Go back where you came from." Ray smiles, says he really likes Grand Island, and is always glad to go back home. It is an uneducated attack, which causes great pain and carries genuine hostile threat in our communities. In one hearing a senator asked how we could know who is illegal. Answer: "They speak Spanish."

Second, we cannot 'un-citizen' a person born here, as some want us to do with babies. The U. S. constitution declares them citizens.

Third, those who entered illegally break no law by living here. Local police officers cannot arrest someone who is not breaking the law without breaking the law themselves. If residents have not been judged guilty in court for other action they are not criminals. If

Hispanics commit a crime they are arrested, go to court, are subject to the penalties, and will be deported if their papers are not in order.

The author has crossed a border and broken federal law -- was not caught, so am not a criminal! We grant that to whites. The situation was crossing the border as a tour group left Israel. While we were there, the next country on our trip declared that anyone with an Israeli stamp in his/her passport would be stopped. Under instructions from our consulate, the guide gave us razor blades so we could cut that page out of our passports, mutilating a passport, which is a federal no-no. If the Israelis had known the pronouncement was coming their custom agent would have stamped a small separate paper which would fit in the passport and could be easily removed. Also illegal.

Our current bishop, caught with a group on the wrong side of a Mideast border, grabbed her suitcase and, under cover of darkness, with the others made the desperate walk to cross the border to safety. Would any one of us object?

As we in her flock consider her story, we hold our mental breath, not for the breaking of someone else's law, but for the risk. The group could end up for months in some remote jail. It is a real world out there, and our government is not always our protector. Breaking a minor foreign law is a risk, not an issue of patriotism.

Fourth, the Nebraska constitution requires us to educate every resident. It does not say "except those who do not speak English" or except those who are retarded, or except children of parents who broke a law, or except those who are disliked by their neighbors.

We educate their children, as required by law, put there for my grandfather, who became a teacher, and for my father, who knew no English when he started to school.

Fifth, they pay taxes. 'Illegals' have income tax withheld, get no refund. They pay full Social Security taxes, into your and my fund. They have contributed billions to our S. S. Trust Fund, with no possibility of benefits from it. If they were white we would thank them. They pay sales tax, property tax or rent, excise taxes, gas tax, etc.

To get honest, Nebraska research shows that an illegal immigrant pays $80,000 more in taxes, in a lifetime, than is received in benefits.

Sixth, they want to learn English, as did our pioneer immigrants.

The writer is a citizen because he was born here, even if his father had to learn to speak English. His great grandparents were here for fifty years, were loyal Americans, and helped build the frontier. Great Granddad even laid tracks for that first transcontinental railroad. Neither spoke English, nor did they feel any need to, nor did their community or church feel they needed to. Whole towns were settled in Nebraska with the agreement that English was optional. In many Nebraska communities until World War I, official records were in German. Currently, we have sixty languages spoken by Omaha school children, who do want to learn English.

Seventh, they come to work, as they have done for decades. We understand why they come. They love their country. Hundreds cross the border every morning, and go home every night -- for work.

Mexicans come here to work, as did my great grand parents. For decades they have taken hard, low paying labor, to do anything to survive. As did my great grand parents. One way it has been said: "We sought workers and humans came."

Eighth, they do not come here for welfare.

People fume to senators about how Mexicans come here to get on welfare. Badly informed nonsense. The last place an undocumented person will go to be checked out is a government office. A letter to the editor, from an obvious fat cat, says he would like to trade places and have his taxes reduced and all these benefits lavished on him. The chances he would be willing to exchange legal situations? Zero. If he did switch he would be surprised at how few benefits there are. (Emergency rooms and a safe workplace are the two laws.)

Why would we be shocked that a father would risk his life (thousands have died) to use that method to provide for his family? Some would consider him a hero, not a bum. There are Mexicans who create fake IDs, like our youth, or who drive drunk without a license, like thousands of our adults. Arrest them all. But do not demean their values. Most Mexicans are here to work, at a tremendous personal sacrifice.

Ninth, most are very poor. They are desperate for necessities, for food and clothing.

This does not ignore the risk of crossing the border, but shades of Victor Hugo! In that time, the majority community threw a father in prison for stealing a loaf of bread for his family. Would any caring father, in a family where the children are desperate for food, risk crossing the border at night to get a job? Yes. Would he prefer to stand in line for that job? Yes. The problem is, there is no line for Hispanics. (If he is a Swedish immigrant, walk right in.)

Tenth, crossing the border illegally is not a crime and cannot be punished. A violation of immigration is <u>not</u> in the criminal code. It is in the federal civil code and federal courts have ruled there can be no penalty. The offender can (and should) be deported, but by law we cannot call that a penalty, or give a prison sentence, or levy a fine, or confiscate property.

Eleventh, enforcement of the immigration civil code is a federal "preemption." meaning that only the feds can do it. States and cities are blocked from enforcement. To try one of many clever end runs is not constitutional. (We could "Obey the law!")

Twelfth, our economy is benefited by immigrants.

A Canadian researcher confirmed that race problems continue, but with some old false assumptions doing the most to hold us back. He told us "Immigrants will make you rich." That has been true for 200 years and has not changed. This is not the shallow thought of 'cheap labor' but the reality of recognizing new assets which can produce results.

Minneapolis understands that, is developing its immigrant population, and is going great. The researcher and others emphasized that creative/diverse cultures have a major correlation to growth.

We honored a high school senior, Hispanic, for his remarkable achievements. He is obviously bright, socially at ease, speaks without an accent, and loves our schools and state. He is grateful. But he came to this country only 8 years ago and feels Nebraska attitudes are that he should go elsewhere to school. He will go to Pennsylvania for a business masters. We groan at the thought of shipping out a young person who feels he owes so much of who he is to Nebraska. We are losing an economic asset. Is there no way to claim him?

Thirteenth, instate tuition is for our benefit, not the students.

A breathless moment came as we passed instate tuition for immigrant youth over the governor's veto. It was the right thing to do, but it is admittedly hard for the public to understand. The bill treats all our kids the same, which the constitution requires. These kids, our kids, who in ten years will be our adults, now have a better chance to become trained for a productive job. Economics is why the vote passed. Term limits helped. This was the last vote for 21 senators so they could do the right thing without a worry. 6-15c

These youth are all on track to become citizens, or they do not qualify. How can they do that? Strangely, the IRS will issue immigrant workers a number so their tax withholding can be sent in. With several years of records showing steady paying of taxes, the person here illegally can then apply for permanent worker resident status. Imagine! Back door, but the legal path we Americans ask them to follow.

The emotions on tuition are real, but the content is fake. No college in the state even knows whether an applicant is not a citizen unless that person voluntarily says so. Colleges and universities have stopped requiring social security numbers, the quick way to check on citizenship, for reasons of identify theft. Hackers can get into college computers and steal such info. Then the school is liable. Even if they checked with S. S. numbers there is such a high error rate in the database it cannot be used as proof. Schools do check residence. If the young woman has lived in Lexington for ten years, she is accepted as a resident. Period. There also is no law that a resident must be a citizen. The tempest is teapot size.

Fourteenth, Mexicans bring strong family values.

Mexicans consistently bring strong family values, as did my ancestors. However, my Mother's Dad did not prove values by sending most of his income back to his Mother in Denmark (as she instructed).

Values? The Mexican loyalty to family and community puts us in the shade. They have a higher ratio of marriage among young adults and a lower ratio of divorce even with the huge pressures of separation. They exhibit a higher support for their businesses and community. Blacks and whites will typically go sailing past a friend's or neighbor's business to save a buck at WalMart. Mexicans could teach us about community.

<u>*Negative factors*</u>

First, a law has been broken. Entering the country without proper documentation or overstaying a work/student/travel permit is a violation of civil code and is subject to deportation.

Second, expectant mothers will try to come for an emergency roomdelivery, pick up the child's birth certificate and return home. The child is a full citizen. That is not fair.

We do understand. Imagine being a pregnant woman in a family desperately poor, in any country offering no hope of having enough food, and without hope for health for your baby. Would you slip through customs at some port in order to get to a hospital where they, by law, must deliver your baby and thereby give it citizenship in a more hopeful country? Any mother would break the law if that were the way for her child to have more freedom.

Third, a few undocumented persons drive drunk and commit crimes (as whites do). Some create problems, are a clear danger, are irresponsible, and must be deported.

Fourth, splitting a family, when we deport the parents and keep the citizen children here, is very expensive for us unless a family member takes them.

We sometimes deport parents and do not look for citizen children, leaving kids to become wards of the state. (We surround these persons with our craziness in law, and wonder why they look for a way around our law.)

Fifth, English as a Second Language (ESL) classes have a 1 to 8 teacher:pupil ratio, causing teacher cost to be twice other classes.

Sixth, some communities have been overwhelmed. Communities can be devastated when immigrants, legal or illegal, dominate the workers in a local plant where the employer does not pay adequate wages. For citizens, tightwad employers even tell them the company's health care is from the government. Schools may carry a load far beyond the size of the tax base, which affects the state funding formula.

Seventh, employers recruit foreign workers and often misuse them when the worker is in an intimidating position and cannot respond. It is a business bonus: "illegal" workers cannot object to wages, conditions, or callous treatment, because they then can be deported.

It is one more form of slavery. For African slaves, you had to put up $1,500 for a strong male and if he died you lost a lot of money. For Irish, you paid a dollar a day and if they became ill you did not pay them. If one died you got another, free, for a dollar a day 'fee.' That is about the equivalent of what we pay our immigrant slaves today, and when you think about it, explains why high paid CEOs recruited them to come and are urging the president and congress to figure a way for them to stay.

Or, we avoid taxes by "contracting" them off of records. How in God's name do we lay our problems of attitude and non-action on the Mexican worker? We regularly find ways not to pay what someone is worth to us, whether it is on our roof or packing our meat.

Eighth, a driving permit could protect us, but is missing.

Those who came to study cannot get a Social Security number, so in Nebraska they cannot get a license to drive. They do drive, especially if they get a job. We would like to offer driving certificates, which would allow us to check for English competency (street signs) and would put more pressure on them to drive responsibly. But that is labeled helping unidentified "Hispanic" criminals.

As noted several times, Nebraska senators do not diminish in any way the serious problem of persons entering the U. S. illegally. This is a huge challenge to our system. We must enhance conversation about the problem parts which we created through the breakdown of the "guest worker" program. If we could actually converse about it, instead of shouting insults, we could make progress on both immigrants and low paying jobs which are such a large drain on public funds.

Also, we must admit our treatment of <u>legal</u> immigrants is shameful. We are embarrassed by the repeated stories. Earnest newcomers are charged large sums of money ($7,000 for a college professor recruited from Canada), snarled at, ridiculed, rudely treated in waiting rooms and crudely greeted. We reject scripture that requires that a foreigner is to be treated as a relative in our home.

Cultural and personal values

The gap in our thinking comes from failing to examine culture -- all of it. Black leaders often complain that Whites know little of their culture. Yes. Whether the culture is Black, Mexican, Chinese or Danish, we do not learn about it. We pick a small part, usually negative, and blow it up to fill the whole screen. We crowd out values, convictions, commitment, and the sense of community.

Anger against immigrants is not new. The Irish who came to frontier Omaha were told, in shouts, to go back home. Many were 'undocumented,' having walked across the border from Canada, which, like Ireland, was a part of the British Empire. (They feared they could not pass the health check at Ellis Island.) We hypocritically pontificated against slavery. As noted, Irish, considered another race, were our slaves and a better deal.

Ellie Weisel, the Holocaust survivor, has visited Nebraska and traveled widely sharing his great wisdom. He reflected about that time when it was human to be inhuman. He lifts up the key: bold respect for the dignity of another person. That is at the heart of our statements of faith and the work of a community. He also pushes our minds to resist a focus on the "otherness" of another.

If racism were not involved, we would still seek to control the borders and deport those who are caught. We must do that. But we would be doing it in an even, easier way -- not making up emotional "facts" about folks with a different appearance.

When Black Power was scaring folks in the 60s, a wise woman with light skin said, "Why fear Black Power? It could not be worse than White Power." How about Brown Power? May the day come when we put our power together, to give respect to every worker, every child, and every adult.

The Lynching Tree

Spiritual values do come to us as we consider racism in our community. Adding to a national sense of who we are is Dr. James Cone, on faculty at Union Seminary and a celebrated scholar on African culture. He states simply that no Christian can understand the tree of Calvary until thinking through the lynching tree.

Both had an innocent person killed by the dominant society. Both had a birth that was heralded by great hope. Black pastors at baptism may ask, "Could this be the one who will save our people?" The murmur from the congregation is as much resolute faith in God as it is hope relating to what was literally said. Both Jesus and the black man on a rope were helpless against overwhelming odds. In neither case was the public innocent. The promise of new birth is in both. We have witness from lynch victims who believed that God would triumph over the event of physical death and humiliation.

That night, the hanged man's family and congregation would quietly sing words and thoughts with undeniable power. "Steal away to Jesus." "Swing low, sweet chariot, coming for to carry me home." "Step in the water, for God's going to trouble the water." "When I get to heaven, going to put on my shoes and walk all over God's heaven." Also, Christmas carols: "On the blessed tree blooms the reddest flower." "It came upon a midnight clear." 7-J

The crunch for believers in this is that none who watch is innocent. We continue to lynch, using new technology, knowing full well that some of those we execute are innocent. They are not truly innocent, of course, just as none of us is truly innocent. Professor Cone believes that until we acknowledge that none of us is innocent, and talk about it (!) we cannot fully understand death on the cross. The most important piece of this is that he is <u>not</u> trying to drive us to a giant hand-wringing session. He is longing for us to finally move on. He believes that <u>when we recognize that we are not innocent</u> we can join hands to become a new people, moving toward the shining city on the hill.

Dr. Cone is helpful. If we take a good look at the lynching trees we can possibly own our lack of innocence. Those who consider themselves pure will not get on the train. In most cases, the man being lynched knew that was not the measure of his worth, of his humanity, of his life. He firmly believed that time is God's, not the mob's. The dying man had no apologies to his Maker. Time, like the loops at the end of the rope, was yet to be uncoiled.

Can we change?

We have great hope of change. The African-American Empowerment Network announced a broad coalition of Black leaders who will initiate new discussions on jobs, housing and education for their people, especially young people. A powerful group.

The Omaha Chamber of Commerce had its first public meeting this week to plan the redevelopment of northside Omaha -- complete with close to a million dollars of money pledged for staff to help it happen.

Plus, the new Nebraska Teacher of the Year has organized a group of educators to lean on the Feds to bring "No Child Left Behind" up to a mode which will truly help educate our kids.

Building Bright Futures is the most daring solid proposal for changing the future of low-income youth that we could imagine.

Four major initiatives! They are well beyond our dreams. 7-17

Legislative actions

The hearings for three immigrant bills had such animated observers the chair had trouble keeping order. Senator Chambers made a request in the hearing we have never heard before. He asked that he be granted the respect to state his thoughts. One of three fellows, still steaming outside the room, said, "I just wanted to tell Chambers to stick it up his nose." We should credit the men with cultivated, sophisticated thought.

In the hearing to require agencies to obey the law, one senator asked if there is an agency that does not obey the law. No. This is about illegal immigrants receiving benefits. No one has identified such benefits and other states which have gone searching have spent many times more money than was found. The benefits are prohibited by law, except for education, which is mandated by our constitution. Should we pass this bill to outlaw benefits and fool folks into thinking we are big and bold? It is dishonest.

Prominent politicians stir the false brew in an election year. Their effort is to invite candidates and the public to use explosive words and images. One leader: "Nebraskans are going to be very upset .... (they) do not want their hard-earned tax dollars to pay for benefits for illegal immigrants." That, of course, is already law.

A witness in the hearing protested that two Puerto Ricans crashed into one of our families, causing death and injury. Should be deported. Well. Puerto Ricans became U. S. citizens 90 years ago, to help supply our army in World War I. Hey, they look Hispanic.

That did not stop the chaotic talk, huffing and puffing. Our chair stood tall when he withdrew his offer to talk some more. "We are shouting, not talking. Time to move on." Thank you. However, we continue to get bashed for not passing a worthless bill. 8-9

The committee immediately killed two of the bills. High jinks came the next day as the governor and attorney general held a press conference to chastise the legislative committee, in very strong terms.

Committee members were the voices of reason. Senator Chambers held his own press conference to set the record straight. The two leaders accused Chambers of calling them racist. He did not. He said they are riding a wave of racism. Precisely.

We are all frustrated. Senators are steaming. We get every kind of email, from thoughtful to ugly vulgar claptrap wrapped in the flag, criticizing us for throwing $$$ to so-called aliens. And the Feds tell us continuously it is none of our business and we are not smart enough to investigate the matter -- so bug off.

We understand emotion is warranted by the trauma in our communities. But the shouting, disrespect, stick it up your nose -- the blue prose and ugly pictures -- are plain racism. We are better than that. 8-8

Most people in Nebraska are products of immigrants, many of whom did not come here legally. Never a word about that. One third of our current so-called illegals flew in from other countries. Never a word about that. A few are rich Mexicans. Never a word about that. We reserve all of our emotions for the poor who look Hispanic.

The pain of racial tension in this moment of our national history is that our president obviously passionately believes that we can unite as differing peoples with common goals. Do we believe that?

<u>Where are we headed?</u>

That is the critical question. This has gone from foolish to sinister, especially in encouraging racial fears. Can we move on? Most important, can we get on with being a true democracy, where we talk?

Dr. Baker, (Indian) superintendent of Mt. Rushmore national park: "We have to tell our stories to hear what our ancestors heard. A multitude of cultures come together in this place. They can make us one. If we do not act in response to e4ach other we will lose our cultures. Our grandparents' stories, the stories of our ancestors."

Martin Luther King: "I refuse to accept the view that mankind is so tragically bound to the starless midnight of racism and war that the bright daylight of peace and brotherhood can never become a reality. I believe that unarmed truth and unconditional love will have the final word.

Martin Luther King, Jr. and the writer were born the same winter, so we were both 39 when he was killed in April 1968. He was a fellow pastor with a degree from a Methodist seminary. We were proud he was a major force in rescuing our country from ourselves. Many pastors were doing all we could to aid his cause. Our grief at his loss to the nation was a tough go. The shock of dying at 39 was harsh trauma. Was my life complete? Not. Was his life complete? Evidently. A deep sense of gratitude for what Dr. King helped initiate is expressed in the words from the Black National Anthem:

> "Lift every voice and sing....
> Sing a song - full of the faith that the dark past has taught us,
> Sing a song - full of the hope that the present has brought us.
>
> > "Stony the road we trod, bitter the chastening rod,
> > Felt in the days when hope unborn had died;
> > Yet with a steady beat, have not our weary feet
> > Come to the place for which our (fathers and mothers) sighed? ....
>
> "God of our weary years, God of our silent tears ....
> Keep us in the path, we pray,
> Lest our hearts, drunk with the wine of the world, we forget Thee ...
>
> > "Facing the rising sun of our new day begun
> > Let us march on till victory is won." 8-3

With a heavy heart, we live in hope.

202. Colleges are very suspect. What happens in a huddle? How do we monitor what is taught?

10. Matters of Life

Death Penalty and Life

The death penalty debate provides an excellent example of the push and pull of most legislation. Here you have it all: the legal, the rational, the emotional, the religious, political interest groups, state budget, public attitude, and spins on all of the above.

Background: the bill to replace the death penalty with life in prison without parole has been proposed in various forms by Senator Chambers for over thirty years. It passed once about twenty years ago and was vetoed. It failed to pass in 2008.

How do you kill someone you consider evil?

What a downer. (2002) We have 49 full-grown adults, meeting for two weeks in "special session" to figure out how to kill someone. Our instruction is to add lethal injection as a method of state killing. The problem with the electric chair is that a court has considered it to be "cruel and unusual punishment." (Federal law says we may kill, but not torture.) The problem with lethal injection is that it is more cruel and unusual than the chair, which is no longer legal.

Hello? We are a bunch of folks in a back room trying to figure out how to kill someone. We have the law on our side, since we write it, so all we discuss at this point is <u>how</u> to do it. If you plan to kill someone it will be messy from someone's point of view.

On the Web, put your Google in gear and type in "Botched Executions." You will find 34 in the past 20 years: electric chair - 10; gas - 2; lethal injection - 22. Physicians and medical personnel may not participate in executions, so they have particular objection to lethal injections. The medical method of injecting into a vein was designed to enhance health and life. Use of injection for death is offensive to good medicine.

The lethal procedure has taken up to two hours to find a vein. "Torture?" Or the vein found goes to the hands, not to the heart. Or the offender is allergic to the drug, causing violent seizures, flailing and fear. In one case, the needle popped out and the offender had to call the team back from behind the curtain to try again. Or the veins collapsed. Ruth cannot be executed in this way. A great relief. The blood bank sent her home after over an hour of poking, by experts. Cruel and unusual? They told her to never come back.

We have no evidence that the death penalty is a deterrent. It does impress those of us who do not plan to kill. Gang members usually welcome death over life in prison. However, if citizens like deterrence they will love my options. How about the guillotine, and possibly the firing squad, as better alternatives? Because they are. They give the deterrent promoters more punch. Put it on TV.

No botched guillotine is on record. It works, is low tech and is tested. Same with firing squad, though it takes some supplies (bullets). (Lethal requires several drugs, which we cannot buy without changing the law. This is a puzzle, as veterinarians say they put down dogs and cats with one simple shot -- no pain, no problems.)

If you want to meet the standards of quick, painless, guaranteed, inexpensive and dramatic, the guillotine is the best alternative. We of course would have to build one and some complain about a guillotine being messy. What is wrong with messy?

A firing squad is the surest method and cheap. There is another nearly sure method, not yet considered. Hire a hit man. A hit man is effective, is relatively cheap, and is a surprise to the offender, so is mostly painless. The method fits our society's desire for violence that we do not have to watch. Someone noted that hit men sometimes kill others at the same time. We accept collateral damage. 8-9

Bingo! A major point. We accept collateral damage as "a price worth paying" to get rid of bad people. We have persons argue that we execute innocent persons less than 1% of the time, so it is a price worth paying. Just be sure to kill the right one among others. Incredible. Killing one innocent person <u>by the state</u> is too high a price, by any method.

Our options omit hanging because it is high tech. Frontier hanging techniques demonstrated you had to correlate between body weight and the length of the rope. A light body has to drop far enough to pull the rope tight. But if the rope is too long on a heavy body, it snaps off the head. The smoothness of the rope on the knot affects the time of death, whether blood or breath is cut off first. In some cases they had to shoot the hanging man so they could go home. The reader wanted to know all that, right?

<u>Uneven application of death sentence</u>

(2008) To get to the substance of the issue, is the death penalty supported by citizens of Nebraska? Once it clearly was, but it is now doubtful. A major reason for the change is that research has shown execution is highly selective. Prominent or rich people do not get Old Sparky or New Needle and Nebraskans prefer fair.

A second reason is execution costs us a bundle -- much more than life in prison -- and Nebraskans are not into spending. Years of a private secure room, with double ratio of guards and appeal after appeal in which we pay both sides of attorneys becomes <u>very</u> expensive.

Similar heinous crimes produce widely varying verdicts. Rural counties usually have prosecutors who will not even ask for execution. Execution of a well-known citizen would offend voters. Part time prosecutors may have no experience prosecuting <u>any</u> kind of murder and do not want to be embarrassed in court. A death sentence trial is a strain on a small county budget as well as on the prosecutor.

In summary of a critical point, rural county prosecutors very seldom make a death penalty charge and will avoid that more in the future, to save the huge expense and a lot of work for part-time staff. So, as in the past, for the same heinous crime urban offenders are much more likely to be executed than offenders in rural areas.

We now hire 'cheap' attorneys. We will soon be required by the feds to provide top line defense, since it is a top line penalty. That will more than double defense costs, will further remove low-budget counties from attempting to execute anyone, and will take state funds from schools, where we have budget wiggle room, to pay for our trials that could lead to death row. We are <u>not</u> becoming more civilized!

Women, the wealthy, the prominent -- are not charged for a death sentence, almost without exception. Black and Hispanic males are far more likely to face execution, for the same crime. <u>Plus</u> we will try to avoid paying for a top-line defense for paupers. These three discriminating factors – rural, rich, and limited legal defense funds – have been documented and will add to endless appeals. Some citizens call for a ten-year limit to appeals. That would be one more ground for appeal!

The writer had a little fun with this on the floor. If his wife were to kill him in the most heinous fashion, feeding his parts to the animals, from a front porch in plain public view, she would <u>not</u> be executed. Gold-plated guarantee. She is white. She is elderly. She is woman. She could hire her own attorney. It is simply unthinkable to execute someone like that. Plus, if she arranged to kill me on a porch in a <u>rural</u> county she will likely only be charged with second degree. If you want to kill, here is <u>free</u> solid legal advice. Commit the crime in one of our counties which will not prosecute the death penalty under any circumstances. The death penalty is not applied evenly.

(2007) We have another critical moral problem. How do we justify a system that makes serious mistakes? Nebraska has executed two innocent men. A few readers were curious about details. Nebraska executed a man in 1887 and four years later the 'victim' came back to town. Hmmm. Wouldn't you like to know about their relationship? And how did the 'victim' successfully set up the state to kill his adversary? The other probable innocent man was in the early 1900s, when another man, on his deathbed, confessed to the murder.

7-12

Arguments of "closure"

In the media and on the floor, a few speak often of providing "closure" for victim families by killing the offender. When families buy into that thought they are being seriously misled.

"Closure" for grieving persons is a cruel, deceptive word, in this pastor's opinion. In counseling hundreds of families in grief, one learns that the door on past hurt is never closed. To imply that, even in part, is not only false but hurtful. Families must learn to move on, but if the mental door is closed the memories behind that door can fester. The death of the offender supposedly closes a door. It does not shut out what is behind that door.

The man is dead but the pain he created is still there and to tell persons in pain otherwise is to deny their pain. If they believe our assurance of 'closure' it most likely will block their progress in grieving. For victims of assault, there is a measure of relief if the offender is caught and locked safely out of the way. They wish forever.

The term "closure" was created by lawyers, not therapists. It was intentionally crafted to further the attorneys' arguments for execution. A mother of a victim angrily protested to a prosecutor: "You say that word and I will give you a black eye. It is a cruel lie."

Why? Consider the emotions of victim families, even after the death of the offender.

Loss of control -- over many parts of their lives. Grieving persons operate at reduced capacity. Their minds operate more slowly. They are tired, lose concentration, and have more illness.

Fear -- to leave the house, to go shopping, to drive down the road the drunk driver (also killed) was on.

Isolation -- friends can imply it was partly your fault for being on that road. So avoid them.

Anger at the offender -- for taking away, with no recompense. "He is dead, but his life does not compare to my husband's life."

Anger with the legal system -- which may have operated appropriately, but was incomprehensibly obtuse about "facts" of feelings and opinions. Victims feel ignored.

We remark about victims who forgive offenders, which deflects us from hearing from the victim who has not forgiven a system that is offender-oriented. "They announce the crime as being against the state. It was against me."

Anger at loved ones -- for going to the store that night, in order to buy something we did not really need. Why did he do hurt us so?

Doubts -- about myself. Why could I not protect my own child from all danger? What kind of a Mother am I?

Emotional cycles -- anger/intimacy/grieving/anger/avoiding intimacy. A wonderfully descriptive phrase in the academics of grief is "inarticulable extremities of change." Somehow the grieving person should be led to articulate the terrible change, to say the unspeakable. That is opening a door more than closing it. Say it, accept the memory and truth of it, and then hopefully move on.

Those who have not experienced a devastating loss will point out that many of these grief reactions are not rational. Yes, indeed. But they are real, and for the rest of us to pretend to close a door is misleading. The death of a paralyzed drunk driver who clearly can never drive again, or of a criminal who will never leave prison anyway has no effect on the real world.

Summary: when a family is waiting for someone else to close the door they are being misled from what they can do and must do in order to move on. "Closure" is a clever legal term but a cruel deception to those who are waiting for court action to limit their grief.

Public attitudes are changing

(2002) In one conservative Nebraska district, which would usually support the death penalty, the figure in favor 5 years ago was 85%. This past spring it was 55%. This is the same per cent that Gallup finds nationally in favor of death in the question: "Which do you prefer: Death Penalty or Life in Prison without parole?" As people get up to speed on the legal issues and the costs the percentage will drop more.

The writer's uncle was involved with the first two executions by electric chair in Nebraska. There was a double execution on Dec. 20, 1920, for the same Howard County murder, which incidentally was far less than heinous. Back then, execution was easy.

Uncle Sam's (yes, that was his name) elderly mother was quietly drowned in her bathtub by another resident of Elba, upon the promise of a $500 payment from her son in law. Both men were quickly tried and executed.

"True Detective" magazine, in about 1930, had an article describing the event and lauding the detective work, which was not impressive. The sheriff forced Uncle Sam to stand by his mother's casket at the grave while officers moved all of the other mourners back, to leave him there alone. Hopefully, he would break down and confess to his mother's murder and their work was done. Well, Uncle Sam was of sterner stuff, so they had to go back and examine the tire tracks under her window. If he had broken down, Nebraska would have one more innocent execution. 4-6

(2006) What is a person of faith to do when confronted with choosing to take a life? Most consider killing to be unchristian, but frankly not worth the battle in the legislature. So much has changed that now many of us feel we must make our witness in plainer fashion. People are rethinking old attitudes. European countries do not do it. We have executed over 100 U. S. citizens who were innocent, including in Nebraska. But more troublesome, we thunder at our kids "Thou shalt not kill." Then add, defiantly, "But we can kill." We can do better. 6-1

Lightweight arguments against the death penalty were that those who favor death get a rush and will even party at a killing. A liughtweight argument on the other side: those against the death penalty feel sorry for the offender. That is fabrication. Some say we pastors would be impressed by a 'deathbed' conversion of an offender. Not. If truly converted, good, but that is God's job. We could not evaluate it. Plus, that is beside the point. The person has been declared guilty. The horrific crime stands and does demand punishment in an orderly society. The only relevant question is the mode of punishment.

Another red herring is to say that those opposed think the person 'deserved' to live. A violent criminal deserves to die. Even more, a man who in unimaginable cruelty held a girl/woman captive for 18 years does deserve to die. That simply is not the question. The question is if we want to be a party to killing. Every member of the legislature shares in the guilt of the death, no matter how you speak or vote. The same is true for citizens. Shall we get together to kill someone?

In the writer's district, the public is 2 to 1 in favor of life without parole. However, we have more low income and minority persons who understand the system will not treat them fairly. That is a powerful feeling which we tend to overlook. It must be acknowledged if we truly want effective deterrence.

It is apparent the death penalty is on its way out. The law is less important than public attitude, so we should give the public time to process the complex issues, especially the uneven application, before we change. As a public we are not agreed that we truly want to deter violence or child abuse, or really bad parenting or drunk driving, or Don Imus/Rush Limbaugh violence. Public attitude is by far the greatest deterrence and we are not there yet.

How do you fix the system?

The system is broken -- how do we fix it? That is the heart of the debate. We are evenly divided. Half say the only realistic fix for the uneven application is to remove the death penalty, so that punishment would focus on life in prison where the offender has the rest of his life to regret the terrible deed, where mistakes can be corrected and appeal delays are not needed to allow for mistakes. The other half feels we should fix the errors, force more even application, and remove error in court.

The unresolved part, not tackled by anyone, is how. How do we get a prosecutor to do what (he) does not feel competent to do? How do you remove error in court proceedings, where it is mostly human error? Perhaps we should pass a law that judges and clerks may not be human while they are at work.

We have reactive impulses. Our excuse making and lack of consensus, more than the moral revulsion of killing in execution, is central to this senator's thoughts in supporting life in prison without parole. On most serious offenders, we strongly agree we don't like them. "Let them stay there." Others simply cannot live among us -- cannot be trusted in attitude and actions. We must 'put them away' for our own safety. Prison for life can be an effective punishment option.

The debate is mostly rational. We cannot guarantee the person is guilty, so we execute a few innocent persons. To be sure of the guilt we have nearly endless appeals, often going twenty years -- well past the so-called time for satisfaction of paying someone back for a horrible crime. The penalty is applied very unevenly. In frontier days the horse thief, discovered, was hung. The next day. No exceptions. Usually no court. Quick and sure. It reduced crime. However, now less than one fourth of those who qualify for death are even charged with death as the consequence. We lost any semblance of quick.

Then there remain the questions about lethal injection. It is curious that in a violent society where we kill someone every day we cannot figure out how to kill a prisoner officially. 5-23

Deterrence

The public makes excuses for criminals and does not strongly and evenly support punishment. We hear persons say that the drunk driver needs his license to get to work. The fellow he killed is not getting to work. In Sweden, society has agreed that a second offense warrants mandatory jail and lifetime suspension of driving. They have consensus! We allow violent acts, like random shootings, bullying, and execution to be examples of how we deal with each other -- with little public comment except by hurting families. That is not deterrence.

'Swift and sure' is a major consideration if we want deterrence. Hopefully we can become united in that thought, so we would be together in teaching our young and in dealing with each other. We could agree, and say, that any violent personal response is absolutely not acceptable behavior. We would reinforce that with the finality of the quick echoing click of a jail lock. 7-15

Several interest groups evaluate how to deter crime. It makes sense to most of us that we would be deterred by the thought of death. Obviously, it does not make sense to a gang member who does not expect to live until 25 years of age anyway. A few see it as a way to commit suicide, but most truly fear a lifetime in jail. There is the personal glory in a death sentence for a gang member. The picture in the paper at every appeal or anniversary is an emotional rush for a youth who had no other success.

Statistics are mostly one way. In neighboring states, the state with a death penalty will have the higher murder rate. Nationally, it is over 40% higher. The United States is the only industrialized nation with death penalties in some states and our murder rate is high. A survey of Police Chiefs showed they felt the death penalty had only a 1% rate of deterrence, and that 31% of the cause of murder is drug use.

Religious Values

Religious values are compromised in several ways. Taking someone's life teaches violence. We all share in public killing. We cannot be sure the person is guilty <u>and</u> appeals on unequal treatment will increase.

On the emotional side, we want not to kill anyone, not to set the example for our kids of violence toward someone who has hurt us, not to encourage violent persons, not to feed the anger of the down and out. In the New Testament, Paul is most afraid, not that the Christians will be killed, but that they will kill, not that Rome will do violence to Christians but that Christians will do violence to Rome.

Religious arguments on the floor were mostly opposed to death. The Ten Commandments instruct us not to take a life. Jesus opposed killing, quoting "Vengeance is mine, says the Lord." --Deut. 32:35 f. It was said this meant that punishment is up to God, who does not make mistakes.

All agree religious and moral principles apply, but as usual this is more about personal feelings than it is about the Bible. Right to Life advocates are evenly divided. Some say life is sacred and the commandment not to kill applies to all life. Others state they do not feel compelled by the connection, which upsets their church leaders.

Then we have the "eye for an eye" statements which are clearly personal feelings. Some see the quote as comment on the Ten Commandments, which is really bad Bible. "Eye for an eye" was a part of primitive Jewish culture as a guide to justice. It was the top limit allowed. If someone took your eye you were limited to one eye in return. More, if the offender's eye 'saw better' than yours you could not legally take it, because it would be more valuable than yours. The values of two lives would have to be measured and compared in court. It was a guide for primitive society and Jesus flatly rejected it. --Mt. 5

(2008) We had full galleries in the chamber for the debate this week. Persons were there whose loved one was killed and who find it unthinkable to copy that by killing another person. On the other end is a fellow who wrote that every Christian should be ready to execute every prisoner. "God condemns us for failing to kill these people."

Most churches and synagogues have official statements opposing state killing. Those who deal with juvenile crime strongly feel that the adult example of killing someone who really is a problem to us gives excuse to unstable youth to do the same. Clearly, our example as seen by young people gives up the high moral ground,.

Senator Chambers feels deeply that none of us should kill anyone. "What part of 'Thou Shalt Not Kill' do you not understand?" Opposing that view are persons who feel that to not kill a person who kills heinously is to diminish that crime. Can we elevate life by killing to illustrate our feeling? Some would add that God instructs us to kill. A few state that we kill in God's name. (Both are personal or group opinion rather than solid scripture.)

One more factor does not quite fit the routine debate: some feel the death penalty should apply only to killing within prison. They argue prisoners need killers removed from their cell block just as the public needs murderers removed from the streets. (08 J)

A Personal Witness

(2008) Upon his release, found by the court to be innocent, the long term prisoner witnessed to us that he discovered many persons in his home community who were angry with him for not being executed. "Someone has to die for her murder and you could have been the one."

Are we that violent? Kill someone. Anyone. Blood revenge. In Afghanistan, if your brother is killed in a drive by shooting, you are to kill someone, anyone, in the next village. That is the way gangs think. We enforce their inclination to think that way by imitating their behavior. Kill someone and give us "closure."

Our violent response teaches our kids that violence pays the debt with blood. A "tit for tat" view has dominated our laws while subverting the teaching of youth to respect every person.

Chapter five had the account of the visit to Nebraska by an innocent man who spent 22 years on death row in Oklahoma. You expect the recount of pain about years of anxiety, anger and despair. Not. Observe his thinking after release:

"I was raised a convict. The state took me as a teenager, from a loving home, and raised me as a convict. Your world is family, children, careers, gatherings of loved ones, support. I do not know your world. You are not my friends."

If the courts had been as quick and efficient as we demand, he would be dead. It is far from routine to ponder the tragic consequences of this human error, especially when it is part of our system, our way to kill. We cannot cover our error. What does that mean to us, let alone to him?

In summary of death penalty

(2007) We had excellent, quiet, respectful discussion this week. It is apparent the public attitude is shifting. But, like us, the public is about evenly divided. Following is a summary of every argument heard in debate on the floor of the legislature.

Both sides agree: (more than two sides, but to make it brief)

Our system is not working.

It is a very expensive system.

The seriousness of the death penalty means 20 years of appeals unless the offender gives up and prefers death to jail. That is the case for one execution, which as was wryly noted became assisted suicide.

Swift and sure punishment is the greatest deterrence and execution does not give us that. Gang member types are more fearful of endless jail than of death.

The death penalty is applied unevenly.

All agree that execution does remove the offender from our presence .... that execution makes some victim families feel better and gives a sense of finality to the general public. We also agree that many victim families are not supportive of execution, and some are deeply troubled that they have any connection to killing someone.

For the death penalty:

The arguments are emotional. "Closure" is not likely, but is debated. A factual argument: "The guy would be dead."

Other statements on the floor include that people want it as a way to avenge a particularly heinous crime and give partial closure. Thoughtful persons should want to avoid the possibility of dying, so might be deterred even in a crime of passion.

Against the death penalty:

(The first arguments tend to relate to statistics.)

Death is not a deterrent in any study. Increases violent crime rate.

Effective punishment is quick and this is not. Execution takes up to twenty years, while life in prison begins at arrest. Gang members prefer death to a life sentence.

Death costs the state more. Estimates in other states are that it costs from $1 to 2 million more per offender to execute.

A fact is, innocent persons will be executed. Nebraska has done that twice.

Killing is action that angry youth tend to copy.

Minorities are more likely to be executed.

The poor, and lower social class are more likely to be executed than the wealthy, elderly, women, senators, successful, etc.

Many rural-county prosecutors will not charge the death penalty. They find that death does not have the support of the people. One rural senator complained about a terrible death of a child, from beatings over several days, without remorse of her father, all for wetting herself. The charge was only second-degree murder. 7-15

Life, Freedom and Abortion

Abortion is an emotional issue, partly because it involves the issue of life itself, and partly because we shout instead of talk about it. We are all anti-abortion. Every witness. Life is to be treasured. However, life is not the highest value and our failure to recognize and discuss that clear fact is a major contributing factor in all the shouting and name-calling. Freedom is a higher value. We treasure freedom of speech, of worship, of thought -- as higher than life. Otherwise, we would not send our young to foreign countries to give up their lives in order to protect our freedom. The issue is not simple. Could we talk?

We Christians have a wide variety of opinions, which makes us interesting! All we agree on is that God loves us and we are to love God and one another. The rest is commentary.

This is from Jesus. Again, could we talk about it?

Using abortion as a club

Messing up the debate on abortion is a well-known organization. Its followers are good people, whom the writer respects. We sometimes disagree, but one certainly finds no fault in their conviction. It is exciting to have so many persons affirming life. Could we build on that? They want to reduce abortions. So does this pastor, passionately. For reasons of faith and life!

Though the members of the Right To Life group are clear in their beliefs, key leadership in the organization plainly lacks integrity. They would rather use the life issue as a club to beat someone to a political death than to reduce abortions. This writer knows, because they tried to recruit him to damage a colleague, and perhaps to destroy the political career of someone who clearly wants to reduce abortion but is not "pure." They raise a lot of money this way and ironically will find any legislative "defeat" a good way to raise even more funds from the faithful.

The point of this background is that their tactics helped cause the defeat of the research ban. For example, a senator signed on as a sponsor, read more on the issue, and decided that a blanket ban on research was too heavy. He wondered about producing critical body parts. How is that destroying?

He expressed his doubts to someone. Organizational leadership phoned contacts in his church, instructing them to attack him in church on Sunday as "pro-cloning," an off-the-wall manufactured charge, clearly not true as well as off subject. They surrounded him on Sunday in the narthex and went after him. He was livid.

Other sponsors had similar doubts and deeply resented the tactics. Votes were lost to the pro-life cause. With term limits, all organizations have lost much of their 'clubbing' clout, so senators are more free to do what they think is right.

Could we get to the place where we actually talk about life and its issues, and discuss our questions? That would be a huge step forward for our society. If we had a secret ballot on research in the unicameral it would not even come close. Research wins on its public merits. Right-to-life has announced that research is not an option that 'their' senators may vote for. (01 #14)

The church/state fine line, carefully presented in this book, allows for the person of faith to vote convictions. It does not allow for church groups to threaten legislators who vote their belief, on either side. Period.

The fine line was crossed when we heard a senator had written, to a very few, that the only point to his proposed amendment was to take money away from a Planned Parenthood clinic (which is one of the 14 clinics presently receiving funds). Most of the clinics are public health and a few are large, so the minor percent reduction to the Planned Parenthood facility would have been quite small. But a cut.

Not a serious problem. But his memo was. He wrote that he found it "insulting" that any money went to Planned Parenthood, even though none of it could be used for abortions. He said his amendment would cut their program budget and asked people to pray that his amendment would prevail.

Well, unholy heck, another form of prayer, broke out in our session, with 20 to 30 speeches and a high level of passion. He had plainly, repeatedly, lied to us, saying he had no other motive than to cut public health clinics. Why would anyone do that? My integrity is my most valuable trait. It is sad to see anyone's integrity compromised. The hurt about the room was tangible, which is the point of this account. Voting for the church is recognized, but trying to hide that is offensive.

Several of us have strong objection to the demonizing of Planned Parenthood. The concocted stories about what they stand for are a question of integrity. Disagreement is fine, but keep it honest. Several of us have asked for the cooperation of any who will join with others to help reduce the number of abortions. Planned Parenthood is the only organization to respond. This is not to praise them, but to ask, "Where is everybody?" This group is, literally, 'planned parenthood,' which means to make every conception the start for a wanted child. Their clients are often taught to use abstinence.

Others want to know about contraception, to which some have religious objection. We respect that. However, there are other ways to network to reduce abortions. The 'planned' label obviously cannot be used. Could we talk, strategize, act?

All citizens should yearn for the day when there are no abortions because there are no unwanted conceptions. If we would each use our focus to reduce abortions and value life, instead of demonizing people with differing approaches, we could make dramatic change. The enemy is not someone else. The enemy is us. 6-11

Life is not our highest value

Moral structures have a hierarchy of values. In seminary classes, we each created and stated a hierarchy structure, to have the others punch holes in it. It was a fascinating exercise, and instructive.

The flaw in this particular structure is to flatly say life is the highest value. It is not, in any moral hierarchy. Dr. Albert Schweitzer tried that 100 years ago, but his theory did not hold. Now, in the research ban, we are told that because this cell is life it represents our highest value. We are to protect it at all costs, human or social. This is simply not a valid premise.

Breathing is not our highest value. A soldier knows and lives that. Patrick Henry summarized it plainly: "Give me liberty or give me death." Freedom is our highest value in America. Freedom to do, to move, to speak, to think, to develop and grow.

If life were our highest value we would not go on space journeys. Such journeys risk life, which we would not do for any reason if life is the highest value.

If life is our highest value we would not drive on the roads. The U. S. roads cost us 40,000 lives a year and we evidently consider it worth it, as we do not cry out to stop driving. Nor do we note individuals walking in protest of the loss of life on roads.

In Nebraska, it costs us about 7 lives a year to drive 75 m.p.h. instead of 70. Is that worth it? We have said so. How about a lottery at the beginning of the year, to pick out 7 citizens to die on behalf of our right to drive fast? We would sacrifice their lives on some kind of an altar and thereby gain the freedom to drive 75 m.p.h. We are, in effect, doing that, willingly.

A good number of Americans even consider the right to drive when the driver is impaired by alcohol to be more important than the lives lost. By that we place a lesser value on life. Thankfully, this attitude is mainly in the United States.

If life is our highest value we would not have police and fire heroes who risk their lives in order to protect someone from injury. If life is the highest value, it would be immoral to risk one's life for anything.

If life is the highest value, we would not allow our young men and women to go to war. We have had wars where they fought and died for freedom and we have said freedom is worth the tremendous loss of life. We honor them and do not judge them to be less moral because they did not hold life to be “of infinite value” -- whatever that means.

Life is of exceedingly high value, which makes freedom of exceptional value. How would we dare to reduce freedom for college students who express their ideas, or for the elderly sick who want to end their lives, or for the confused pregnant teenager, or for the explorer who takes on a "crazy, hopeless" venture? We hear that each should have available good consultation. By all means!

Freedom is not absolute

Not one of us is free to do as we please and this is where it gets really interesting. I am not free to walk into you when you choose (freely) to stand on the sidewalk. You have a ‘right’ to clean air, clean water, and clean food and I do not have the freedom to compromise any one of those for you. Freedom is limited by respect for other persons and their value(s).

"Pro-Choice" says you must value and respect the person -- the freedom of a confused 18-year-old pregnant girl to make medical decisions for her body and health, with trained consultation available. "Pro-Life" says you must value and respect the person -- protect the developing fetus in her body. Both value life. The conflict is on freedom. We refuse to talk about it, except to ourselves.

This chapter will document attempts to change the legal definition of a person, which is back to the club, using law instead of dialog. A fetus is life and has value. Ask any expectant parent. How do we honor that value while valuing the mother whose body is critically attached? Until the fetus is "viable" they are one, not two. Could we talk, and together marvel at the miracle here?

Are we waffling on definitions?

We ponder the meanings of a slippery word: freedom. It is spoken often, with stained-glass voices, and with cartoon-like flags flying from both ears. However, one is not sure how many who say it truly love freedom. They love theirs, but not mine.

Those who say they want freedom for Iraq usually do not want it for dissenters in our own country. Many Christians want it, but not for Muslims. A few are adamant that the freedom of a fetus trumps the freedom of an adult. The freedom to smoke or to ignore smoke trumps the freedom to breathe clean air. The freedom to drill an irrigation well trumps the freedom to take water out of the nearby stream.

We also hear that freedom to pray in schools is more important than freedom not to pray. Freedom to carry a concealed weapon is more important than freedom to walk down a street without worrying about how many "good" citizens are carrying guns. Freedom to have air through the hair on a motorcycle competes with the public's freedom not to pay for lifelong injuries which could have been prevented by a helmet. 5-19

Do we waffle on defining life? Not really, because we do not define it. What is it about life we are to protect? Awareness is central in any definition.

The heart of the "life" discussion (not abortion) is what is the meaning of life before pregnancy? A birth of a viable fetus produces a human being. Before that, a pregnancy may become a fetus. But what about before pregnancy? Is a fertilized egg that is not attached to a uterus a human being? A live piece of my thumb in the shell of a female egg is not a person, but could become one. How do we distinguish between live tissue and a human being? (By any legal definition, which is what we are limited to in writing laws, a "person" must have been born.)

Legislating religious beliefs

The fetal tissue bill is tied up in committee this week. Several of us object that it is simply an attempt to put religious doctrine into statute and therefore is not a subject we should even discuss. Imagine -- we may be asked to vote on who is moral and who is immoral. In case you are wondering, the moral position is the one with the most votes. 1-11

Opposition was expressed after my statement that the bill stomps on religious conviction of citizens who disagree with the sponsors, that we are being asked to vote on who is immoral. Worse yet, we are preparing to vote that a basic religious conviction of the entire Jewish community of faith is defective and not acceptable in our state. There were many very quiet thank you's from senators who were forced to vote against their belief and from key staff people all over the capitol. Several staff said they had never commented on floor debate before and they could not now, but "Thank you for saying something we have not heard before."

Someone objected that in the debate we had spoken against Catholics and catholic belief. Not. Never mentioned it, as a catholic speaker quickly pointed out. We said we were there to defend traditional catholic doctrine, that proponents of the ban have put a new bend in it. During WW II we were told on catholic doctrine that life is not a higher value than "Just War" and so catholic men and women could go to defend our country. Obviously, if life is the highest value, as we are now told, no one could do anything that might cost a life.

(2006) Contraception is another sensitive issue that gets tied with abortion. For many Christians, there is a connection and we respect that. But for government policy, there is no valid connection between abortion and most forms of contraception. The issue is used for fund raising by groups, not for light. Hopefully, open debating of cloning will clear the air so we can work together on reducing abortions. Please, could that possibly happen?

Jim Wallis, evangelical theologian:

> *I may be opposed to abortion for religious reasons, but if I seek to pass a law banning the practice, I cannot simply point to the teachings of my church or evoke God's will. I have to explain why abortion violates some principle that is accessible to people of all faiths, including no faith at all.*

Objection to taking life is a principle available to all. Contraception and tissue research simply do not qualify as taking life.

The fetal tissue bill brings out a lot of earnest debate. However, it was totally based on Catholic doctrine. We have no business putting a denomination's product of religious principle into statute and this senator announced one more time he would not vote for or against or to refer. Nothing. He has two or three religious principles himself, but would not try to put them into statute and they should be grateful. Debate was very friendly and respectful, which is welcome.

(2001) There is the tired old saw that anyone who objects to Right To Life legal language is pro-abortion. That is so ridiculous it no longer deserves comment. This senator will stand with anyone to reduce abortion. But that option was not being offered this week. Or, on the other side, we have the same kind of charge, that the adversary is anti-choice, so is opposed to freedom. Not. Could we talk?

Cloning vs. stem cell research

(2007) Cloning is stripping a female egg of its contents and inserting cells. If this produces a viable fetus and the subsequent birth of a person it is called "reproductive cloning." Every senator is opposed to that, but how can it be called anti-life? It is life.

If used for research, cells grow as they will and come to an end, or provide discovery of new information and then come to an end. Many oppose creating a cell/life for new information. Others see this as honoring life by exploring its mysteries. Others want us to say the cell is a person. It is a form of life, like the cells in your thumb, but it is not a person and it will never become a person.

There is a third possibility in cloning. The manipulated cell can become a body part, as a liver or heart. It is clear that is in our future. Using the person's own cells will provide an organ for transplant without rejection. Rejection of "foreign" tissue is one bugaboo of transplants, so the prospects are intriguing.

The bill in its first edition prohibited all three options by banning use of the female egg for any manipulation. This could affect other cell research.

Cell research is one apparent key to restored life for many paralyzed citizens. Wouldn't that be a day for rejoicing!

Research looks at God's creation, to discover more facts. The spinal cord of our son is severed between his shoulder blades. One hope is that a collection of his own cells, inserted in an egg, would begin cell generation and heal his spinal cord. Like his cut hand will heal. The medical fact is the spinal cord of a fetus will heal if it is cut, but not after birth. Why? A great mystery. Inquiring minds want to know. Could we possibly train or trick spinal cord cells into regeneration? That is a subject of research.

The point of research is discovery

Central to research is the inquisitive mind. What might we find that is new to us? Do we want more info? Would God not want us to learn more about God's creation? Inquiring minds should want to know.

It is mind boggling to declare we do not want to know how the body functions, which is what we say when we ban research on the body. In the search, we will learn more about this marvelous creation, our body. We have already learned secrets we could not have imagined. Life is not diminished by our discoveries in creation, but rather wonderfully lifted up. Now, even the cynic has to marvel at creation.

The hardcore attitude is said by some to represent God, but it reflects more a lack of understanding on the nature of research into God's creation. Confusion on research is to be expected, as a true researcher is a unique person, often not understood.

Ruth's Dad, Bob Wallis, was a researcher on insects for over forty years, for the U. S. Dept. of Ag. Bob examined the life cycle of a creature so flimsy in its flight stage that wind currents carried it from state to state. If it were not for the potato psyllid Lowen and Ruth would have never met, because that little varmint brought Bob and his Ruth to Scottsbluff and Nebraska for 17 years. Humbling. Without that insect, our Doug and Jo would not exist. That is a mystery that far surpasses research on embryos. Should we criminalize thinking about it?

True research includes a basic assumption that it may take you to facts not known. If Bob knew where he was to come out he would not have come out with new knowledge and would not have saved millions of dollars of crops in Nebraska. He was intent on discovering the unknown and received a distinguished service award for putting money into our economy. His discovery continues to help our state budget, which we senators do appreciate! 7-11

This father would have given his life in the crash event if there was some way it would have protected Doug from being paralyzed. In a minute. You add your own illustrations.

Some day we can join voices to celebrate how valuable life is. To think about the values for which one of us would risk life is not a devaluation of life in any way. It is lifting it up, giving it new meaning. In a moral structure, life with its attendant values helps define our highest values. We had ten hours of Martin Luther King, Jr. celebrations recently. Illustrations from his life and times abound. Several thundered at the audience: "Men and women, black and white, died so that you can vote. Their blood is in the street, for you. How dare you stay home on election day?"

Is voting a freedom value? 9-1

Changing definitions

Legal positions on the beginning of life are directed by Roman Catholic theologians who interpret "unchanging" belief. The problem: they keep changing their minds. In the old days we were told by them to agree that life begins in the fifth month of pregnancy. That included ensoulment -- when the soul enters a new life. Then it was three months. Then, we had to change to "quickening," which is when the fetus moves on its own. Then, we changed to when the woman is pregnant.

There is more. Then, we were told life begins at the moment of conception, before pregnancy, when the egg receives a sperm. Small problem: physically, there is no moment of conception. It is a process, with no life guarantees. Then, soon we come to the implication that embryonic research is tied to abortion.

Are we talking about issues of abortion before there is a pregnancy? How did we get there? When did rational thought leave us as we were led along this path?

Conception is not pregnancy. Many a couple, going through the difficult process of a fertility clinic, will tell you that until the embryo is embedded in the wall of the uterus you have nothing. Not pregnant. Do words mean anything here? Our definitions are so deeply flawed we have lost communication.

Most of us accept that life begins at conception, or whatever someone will demand we accept ten years from now. We just give up. A few pile on by calling it "innocent life," though traditional catholic thought says a baby is not innocent until baptized. Life is exceedingly valuable and precious to each of us. But it is not the highest value for any except the most strong-minded pacifist.

(2007) An anti-cloning bill had press play because over half the senators signed on as cosponsors. Everyone opposes human cloning. (Even God, since cloning is competitive with creation?) So what's the deal? The senators soon discovered the cloning bill is not to stop the threat of human cloning (a straw man), but to criminalize embryonic research by a legal re-labeling of an embryo as a <u>person</u>. Several signers have switched to oppose the bill and it certainly will not get out of committee in that form. A human being is more than an egg in a dish, with a temporary existence.

Again, this senator refuses to vote on amendments which are simply fundraisers. "Look! We stopped cloning in its tracks. Send more money." The God-talk that is tucked into the spin is bad news. Supposedly, this is all tied to abortion, to which God objects. Nice spin, but we are not dealing with abortion. Again, how does one have an abortion without a pregnancy? Can a Petri dish get pregnant? 7-11

Senator Landis did a triage argument. He proposed that if an Alzheimer's patient and a dead fetus were floating down the stream the proponents of the ban on research would save the dead fetus as their ethical choice. O my. That kicked up some dust. Or was it stream-water? 1-15

The controversial cloning legislation passed. Why? It is bad legislation that draws irrational anger that is hurtful to us all. My final vote on the bill was positive because all sides said they could live with it (does very little actually), and, far more important, all promised they would not bring the subject back for several years. Yes. Please.

Fetal Homicide

(2002) We are moving ahead with a fetal homicide bill, which this senator urged 3 years ago. A drunk driver killed an unborn baby, due that week. The mother was killed, the baby was delivered and then died. The law allows no punishment for Zachary's death because he was not yet born. A clear gap.

Unfortunately, a few Right To Life promoters decided to load it up with abortion language. Like defining a fertilized egg as a child. This legislation is not a matter of when life begins. We have agreed life begins with the fertilized egg, and that the crime could apply back to the beginning of pregnancy. But they wanted to call the egg a person, which creates all kinds of mischief, beginning with having to count pregnant women as two (or more!) in a census.

The language remains an "unborn child" which is defined as human life that is now dead. Hello? An unborn child is always dead? (The wording is a ploy to sneak in the word "child.") Since it is impossible in the first trimester to prove that a miscarriage is not taking place, a few of us moved to start the crime with the second trimester. But the majority would allow no amendments. So it remains that an unborn child is defined as a killed fetus. (!) A miscarriage is now labeled a crime if the woman is injured in an accident during her medical crisis. Could we use English?

Celebrating life

(2002) We get "Life is sacred" statements in the mail, urging us to be hateful against anyone who disagrees. Really? Human life is sacred. No doubt of it. The earth is sacred. The colorful little bird at the feeder outside my window has sacred worth.

Actually, these are highly positive thoughts. There is so much to celebrate here. We wrestle with life and death issues precisely because we do consider life to be sacred, of exceedingly high value. We note that in some countries life is cheap, and in some community cultures among us life has little value. We strive mightily against those cultures.

To label research for healing as pro-abortion is outrageous. It is offensive in the extreme to label our Doug and his loved ones as anti-life because he wants healing of his spinal cord. We are in a weird frustrating scene where all persons around the table celebrate life but are reduced to trashing others' value of life.

If we could only discuss life, our discussion would lift the value of life. Together, we could reduce the public devaluation of life – the killing on the street, abuse in the home, putdowns in public. Let's pray for it. Would that we will join with each other to affirm life and hold to account those who would lead us to hold lesser values in our entertainment, our work and our lives. 3-4

Values of life vary

The poet speaks of those "whose fat blood sleeps as it slips along their veins" (Bailey). They are alive, but useless. Is that true life value? As we put our lives on the line each of us enhances value. That kind of life is precious in God's sight, and in ours. (2004 #3)

A mother's life is of higher value than a baby's, or so most consider it. We consider a breadwinner's life to be more valuable than that of one of the children. Loss of a breadwinner on the prairie usually meant the breakup of the family, another value.

Some say a baby is equal to an adult in value because he may be a Beethoven, she may be a genius mathematician. That is imagination dancing, not the real world. If true, we should urge the family, desperately poor, to have all the babies they can because one may be an exceptional artist. Please not. Arguments to not waste an egg or a sperm deny a basic of God's creation: our creator chose to provide an unimaginable surplus of sperm and eggs. Value creation.

228. Kelly's portrayal of the death of Senator McCarthy. The undertaker waits for a man left with no friends.

11. Other Controversial Issues

Gay Issues

The rational debate on the legality of homosexual orientation is actually over. Overwhelming evidence shows orientation is not a choice. Brain and DNA research has identified the deciding factors in sexual orientation, for any of us. Since the person does not decide, the law cannot punish or restrict orientation.

However, the debate continues because of personal opinions about presumed activity that is assigned to a class of persons. Same sex activity is never the subject of discrimination provisions in law. The opinion debate on sexual activity may be about the emotions but it is not about the legal.

Our amendment on homosexual orientation rights has produced interesting sparks. It is rather routine, relating only to prohibiting discrimination in housing, with no real enforcement. But it is a statement of public policy and the real estate association supports it. "It is our present policy."

However, the sponsor of the bill to which it was attached was very upset and said he would pull the bill (his priority) rather than see it pass. The real estate association voted unanimously they continue to be supportive of the bill. Chambers signed on as a cosponsor, which means he must approve of pulling it. So then the sponsor said he would ask that it not come on the agenda.

A majority of us signed a petition that it come up. Could we talk about the legal issue and not his emotions? We did and we passed it.

"He looks gay."

The most frustrating piece was the failure of opponents to recognize that the bill is to restrict discrimination for someone who appears to be gay. How we can justify withholding rights because of anyone's looks is a mystery. The real estate response is encouraging and reminds us some people are thinking. 1-21

There are a variety of opinions around the floor on gays (as well as about fat people, the elderly, and baldheadedness). That is not a problem. Our human nature is to be opinionated. However, our talk confuses. Even the governor, in his veto message, showed total confusion on definitions. In three sentences, meant to be speaking to the orientation amendment, he referred to it as (1) orientation, (2) choice and (3) activity. O my. Which is it?

Orientation is like the hair color a man is given, choice is to dye it orange (which one senator did to boost his local team) and activity is what he does while his hair is orange or natural. One senator said orientation is a choice. We asked if he had chosen his sexual orientation? Silence. We do not decide, one day, whether to be attracted to boys or girls. Or better understood, a boy does not decide he is not attracted to girls.

The house was evenly divided, with the fears of an emotional public expressed. It is really discouraging that intelligent people cannot get past their feelings to look at the words they are using. If we could get clear on orientation we then could discuss sexual activity in a helpful way. (01 #22)

Into the cheery mix of another bill, Senator Chambers threw his small amendment to require that all grant recipients agree not to discriminate against sexual orientation. That is easy, because they each already have that explicit policy. However, he still wanted to say it and you would have thought he threw a bomb. We passed it, barely. Senators muttered that this will stop productive work in this session, the governor will go bonkers and the end of the world is near.

How can this be? If we were to go on to talk about offensive sexual activity, there would be understandable passion. We could express dismay about the actress who reported that, to keep her husband happy, she often went out and recruited another woman to join the two of them in bed. Do those straights have no shame?

It is very clear public policy that we do not allow employers to discriminate against anyone by looks. Period. What is so bad about saying so once in a while? In a nice quiet voice. And then moving on to the tasks at hand. This venting is tiresome and useless. Worse, we are back to trashing a class of people. 5-14

Hateful opinions generate strange ideas

The President of the large Southern Baptist seminary in Kentucky, Dr. R. Albert Mohler (close to a Baptist Pope), has announced that God made some persons gay as a punishment to all of us for original sin. Hang on. We can sort out his weird thought, his way.

First, original sin, according to him, is Adam biting an apple, for which God could not forgive him. (Really? God can't forgive?) This means we are all guilty. Shame on you! Please, this is not Jesus talk. This is from some monks in the Middle Ages who had spent too long away from the sun and had forgotten about God's light and love. (Off to the side, the theory plugs into some Christians' sincere beliefs, which I respect but do not accept. However, this man abuses the theory.)

The more amazing part of Brother Mohler's statement is that he is ready to accept that gays are so by genetic makeup. So how could a good God do this "bad" thing to someone? Because God was punishing Adam and us, that's why. God changed the gene code or messed with hormones and made some of his creation gay. Hang on. It gets stranger.

He says perhaps science is close to identifying the "defective" gene or lack of hormones that cause 'gayness' and perhaps that can be known in the fetal state so that the mother can take action. Perhaps a patch on her tummy will "cure" the "defect" (Cure God's created defect!) Therefore, he says, we should root out God's punishment (and thereby avoid pressure for forgiveness?) so we can get rid of the gay blemish on creation (caused by God).

Love it. Whatever your and my convictions, he stands them on the head. Are you a 'conservative' Mother who discovers a gay fetus? Have a 'liberal' abortion and clean up a bit of sin. Are you a 'liberal' mother who strongly supports gays -- but would not want to raise one? Have an abortion and make the world more conservative. Are you a conservative who is 'liberal' on research? You may discover more than you wanted to know about your fetus. Are you a conservative who thinks only Jesus takes away original sin? Put a patch on your tummy and do it yourself.

Ridiculous. All of this messed-up thinking, which boils over into the legislature, comes from labeling our opinions as God's. "I hate gays because God hates gays." "People who do not hate gays should be punished, for God hates them too." 7-11

"Gay marriage"

The non-news of the week: a court has ruled Nebraska's anti-gay marriage amendment unconstitutional. Well, Duh. It was written to be unconstitutional. It was a copy of a law already declared by the Supreme Court to be unconstitutional. It was a sham managed by a few unprincipled profiteers.

People speak out against "gay marriage." Fine. It is a free country. But God save us from persons who milk emotions to build a self-serving base and collect more money. In this case they planned for two campaigns, one to pass the petition and a second to object to the expected court ruling. We had quotes from these slimy types, who, when asked why they did not go for reasonable wording, said "our people" will be just as upset again when it is declared outside the law and they will then build up antagonism toward judges for "overriding the will of the people." We wonder how courts get a bad name.

Do remember that "gay marriage" was illegal in Nebraska before the amendment. The proposal was to stir fears. The first sentence defines marriage as between a man and a woman. No public problem there. This senator agrees and most courts agree. "Gay marriage" is in quotes because it is confusing language. Words have meaning. We know what marriage is, so should come up with another word for a same-sex contract with identical benefits. That may be impossible, given the hundreds of references to marriage in statute. Do recognize there is room for discussion here. That would be good.

The second sentence declares, among other things, that same-sex domestic partnerships are not valid under law. Let's see. That would invalidate the contract a father and son draw up on how they are going to manage their farm. Or prohibit a mother and daughter from a shared agreement on their Living Wills and how they want to be cared for in illness. Or block a gay couple with joint home ownership from going to court to protect their property. The judge said it would place restrictions on roommates, tenants, foster care parents and shared living arrangements (as, a woman caring for her Aunt).

Our legislature tried to pass a statute that would enable two persons of the same sex to contract with each other to make hospital decisions if one were incapacitated. Our Attorney General said the gay amendment prohibited even discussing the proposal in the legislature. (That is the same Attorney General who says we must object to the court's ruling. But he prohibits us from talking about it. Help!)

The judge said this amendment amounts to a punishment of a class of citizens. "It goes so far beyond defining marriage that the court can only conclude that the intent and purpose of the amendment is based on animus (feeling of animosity) against this class" of citizens.

How about some animus against those self-appointed organizers who are using good people to stir up false fears, get signatures, collect funds and promote the idea that the world is about to come to an end? Send money! 5-19

Marriage ceremonies

A most joyful part of this pastor's work was preparing for and conducting hundreds of weddings. My preferred ritual is several centuries old. It was good to be able to say to a couple, "This ceremony is similar to the wedding ceremony of your great-great-grandparents, wherever they were." Here is tradition, family and community. We think about all that as we examine the nearly universal service of 100 years ago.

However, the ceremony does not come from the Bible, or even go very far back in the church. Church weddings are no more than 500 years old. For the first 1500 years after Jesus, marriage was a civil contract only. If a new couple wanted a blessing of their marriage they would ask a priest, who could do so on the steps of the church, not inside. Marriage was not within the church. That was by law.

We have evidence there may have been isolated blessings of a couple, both hetero and same sex, in a few congregations. It would never have been considered a legal marriage.

Also clearly, the current marriage rituals are conducted with two components, a civil contract and a religious ceremony. Couples may choose one or both. This pastor has conducted ceremonies which were church only. If a couple wanted only the legal ceremony they were sent to a Justice of the Peace. A few countries do not allow both ceremonies at the same time. Civil and religious ceremonies are separate and not equal. Scripture does not guide the marriage contracts of the state. It has never been the church's business.

A few ask this pastor if he ever married a gay person. Well, yes, of course. Every pastor with hundreds of weddings has done so unknowingly in regular weddings. Our society 'orders' everyone to marry. Most gay persons probably marry. One would hope the gay person would share with his/her beloved that sex will not be fun, but that they will continue to love each other, and to have children. So there will be limited sex. Because they are deeply in love, they often become a model family. Certainly gays are as good at parenting as anybody and it is not the neighbors' business.

The pastor may find out about it later if the man begins to abuse his wife because he is not getting "enough" sex "from" her after the children are born. We know it is easier for lesbians to "pass" and there certainly is a wide variance of interest in sex among us. Those who use the scriptures for a selective purpose ignore that many gay persons, as many straight persons, do not engage in sexual relationships. They may be married.

"Defending" marriage

A few agitators claim to be "defending" marriage against the "gay attack." We read that, "Gay marriage will destroy America and all we hold dear." Such puffery is effectively deflated by a recent Atlanta Journal cartoon. The terrorists are in their cave, plotting the end of America. Their plan: "We will sneak in and marry each other." We have hetero couples who are compromising marriage quite well, thank you. They do not need help from gays or terrorists.

Political voices that claim to tell us exactly what God is thinking today want <u>their</u> concoction to become law. In supporting "Defense of Marriage" legal actions, they say the Bible established marriage and directs wedding ceremonies. Not even close. The Bible does not instruct us to marry, or to marry before having children.

Marriage was a <u>cultural</u> custom in other civilizations, both in Europe and the Americas, preceding Israel by thousands of years and was continued as a part of Hebrew culture.

The Hebrews people tell the story of creation in a beautiful way. A man and woman leave their homes and "become one" in order to produce children. It was not called marriage. For most couples, the creation story becomes their story and means establishing a new home. However, many couples in biblical times did not leave one parent's home. Also, Solomon 'became one' with 700 wives, plus concubines. When we call polygamy anti-marriage we are objecting to selected scripture, which supports multiple wives.

Also in ancient Hebrew tradition, marriage was more like a property contract and the wife was owned by the husband. The man could dissolve the agreement, but the woman could not. The man could make other such contracts.

The woman would be guilty of adultery if she allowed another man intimate contact, and that man would be guilty of adultery, which was the violation of a man's property. But the husband did not commit adultery if he roamed far and wide in sexual exploits -- as long as his new partner was not some one else's property. This is our model of marriage?

Pastors, and cartoons on weddings, will mistakenly use the line, "I pronounce you man and wife." It gives away a lingering attitude. The groom <u>was</u> a man before the wedding, so is he adding property? Emotionally, when does he become a husband, a true partner?

Several scriptures certainly assume marriage as a cultural custom. It was a contract including payment (a dowry) for the bride, and was celebrated in a home, not at the synagogue. Every healthy adult was to produce children. We assume Jesus did not marry, but he attended a wedding (in a home), even making some very good wine for it, and he used a wedding setting for a parable. In speaking of family, Jesus was more likely to speak of wedges and tensions which divide families. Jesus was very direct in confronting the hurt to women, as declared property, by condemning divorce by a man. Frankly, Jesus left no room for "Just breaking up." (Matt 5:31,32) If someone really wants scripture for the defense of marriage, why not take that one and complain about divorce? We do not do that.

The proponents/opponents of civil union between the same sex are examples of serious offenders in the abuse of scripture. A few would say that if two men love each other, and have a commitment to each other, scripture would say they should be married. Not any more than hetero. Far more agitators would say that scripture prohibits a same sex couple from a committed relationship. No same sex scripture even_mentions love or commitment. That judgment is in the mind of the reader, as s/he looks for scripture to back an opinion.

We can define marriage as a contract for a man and woman, as legislators usually prefer. This does not prevent the state from finding a good term for a contract between two men or two women, where law allows it, with identical benefits. There is much to commend a contract, especially when children are involved. They need a stable home, which it is in the interest of the state to provide. Prohibition of legal standing puts a couple in jeopardy in several situations and is therefore a harm to a stable community. Scripture guides us in family life, but does not direct the civil contract.

The point of the actions of Nebraska and Congress is not about existing marriages but is to prohibit selected civil rights for a class of people. According to our Attorney General, the Nebraska defense of marriage amendment prohibits a gay person from advocating for his/her rights with state legislators. Free speech is denied. They may not talk with senators about rights.

Really? How can this be? There is not another person in or out of Nebraska who is prevented from talking with a senator -- not a felon, nor anarchist, nor terrorist, nor member of a weird religion or party. "God's commands" come to this? It is an insult to God.

Scripture and Sexual Mores

We have a right to express revulsion about homosexual activities, and a right to debate theories that our sexual orientation may be chosen and therefore is an act subject to law. Just do not blame God for these opinions, or pretend scripture is the source. Biblical writers never heard of a concept of sexual orientation, which was developed centuries after they wrote. Scripture has no reference to homosexual orientation or to a loving intimate relation between two men or two women. Plainly, loving gay couples are not known or assumed by any scripture reference. Period.

We find ten scripture references (15 verses) to same sex activities. All assume the activity is between heterosexual persons. For example, the men in Leviticus and in Paul's writings are assumed to be married. In the Hebrew culture, all potent men were expected to marry and have children.

Two passages have direct statements. Paul speaks his outrage to and about men who are married, plus have a mistress, plus seek mutual masturbation with other men. He calls it "lust." Yes! Paul is devastating in his comments. Anyone who reads Romans 1-2:3 with no pre-formed opinion would recognize the point being made. Paul decries those "whose evil ways prevent the truth about God from being known." (Romans 1:18)

One way is by worshipping their God-given bodies instead of the Creator. This is sin, because it obscures a clear vision of God with a focus on one's body. Heterosexuals can do that! The same scripture lists other serious ways to obscure God: with greed, vice, jealousy, murder, fighting, deceit, malice, gossip, insolence, pride, boasting, disobeying parents, not keeping promises, or having no kindness or pity. "They deserve to die." (Romans 1:28-32) How about organizing movements to object to all these sins? Jesus is crucified again when lust kills love, or when selfishness and pride overpower caring.

Lust fogs the mind and is sin. It is the lack of control, the using of another person for self-gratification, turning away from productive use of life energy, shielding one's intellect from the power of God. Some of it is same sex but most of it is opposite sex -- in scripture and in life. Paul makes one reference to women (Romans 1:26) in an act that is 'not by nature,' but the subject is still lust. Would that we could skip our proof-texting and join wholeheartedly in publicizing his thoughts about that which obscures God: that whole list of sins. We abuse scripture when we detract from the central message. Thereby we give excuse to those ignoring the message.

Leviticus 18:22 brings a very different setting. The prophets vehemently fought for the belief in and practice of One God. Any compromise brought impurity, which was called an abomination. Leviticus is a book of rules to guide priests in temple rituals. Lifting verses from that context changes the meaning, as the original intent is part of the message.

For example, the literal translation of the first same-sex passage is "(No male shall) lie the lyings of a woman." Don Hanway points out "This is not a moral violation but a violation of purity according to the Hebrew thinking of that time: one's maleness is compromised (diluted) when one assumes the woman's role in the sexual act. It is akin to mixing two kinds of seed in a field or two kinds of fiber in cloth -- behaviors which are also ruled out." This is not about sex, but about pretending to be a woman. It is a sin similar to raising hybrid seed corn, another abomination according to the priestly code scripture.

In addition, on this text, there was the problem of doing acts of devotion to a foreign god. Married men, with families and a farm, were to trust that Jehovah would produce crops. However, some farmers heard that a Caananite goddess had a reputation for enhancing fertility and may help crops and herds produce more. So what could be harmed by covering all the bases? Devotion to One God, that's what was harmed.

The offending men crossed the border to the temple of the goddess where they were directed in mutual masturbation, collected the sperm in a small dish and placed it on the altar. They then did "the dance of the burning corn" around it and went home to watch their crops and herds grow. Were these gay men? Were they in love? Were they establishing a union? Were they being disloyal to their wives? Not by any stretch of the imagination. Was it an abomination? Yes, without any doubt. It was flirting with a foreign god, diluting allegiance to Jehovah, and harmful to the Hebrew community. (The prophets also felt masturbation was a wasting of the sacred seed needed to build a nation. In their minds, a woman had no seed or egg, so sperm was the seed to be conserved.)

Same sex affection is not a theme of scripture anywhere, though persons like David and Jonathan acknowledged it. A Lutheran bishop put it simply. "God does not care about humanly devised categories that label and demean those who somehow do not fit our norm. God made all of us and did not make us alike."

It is an extreme disappointment to this pastor that more Christian denominations with Biblical authority as a central premise have not stepped forward to speak openly about the above understanding of scriptures, which is consistently taught by Biblical scholars of a variety of backgrounds.

Again, a few persons express negative attitudes toward gay persons. However repulsive, it is personal opinion. It is hard listening to the diversity of attitudes, but we strongly affirm the right to these expressions. Listening is helpful in a democracy as we make up our minds about what is best public policy.

In summary, please note this writer has not commented on same sex relations, whatever that is. Two men hugging on a football field is a same sex relation. When we throw in words we do not define, like "intimate," how can we have intelligent discussion? Also, not a word has been written about support for heterosexual "private" practices. O my. Would someone expect us to bless Madonna? Or every birth? A few marriages are legalized rape. Man to woman abuse is a major (sexual) assault on our society.

We believe marriages may be blessed by our creator. We could affirm loving relationships as strongly as do our beloved scriptures.

Summary

The saddest note: the debate diminshes the wonderful gift of sexuality, which is an important component of who each of us is.

Discrimination against gays is an important subject, certainly, but one wonders, "Why does this continue to be such a big deal? Why do we talk about it this much?"

We are created with all sorts of physical and mental conditions and we generally get along with them. This kid wanted to be a star basketball player, but after reading the smiles of the coaches and other team members he got over it. Would love to be an artist, but even my stick figures overload the imagination. God created us differently.

Someone is handed a gay body/voice/wiring and we can observe that this guy really has no interest in dating girls. However, persons will go ballistic with no more than that, and their imaginations -- to go on. One testifier said that every gay person is a predator on children or is trying to recruit others as predators. Hello? We have crime after crime after crime of men's assaults on girls and women, but it does not mean that all men are like that. Follow-up questions indicated he probably had never knowingly met a gay person.

We find some of the same fearful political statements in our history. In 1900, Bert Martin, from the panhandle, was sentenced to prison for stealing a horse. In prison, they discovered he was a woman. The governor was outraged that "a sexual monstrosity" was anyplace in the land. "It" was so serious a threat to prison morals (!) that he released the man early, presumably to go back to his partner and help her raise their child.

That is strong personal opinion in search of a scripture, but we do not read that he found one.

There is good humor in it all. A pastor-type, in a hearing, said that gays are a huge problem in our society. Then, unbelievably, he said he would support this bill if discrimination against gays presented a massive problem, but there are so few that we should not bother.

Reverend Chambers (this senator loves to call him Reven'r) charged to the questions. Brother Ernie asked him, a pastor, if he remembered how many it took for Jesus' promise to be in the midst of them? Quiet answer: Two or three. What, cries out a shocked Ernie, does there not have to be a multitude for Jesus to pay attention?

The next is sheer scriptural genius, given the theology of this pastor. Ernie asked him how many it would take for Jesus to be willing to be stretched out on the cross and crucified? Would Jesus willingly die for one or two? Or did it have to be a multitude?

This is fun satire and the dude brought it on himself with foolish opinions. But why does the whole process of legislation have to grind to a stop to let someone's imagination churn up dust? For individual rights, yes. That is a big deal. But for the rehash of feelings of someone who despises another person he has never met? How much longer does this have to go on?

Driving Under the Influence (DUI)

Issues of church and state come together in alcohol-impaired driving. So called "drunk driving" is more likely to kill or injure a person under 25 years of age than all other risks for that age group combined -- disease, defects and accidents. In Nebraska, we kill over 100 persons a year in this way. Persons of faith are adamant in protecting life, but have shown surprising indifference to these losses, which are completely preventable! To be quite frank, we have not seen any church or synagogue object to the death and mayhem, except at funerals. There has been no resolution opposing this type of violence, ever, and no religious task force to change public attitude. Public consensus lags behind law and is the holdup to progress. Many citizens give tacit permission to drive impaired.

This senator did not go to the legislature to tackle drunk driving or to complain about Christian indifference to antisocial behavior. However, he was sensitive to the legal issues, having lived them as a victim family. He saw the gaping loopholes that past legislatures had put into law. Part of his job, as a person of faith, was to work on those gaps in order to prevent loss to more families.

The Nebraska law is forever changed in the last few years through the effort of many, and more citizens are expressing greatly increased outrage at the mayhem. Lives have been saved.

As a couple, we have been a part of a group that has literally transformed the landscape for impaired drivers. Loopholes are mostly gone, penalties are greatly increased, prosecutors have tools which will work, and judges who care are able to enforce stiff penalties on a repeat offender. With help from groups, friends, officers, prosecutors, and on, we have drafted and passed dozens of bills.

It was never easy, but frankly, if you can show that a bill will reduce the number of drunk drivers the legislature will back you. Senators are ahead of the public and are very upset with the mayhem. We are grateful to all who helped!

Personal involvement

The Kruse family persistently objects to the mayhem because our son and his wife, Doug and Lisa, were injured in Omaha by an alcohol-impaired teen. Three laws were broken that day, with no arrest of any of the adults involved and no effect on the liquor license of the illegal sale. (That is a system which protects its own!) Adults got the teen offender drunk and adults asked him to drive because he "had nothing to lose" like a license or family or reputation. His friends snookered him, which is typical of those avoiding the law.

On a personal note, Doug and Lisa are faculty members at Rutgers University in New Jersey and live productive lives. However, they live their lives under severe restriction, as Doug is paralyzed, needs two hours to care for his body every morning, and has given up many activities he greatly enjoyed. It never ends. For openers, they have managed great stress, which many couples find too much to handle in marriage. They have required millions of dollars in medical-related cost to get this far. A chunk of that comes from our family, especially from the two of them, but most of it is paid by you.

Doug and Lisa are highly committed social-issue persons, giving their lives to improve society. They would gladly shift these medical dollars to schools or health needs. We could help that to happen if we agreed to declare that drunk driving is offensive to neighbors.

Public costs of driving impaired

(2001) Alcohol and driving impaired causes over $300 million in losses in Nebraska every year. That is a conservative, professional estimate. Driving impaired is expensive for the community. Persons of faith are able to think of better ways to use that money.

Injuries and death from drunk driving send innocent victims into bankruptcy (the innocent pay most of the bills), their children into a different life with loss of dreams, and whole families into depression. Again, every faith group is aggressive on behalf of healthy families and has a natural interest in preventing impaired driving.

The outrageous gap in funding is on public costs of alcohol. We need at least $50 million the next two years for teachers incentives. We have four sources: Property tax, sales, income, and sin. "Sin taxes" -- tobacco and alcohol -- are way down from paying their way. We are hesitant to appear to apply the revenue to teachers, though they are hurt by funding the subsidy. Our direct costs of alcohol are at least 4 times our income. We spend $300 million or more on direct costs of alcohol each year, and collect only $70 million taxes. Removing this deficit would clearly help teachers. Tobacco also costs us dearly in care for elderly who are ill. Ironically, tobacco does help Social Security funds because many users die early. 1-18

(2003) A big revenue piece also available is to increase alcohol tax. For beer, we tried to add 2 cents a can. We were told that would be an "astronomical increase." One dealer said it would be the end of beer drinking in Nebraska and put hundreds out of work, crippling the state economy. A senator said on the floor that several businesses would close. The nonsense worked. We voted to protect beer and avoid disaster.

Meanwhile, back on this planet, we can find no one who would be hurt by the increase and it would put $20 million on the table. One senator would rather cut $10 million each from the university and from K-12 education. That is a fascinating proposal for a discussion of priorities. Is cutting our kids' education more important to us than raising a can of beer by 2 cents? Will 25 votes support this strange trade? If they do you can be assured we will be doing all we can to add to public embarrassment for protectionist senators.

(2006) A few of us dropped a rock in the pond, to increase alcohol taxes by 630%. The splash is about right. Mostly on radio.

"So what is this about?" they ask. It proposes to set up a fund to pay for all of the costs associated with alcohol-impaired drivers on the roads in Nebraska. We would pay for the medical costs, death costs, loss of income costs, property damage costs.

"How much will this raise?" About $140 million a year. "Doesn't that seem like a lot to you?" O my yes. It certainly is a lot. But that is the bill we are already paying, through insurance, personal losses and taxes.

"Is alcohol the sole cause of the losses?" No, the person who chooses to drive after drinking is also a cause. But without alcohol there would be no such losses. We expect that a product should bear the cost it creates in society. We have recovered some of our tax losses from tobacco, so it is alcohol's turn.

"Do you think that the person who drinks responsibly should pay?" Do you think the innocent party who is hit and whose family is devastated should pay instead?

There is a small problem with all of the above. It does not nearly cover all of the costs, especially the domestic costs that alcohol causes taxpayers. The total is well over twice this figure. When taxpayers get upset enough will they ask for protection from a very expensive subsidy??? Or will folk change their tune and say they like paying increased taxes? 6-3

Public attitudes on DUI

Public attitude is what we are thinking about. We excuse, even give tacit permission, to driving while drunk. As noted in the neighbor chapter, citizens of Sweden do not do that and they suffer none of our losses. We are not that neighborly.

Senators care about impaired driving because it is such a huge cost. However, we get only modest support from citizens. Hopefully, the day will come when all senators will be reminded by the public that alcohol impaired drivers cause more mayhem than any other single factor in our society. 3-14

The public and some attorneys often excuse the drunk driver in a crash, saying that he was drunk so he could not help it. Hello? We have to get under the public's defenses on .08% BAC. This is serious drinking! Opponents say that it will ruin restaurant business because the new limit would be invasive of social drinking. They go on to say that persons who intend to drive will greatly reduce their drinking. We could hope.

The Lincoln Journal had an article starting off with something like "Senator Lowen Kruse, 190 pounds, spoke at the .08% BAC hearing yesterday about his beautiful body and how much alcohol it would take to be over the limit."

Well. he was on the floor the next week, to object that his weight was published in the paper. He could get over it if every other member's weight is published. He went on to say that until the article very few commented on his beautiful bod, which is surely an oversight.

On the bod thing the serious point is how many drinks it would take to put someone of average weight over the limit. The answer is 9 drinks in a social setting. One more to be arrestable. Another one if the person had some food with all that alcohol. We voted for .08%

BAC, which would reduce the limit by one drink. That's it. Only exception is over 250 pounds (a two drink reduction). The bottom line: ask if anyone present thinks it unreasonable to ask drivers to cut from 9 to 8 drinks before driving. Hello, real world?

The opposition likes to ask, "Is it possible that a 120 pound woman (always a woman) who has a glass of wine before and after her meal will be thrown in jail??" No, it is not possible. It would take five drinks in one hour for her to be arrested (but not jailed) under the new limit. Her reduction under .08% would be the same: one drink.

When we asked others to define social drinking the answers varied from 2 to 3 drinks per hour. So take three drinks per hour, which requires three hours for nine drinks, plus at least half an hour for the alcohol to get into the blood stream. In actual experiments on the matter, not going by the charts, a 140 pound person with food took 9 drinks to get over the .08% BAC. We have here clear evidence that this senator only weighs 140 pds. Beats dieting. 1-1

Legal challenges which were won

We passed a bill that will allow 3 hours for an arresting officer in an alcohol-impaired driving situation to get the blood sample. If taken within 3 hours, the sample will be considered per se evidence of alcohol impairment at the time of driving. Judges and prosecutors need a definite standard to shut down game playing.

In the midst of conflict there is humor. We had only one person in opposition, the El Honcho for the Trial Attorneys Association. He said this could hurt an innocent person, and told how. This person drives home and for some reason is driving erratically. When he gets home he proceeds to start drinking, and after he has been drinking for two hours the officer who has been informed by a witness of his manner of driving arrives at his home, arrests him, takes him for a blood sample and he is convicted of DUI.

The attorneys on the committee did their best to hide their amusement while asking if this was an actual case. The very impressive-looking attorney said no, but it certainly was possible. Would an officer enter a home and arrest someone for a driving infraction while the person is not driving -- and whom the officer had not witnessed driving? Get real. 1-9

Nineteen loopholes were plugged in our efforts over 15 years. Most gaps in law were put there intentionally by lobbyists. For example, an offender could drive onto a grocery parking lot, with police in chase, and not be subject to arrest on 'private' property. A bar tender could serve a teenager with no accountability for damages the teen then caused.

A person could have convictions for a dozen DUI offenses but still be charged with first offense. Penalties were light and did not always come in a predictable way, so that different courts would provide a confusing wide range of penalties.

Now, social hosts who allow teens to have a keg party in their large home are liable to a judgment which could easily claim that expensive property -- and more. One father drove across the state to testify on the bill. His daughter never drank but ended up one night at a house where the parent provided all the drinks teens could handle. The girl was led to try drinking and quickly realized she could not safely drive home. The host panicked and forced her to leave before her parents could come for her. She rolled her car down a steep embankment on a stormy night. She lived, through some miracle. While she was being treated at a Scottsbluff hospital, two more teen girls were brought in, individually, from another home party. The one appeared to be dead, with no heart or breathing. The staff revived her, but they did not know if she had brain damage from the lack of oxygen.

We decided to include the merchants. That bartender is the last person to see the intoxicated person and can, with training, make a winsome offer to find a ride home. But bars have lobbyists (!) and they are very clever as well as deceptive. We want to motivate bar and package owners (and grocers and other sellers) to train their servers/clerks and ride herd on them, checking to be sure they follow the regulations. 8-14

To be fair, we have had many trial attorneys over the years privately object to their association's attempt to protect their loopholes. "Please, take away those loopholes so I can talk straight with my client, who is putting my own children's lives at risk." 3-8

Can teens receive communion?

This was the ridiculous fuss in the legislature, possible only because we the public are not quite ready to say that teens ought not to drink alcohol. Recent research clearly shows that serious drinking by teenagers causes permanent brain damage through delayed brain development during growth years. It is a no-brainer (pun intended), not a subject to play around on. If we do not care about teenagers we should care about public funds twenty years from now when we are spending tax dollars to accommodate persons with lowered brain power. We recognize that most bar owners are not a problem,

The evidence is clear. Brain damage is visible to the naked eye in an autopsy of a drinking teen killed in a crash. One researcher said, in shock, the young person's brain looked like the brain of a 70 year old. Watch your language. 1-10

The news items relate to where minors can drink. At present, church and home are the only two exemptions in location. Clearly, public policy should be that teens not be allowed to drink anywhere. A few Christians are contending that communion is drinking. That is ridiculous, but we changed the language to make it clear.

However, it is not simple and several lawyers have wrestled with it. Present language allows teens to consume alcohol "on the premises where religious services are held..." Perhaps it is good legal language -- but it is misleading English. It allows Senator Chambers to say we are hypocrites when we say teens should not drink, but they may get drunk at church or at home. The language must be changed.

Staff members enjoyed discovering that Kruse was a sponsor, five years earlier, of a bill allowing minors to have a sip of wine in religious ceremonies. Before that it was assumed that receiving communion is not drinking. However, churches asked for specific exemption for any church activity, to which Kruse foolishly agreed. This gave Senator Chambers the opening to say that churches want to get teens drunk. 7-5

The bill to restrict the use of alcohol by minors to zero was the center of a flap that had every senator getting emails. It is a tempest in a teapot, which occurs often. This senator received over 100 messages on wine in religious ceremonies. That is drinking? The law has never considered it so, for anyone. Not one Jewish family asked if the bill affected Jewish Passover meals in the home, when a glass of wine (or grape juice for young children) is shared with the meal to express thanksgiving for the fruit of the vine from God's good earth.

Four denominations regularly use wine in ceremonies. Only two objected, but they made up for the rest. There is no proportionality of responses when church folk get noisy.

To balance the witness, one older man said he had gone to mass regularly for years and had not received enough wine in all that time to cover the bottom of a glass. (Many priests use only the wafer except on special occasions.)

Two older Catholic men marveled at the fuss, offering the general thought that we should, in law, ignore the minimal use of wine in ceremonies. Each said he was a hopeless alcoholic until 20 years ago, when he regained health and has not touched wine since. One sat there, looking down at the table for a long time, then said, "Don't these people have anything else to think about? Have they heard of world hunger? Child abuse?"

This pastor of course is opposed to any law that would compromise a religious ceremony. The technical wording is a distraction from the main point: stop teen drinking. We should question the mixed message sent by a priest who, as one parent complained, tells teens not to drink but forces an altar boy to drink leftover wine. There are better and acceptable church alternatives but that is for the church, not the senators, to say and do. For example, Jewish leaders say scripture does not require wine for children. Also, every church serves the valid Eucharist to pregnant women and recovering alcoholics, without wine. So it is acceptable Eucharist. Again, the modes for communion are for each church to decide.

There is humor here. A Missouri Synod Lutheran, who supports the ban on teen drinking, says it really is not an issue for them. They put wine in the cup and God changes it to blood. Arrest God.

The new law addresses only the minor, not God or the servers. At present a priest, pastor or rabbi can serve alcohol "on premise" and that does not change. We waffled on alcohol in the home, though most of us consider that moot and not a matter of law. Every parent is prohibited from serving alcohol to a child's friend.

These are not questions which someone dreams up, nor are they anti-alcohol. Nor are they, as some have said, this father's emotional reaction to Doug's injury. Our son was hit by a minor impaired with alcohol he and others purchased illegally. It is law, not alcohol. We are dealing with our consequences but certainly want to protect others from the sad loss.

The specific issues come from local law enforcement and the state patrol. When they raid a teen keg party, for example, and witness kids who are obviously drunk, the kids know to say they were drunk when they left home and so they cannot be arrested. That is not acceptable if we want a clear message for teens.

As a horrible example, one fellow called the office, said the senator is over reacting. He would rather lose his son than force teens to quit drinking. O my. Right away we know he does not have a son. We will bet he hates taxes even more than kids, so how about another fact? An extensive study concluded that drinking by minors costs $435 million per year in Nebraska. Wow! Think we could use that money to a better purpose? That is equivalent to 20% of Nebraskans' property tax bill. Think we should stop it? Remember, it is adults, not kids, who cause the problem. 7-2

In the floor debate we had a series of "Well, yes, teens ought not to drink, except..... " It is dispiriting to see leaders offer teens excuses for not following the law -- in the army, working hard, celebrating. Teens can think of enough excuses on their own. Leaders set the example for attitudes.

Do understand, those are scattered voices on the church flap, not the consensus of the legislature. We expect to come together to declare that minors are not to drink alcohol. This waffling sends messages. Add to it the advertising of alcohol that targets kids more than adults. Kids see ten times more alcohol ads than do adults, which makes pandering even more dangerous. 7-20

The good news: senators are 100% together on something! We have united in recognizing that the meth drug is a powerful enemy of our citizens. We must develop solid plans, but it is clear we have the political will to do "the needful," as the old-time preacher put it. 5-20

Those who ignore impaired driving have an attitude and need a very firm, consistent message. Like a child. Let's hope the message comes through. Bottom line, the public attitude toward driving after drinking is more important than laws. Hopefully clear laws will help us join in a clear message, and hopefully persons of faith will aggressively pursue life and health for their neighbors. 5-22

Gambling

Moral questions

Gambling is a moral issue in almost every religious group. How does a senator of faith respond in voting?

We grant that gambling is bad for society, breaks homes, ends careers, reduces income and sales tax, creates homelessness, hunger, neglect, and family abuse, and depreciates the thought of working for a living. Do casinos hurt our people? No doubt.

However, is a bill on gambling a moral issue for the Nebraska legislature? Probably not. We have gambling and its ills already. We are not voting on whether to gamble, but on how much to gamble.

Moral issues are involved in considering expanded gambling. The cost becomes the moral issue. Strictly the bucks. Increased gambling will cost us more tax dollars and we are already in a deficit. Many studies have been made of the public expense involved. They range from $3 to $6 cost for each $1 received. If we thought we could pull 2 Nebraska gamblers in Council Bluffs back to N. for each new gambler in N., the 3:1 ratio would have us break even. The estimates, from very clear-eyed people, is that we will not be so lucky as to bring the two back to Nebraska.

Left out in these measurements of morals is personal and family pain. Is health of families a moral issue? 2-6

Loss of public dollars

South Dakota contracted with Deloite and Touche to do an audit on the video slots they approved a while ago, to determine actual dollar costs. They reported that the state lost 640 jobs and went in the hole $104 million a year. The Governor said approving video slots proved to be the worst decision the state has made in recent history. However, those receiving the slot dollars have so much funding they can overwhelm the truth when the voting comes. Poorly informed voters are not able to reverse a popular innovation. Another state did a similar audit and the people did vote the slots out.

How does gambling cost so much? First, the state receives less of the gambling dollar than Las Vegas. When a million dollars is sent to Las Vegas it is taken out of our local economy and reverses economic development. It is gone. We lose the tax on the income as it was spent elsewhere, and we lose the sales tax. Bankruptcies and broken homes cost the state money. We are required to care for the children who become wards of the state. Lottery and Keno, which pay the state much better, are reduced by casinos. Keno probably could not survive.

At the Pine Ridge reservation the local government gets all of the revenue, and they are poorer now than when they started it. It is the second poorest county in the nation. Gambling revenue, pure and simple, is a tax on the vulnerable. It is a 25% sales tax on each quarter that goes into a slot .... and the city still cannot pay the bills in Pine Ridge.

(2002) There would not be a snowballs chance of passing more gambling on the legislative floor, because we know about the costs. So what can we do when bar owners are starting a petition for citizens to vote? A petition that "limits" video slots to 300,000 in Nebraska? That would put into the constitution a guarantee of profit to bar owners? (Hoo boy, would farmers, restaurant owners or small businesses like to write their guarantee into the state constitution?)

Any major change has to go to the vote of the people, so there are also those gambling operators who piously proclaim "Let the people decide." They really mean, "Let our advertising decide." The problem with that is every one of their plans will take more dollars than it produces, by at least double. Are we really obligated to let people vote on a terrible idea, especially when the complex finances are not understood by the people? (02 #5)

We do not expect the legislature to come up with a safer alternative plan that will pass. We have bar owners, keno operators, horse tracks, pickles, Ameristar and Harrah's all scrambling for an advantage and trying to block the others out. Depressing. If we cannot control the madness we are headed into a very expensive future for Nebraska, with increased taxes. (Note: the public petition vote failed to pass.)

How about a casino in Omaha?

(2004) The bottom line is that casinos cost us money. We cannot afford even one. They have 'purty' lights on the outside, bells on the inside and cushy carpet underfoot. Nice. But we are broke and we can find no reputable study that shows a net gain on taxes.

That does not make sense to a lot of folks, since there is so much money there. But one-third is sent to Las Vegas and the rest will not pay the bills. Dr. Ernie Goss, Creighton economist who has studied it as it applies to Omaha, stated: "Few areas in the U. S. can realistically boast that gambling actually contributes to overall economic development." The only possibility for breaking even is one "destination" casino in downtown Omaha. "Destination" means that folks will flock in from other states because our casino is so huge and glitzy that they just have to see it. We cannot imagine that a million people in Minnesota and Kansas are going to get sucked in to coming to Nebraska on a regular basis. If the customers are only Nebraska and Iowa, it is a loser.

What screws up people's thinking is that it seems common sense that if we pull the Nebraska dollars going to Council Bluffs back across the river we will have $$$. Not. If we pull half the trade away from the three casinos over there, we will get $30 million in net revenue. But no more, as Omaha is not a place one flies to, to gamble. The $30 M. will be used up in increased Medicaid alone.

There would be extra jobs in a large casino, for Nebraskans. However, one casino, Dr. Goss reports, would drain 2,294 jobs away from surrounding counties. Part of that is because money is going to the casino, which causes a loss of local spending. One casino in Omaha, a big one, will suck out of the economy $145 million a year in gamblers' losses. That comes out of revenue to our businesses. If we thought we could bring an outfit to town that contributed $145 m. a year to our economy, would we be excited? 4-5

Simple facts.

"Look at all the jobs a casino would produce." Most of the jobs in the Council Bluffs casinos are Nebraskans.

"Look at all the supplies to be purchased." Most casino purchases are now from Nebraska.

"Look at all the money." If that is Nebraska $$, it is reducing local sales by that amount.

"Look at all the sales tax on products." We lose more sales tax than we gain. Gambling is not a product. Fewer refrigerators will be sold.

Our friends in Iowa do not think they are making money on their casinos, but it is the devil to try to close them. Casinos shift money around, big time. Those on the receiving end have enough clout (and money!) to keep the cycle going. The transition back to normalcy would be painful, even though it would save money. Council Bluffs taxes are going up a chunk this year, and they will cut some fire and police personnel. In fairness, they are doing extra things in C. B., because of the casino action. 3-9

Kansas chose to own a casino. It will put $$$ into the budget, but will cost them over the long run (see S. Dakota). The loss will be reduced to about 2:1 because they own it.

The Omaha Chamber backed off a supportive stance to a neutral position. Businesses are the main ones to be hurt financially. We have looked at all the studies. Not one of them varies from the conclusion: casinos are a net loss. There would be some value to have this asset, a hotel and casino, by the convention center. But who will pay the bill?

Other Controversial issues

A really tough dilemma is the proposal to allow the Indians' request to have casinos on their property, as economic development. Economic development it is not, even if they are desperate for money and jobs. The casino cash cow is expected to last only about five more years. However, they are sovereign nations and are deeply offended that they have to ask permission. That, they say, is only because of broken treaties. Where is Solomon when you need him? Solomon would figure out a true economic development project, but that of course could be paternalistic. 1-4

Quite aside from the adversarial fuss, how can we understand the person who does business with someone who openly promises to give back less than he/she takes in. If you keep coming you will be broke. What is so great about that? The biggest owner in Las Vegas was asked if he had ever heard of a big winner. "Never."

Plus, it now becomes apparent that the slots are dishonest. They are not random, not a roll of the dice. They are computerized to stack the deck. The player is not spinning a roulette wheel with an equal chance on each number. The computer has programmed it to stop next to the winning space, more than any other space. Again, try to imagine why anyone would roll dice with a computer in charge. 4-Oct

254. Macho men are needed to make tough decisions in the hearings. Pocahontas cannot be trusted.

12. Prayer

<u>'Let us be in reflection and prayer'</u>

O God, quiet our minds in this place, that we may marvel at your creation and give heartfelt thanks for those who join with us. We gather to do your work, to do our work, to do that which will be a blessing to our people. We cannot do this on our own, for we do not know it all. We are cantankerous at times and we often are poor listeners.

We pray for your gifts of wisdom, patience and courage. We give thanks for our staffs which give us support and for our citizens who yearn for the evidence of your blessing. God of all nations, help us to be your people. Amen.

Every morning that the body is in session the legislature opens with prayer, before convening. Volunteer pastors, religious leaders, and senators lead listeners in their prayers. The practice is strongly protected by the senators as a way to acknowledge our dependence on God and to help all who will pray to focus on the day's work before opening for business.

Guidelines for prayer are clear. One, the time will be brief, under five minutes. Two, reference cannot be made to subjects up for debate, or to partisan issues. Three, the prayer is to be nonsectarian. The first two are observed almost without fail, but the third is compromised. Prayer is to be for <u>all</u> citizens, but those who pray are usually Christian and many will use their exclusive language.

The usual words that cross the line are signing off a prayer with "in the name of Jesus." Sometimes words like that will include reference to Jesus as "our Savior." The improper language comes from routine thought, not from an intent to offend. Pastors know better. Senators impress this pastor with how many get it right. They find all kinds of ways to "sign off" while respecting the personal faith of all citizens.

One pastor said he could not pray except through Jesus. He claimed he would lack integrity to be silent about Jesus. Sorry to hear that. That is his choice and is his right. However, then he should not pray in a public place. We want <u>all</u> the people to be able to say "Amen" and none of us believes God receives only the email Jesus forwards.

Other problems are few. A pastor explained to God, at some length, how to gain salvation through the only source available: Jesus. One does wonder how God became so limited that God cannot provide salvation for Jews and Muslims.

Another asked for a blessing of his community ministry, described in some detail. All that was missing in this "hearing" was the concluding request for funds. We were quite sure he was not preparing a request of God.

Another pastor (who also was not invited back) informed God about God's plan of salvation, in which God saves those who believe in Jesus but sends Jews and Muslims to hell. Besides excluding selected citizens, telling God what God does and then spinning it to bash the people you dislike is not prayer. In a congregation it is a form of sermon. In the legislature a sermon is out of order.

A leading Southern Baptist pastor has asked his congregation for prayers that his enemies die. Is God a hit man? The pastor's declared enemies are those who believe in the separation of church and state.

His 'enemies' discovered he is telling people how to vote and so turned him in to the IRS. This soul needs <u>real</u> prayer.

<u>Our prayer reveals us</u>

When the author was a supervisor of pastors, evaluation of belief and skills was essential. He found the fastest way to get dependable information was to listen to a pastoral prayer (better source than a sermon). Prayer shows where one's heart is and it exposes shallow or inconsistent theology. Lazy persons tell God to do what they are not motivated to help do. True attitudes toward one's own responsibility are exposed in prayer.

Our beliefs show more in our prayers than in our statements. Prayer in the legislature teaches all of us more about prayer. This pastor of fifty years had developed his own habits and was challenged in a new setting to be clear about what we pray. There are <u>God</u> jobs and <u>our</u> jobs. Both are appropriate to prayer, but the focus should be on what <u>we</u> are to do. Most believe we do not change God, but certainly <u>we</u> can be changed.

We can praise God for our natural creation, but are most presumptive when we direct God on how to operate nature, or when we tell God how to rescue us in our own job. Thoughtful prayer in the legislature does help sort out what is our job.

We could, for example, pray: "God, get us more dollars for public school education." Two problems with that. One, it is not God's job to prioritize our budget. Two, this is using prayer for lobbying purpose, to hit the opposition who wants the funds for health care. Rather, we could pray: "God, help us to study the needs of every program, to listen to one another, and to reflect on citizen concerns. Give us the wisdom and will to establish priorities which will be a blessing to our people."

Or, we come close to praying: "God, send more water in our river to Kansas, so they cannot sue us." Not God's job. Instead, we could pray: "God, your creation has given Nebraska more underground water than nearly any place on earth. Help us, together, to be good stewards of water so that all will have an adequate resource."

Or, we may pray "God, keep these kids from shooting each other." That is not God's job. Rather, pray: "God, help remove the violence from me, from my neighbors, from my church, from my city." When the violence is removed the shooting will be greatly decreased. St. Francis is a sound teacher:

Lord, make me an instrument of Thy peace. Where there is hate, may I bring love. Where there is offense, may I bring pardon. May I replace error with truth, doubt with faith, despair with hope, darkness with light. Make me not to so crave to be loved as to love. Help me to learn that in giving I may receive. Amen.

A created example of personal prayer, 'inspired' by an ad, makes the point more clearly. "God, give me a WOW body." Not God's job. God already gave me/you a WOW body. Your body is a bundle of miracles, beyond the full understanding of the best-trained physician. Our job is to care for that body. Would prayer help? Yes, especially if it is in community. There is power in a congregation praying for fitness and health. We do not know how God connects us in spirit, but we have witnessed it. There is power in community prayer.

Dorothy Solle, a marvelous theologian, wondered how we lost our way to communicate clearly about God. Old formulas, stated without thinking and in terms the public (therefore we) cannot really understand, are part of the reason.

A "Prayer For the 21st Century" demonstrates clarity *(Ed Kail)*:

This is your land, O God of all Creation, the land by which You give us daily bread.

This is our land, but only as a trust, Lord. We are your stewards, here to do Your will. This is our land, but not as our possession; though we may tend it, it is Your land still. This is our land, our place of earthly labor.

Our land to love, conserve, preserve and till.

You give us life on farms, in towns and cities; all bound together, one community. But sin and pride and greed for wealth and power threaten that life, destroy our unity. Our life is sacrificed to idols, to gods of war and "prosperity."

Let righteousness roll down like living waters, and justice like an ever-flowing stream. Let us be neighbors, caring for each other, working together to preserve the dream: a life on farms in towns and cities, God's land and ours, community redeemed.

These are personal thoughts. Hopefully no one is offended by frank comments on how some ideas sound in the legislative setting. We do have powerful, effective prayers which show deep thought, and concern which is carefully focused. Most prayers are an inspiration, including Sen. Cap Dierks this week: "God, we are here again and we need blessing and guidance. Amen." 2-4

An early lesson in prayer -- and God

A farmer taught this farm boy's confirmation class in a country church. He was also a German theologian. He struggled with English. "I could say it in German. It is so beautiful in German." Gratefully, he was able to put profound thoughts into simple language.

Mr. B. was always teaching. One summer after Church School the men and boys were in a circle on the grass, per custom. A drought was fierce and corn had no more than two weeks of life left. One of the men asked, "Mr. Bernhagen, if we had a prayer meeting for rain, would it rain?" His quick answer: "Yes."

However, he continued, we ought not to do it. Every one wondered why not, which is the perfect teaching moment. "Because not everyone would come, and those who came would not bring their overshoes." Unpacking that, we were given two basic lessons. Prayer is not simply words. Prayer by everyone has more power.

There is no doubt about Mr. B.'s belief regarding God and rain. He did not believe God manipulates the clouds, moving rain away from those who do not pray, to those who do. He had a point to teach, and he did it. Our thoughts on storms and accidents are a test of what we truly believe and how we will act.

Our son was not picked out by God to be hit by an alcohol-impaired driver. That kid, and the seven adults who fed him alcohol all day, were exercising the freedom which God gave them, but in a very destructive way. Those adults not only cruelly changed Doug and Lisa's lives, they destroyed who that young offender could have been. He continued to drink and offend, ending in prison.

Since we have lost so much to a drunk driver, we have been asked the Mr. B. question. "If we all prayed that drunk driving would stop, would it stop?" Yes, without a doubt. When a community prays together that drinkers do not drive, it will stop. We know that because Sweden has prayed that -- with everyone in the nation agreeing they are not going to do harm to their neighbor in this careless way. It is their prayer and it has power. Drunk driving stopped in Sweden.

In a crash that spares our loved one, we are likely to thank God for being with us and protecting us. That is misleading, but legislative prayers have done that. What about the ones who died? Was God absent from them? We do not believe that. As a former farmer, one remembers seeing an angry storm cloud coming and yearning (praying?) that the hail would miss us. Did we prefer it hit our neighbor and would God get credit for that? Did God send the hurricane to one city because they were not praying (as some TV pastors have said), and not to the neighboring city on the gulf coast because they are more righteous? We do not believe that and should not pray that way.

To be clear, our family has no doubt that prayer for Doug's healing had a powerful effect. One nurse in particular that first night manipulated the breathing to save his brain. Her steady (black) hand skillfully kept the oxygen level up. Was Dora praying? You better believe it, and she, with other emergency personnel, gave Doug his future life as an academic. Prayer connected with dedicated medical efforts to rescue his brain. Hallelujah.

We in the legislature do not direct God to make it rain. We need rain and are grateful for rain, and should say so, for that is a part of a marvelous natural world. This senator had to sort rainmaker out quickly one morning. But he blew it. Fame and fortune could have been his with one short clever sentence. Thought it, but did not say it into the mike, for all Nebraska to hear.

Several of us can be counted on to punt when the pastor of the day does not show to open with prayer. Walk forward slowly and think. One of the senators on the aisle whispered, "We need rain." Would that be a legit prayer? Yes, if stated that way, for we do acknowledge our needs in prayer. So end with: "Lord, we need rain. Amen."

Well, it was the day after a big fracas, which brought to mind some serious thoughts for prayer. With that in mind, the pary-er forgot to include the need for rain.

Within the hour it started to rain and it rained for four days. Beautiful, slow rain. Five inches many places, three inches in the panhandle. Wow! Blew it. Everyone would have given a senator credit, even if it was not appropriate prayer. Being a rainmaker in Nebraska is just above being governor, next to being a Big Red coach.

We tip our mental hand, like the fellow this week who prayed for blessing on every elected official "on down to the county commissioners." Hey, they may not think they are the bottom of the feeding chain.

A Prayer that struck a chord

Basic prayer is praise and thanksgiving. Most pastors begin that way. Isaiah 6:1-6 provides the classic pattern of prayer most pastors are taught, with a four-part outline that always works.

1. Praise. We read "In the year that King Uzziah died, I saw the Lord sitting upon a throne, high and lifted up….."

2. Our human failing. The view of such glory causes us to see the contrast with our humanness, our need, our failing. The next lines are poetic: "Woe is me! For I am lost; for I am a person of unclean lips, and I dwell in the midst of a people of unclean lips ... (yet) my eyes have seen the King."

3. Renewal. It can be said many ways, but in the wonderful image of Isaiah the coals from that high altar are brought to touch (our) lips, to forgive and renew.

4. Dedication. God asks who will go for us: "Then I said, 'Here am I. Send me.' "

The writer was startled to discover he gave his most famous prayer last week. People have been commenting for days. In all humility, that never happened for a Sunday morning prayer, however fluent or thoughtful -- or even spiritual.

An unusual circumstance was the setting. As we begin a two-year session we have not yet elected officers. Since it was the opening of Senator Chamber's last session, and he had seen many of them, leaders decided he should convene us. Senator Chambers, who strongly protests that we open with prayer and who has not been in the chamber for a prayer in anyone's memory, was going to have to ask for prayer. Everyone was nervous, including Senator Chambers.

The clerk's office lines up pray-ers and privately asked this pastor to be ready for whatever might happen -- to be prepared to punt. As pioneer pastors warned each other, "be prepared to preach, pray or die at a moment's notice."

This pastor soon discovered that "Brother Ernie" was just as nervous, for he had only one chance to do the opening tradition right and he wanted it to go well. He came over, also in private, saying he would call for a time of reflection and then introduce me, confident that we would be led in a non-offensive way. He spoke of my being open to all faiths. His praise was appreciated and sincere, but not necessary. My response: his time of reflection would simply be extended. He seemed relieved, which was interesting in itself.

Out of respect for Senator Chambers and for all who would pray, the writer extended the "time of reflection" into a "directed prayer." Four suggestions to the listeners for their own prayer were each followed with a moment of silence for individual thoughts.

The outline of the directions for the silent prayers was from Isaiah.

"Pray about what you praise God for." .....

"We are human and fail. Pray with God about that." .....

"God forgives and renews us if we ask." ......

"We are renewed for a purpose. What will you do now?" .....

That was it. The whole thing. As modest an offering of rhetoric as one could imagine. The place was absolutely silent. Several senators wondered what might happen next, still fearing possible tension. No need for apprehension. Afterward, Ernie was profuse in his thanks for the prayer time.

Dozens of persons phoned or wrote, or stopped to talk in the hall. One secretary said she was in tears at her desk as she realized that all of these people are truly praying together. The community in prayer has power.

Prayer exposes flaws

Sen. Chambers is not really against prayer, but is deeply offended by those who piously tell God what a good man Jesus was and give no credit to Buddha or Gandhi. Agreed. How can any pastor feel obligated to tell God that God is limited in any way? Poor God.

Some prayers just plain bash. It is the "Lord, thou knowest my neighbor is a bum" prayer. When you hear a leader say in prayer "Thou knowest" you can know (he) has stopped praying and gone to preaching. "Lord, thou knowest that Republicans should quit being selfish." "Lord, thou knowest that Democrats should quit being generous with other people's money."

"Thou knowest" is not prayer. But a greater offense is happening. The speaker is dressing up a lie as prayer. This senator became well acquainted with quite a few Republicans and thereby came to know many generous persons. Likewise, it is not hard to find Democrats who are plain stingy. We have heard trashing prayers like that, but thankfully not in the legislature.

Dr. Tex Sample, internationally known theologian, tells about a young man from his small town in Mississippi who felt called to be a pastor and who became a recognized Baptist Biblical scholar. He came back to visit his family and this day was in the home of a salty, racist, angry (white) uncle. They were watching TV, when a nationally prominent black pastor whom the uncle despised came on. The uncle said the man should be shot and if he came to this town "I would do it. I would gladly kill the man."

The pastor challenged him, that he did not mean that. "Oh yes, I do. He is a disgrace. The world would be better off without him. If I had a chance I would kill him." Then, the pastor responded, you should go down to the church and pray that. The man responded in disbelief, said he could not do that. "Yes, if that is what you yearn for you should pray that God would help you do it."

His response (continuing to clean up the man's cursing): "No. Jesus would not buy that." Though he yearned for an outcome, he knew that this anger was <u>his</u> flaw and was not in the spirit of Jesus. He could not pray it.

The flap of the week was an opening prayer that was way out of line. The pastor acted more dull than one suspects he is. In supposed prayer, which he later said he had worked on for several days, he informed God how sinful we are as we ignore God's clear word on abortion and evolution. The pastor of course left no margin for error in the premise that his thoughts <u>are</u> God's thoughts.

My favorite piece of his prayer came as he instructed God on evolution. Picture (a forgetful) God on her pearly white throne, asking assorted angels "How did we do creation? Does anyone remember?" ("We" is from Genesis 3:22 -- creation was evidently a team project.) Fortunately for God's team, right then comes this pastor to the rescue, reminding God how to create the correct way.

There is a lot of room in the legislature for varying religious opinions, which we can celebrate, but at least once a week the words chosen do take one's breath away. We have patiently listened as the pray-er asked God to turn the economy around, make the farmers prosper (no mention of Enron or the banks), or make each of us holy. We have ordered (!) God to bless the animals, the children who study, faithful officials, the widows and orphans who are dependent on state funds (which we are cutting), and to bless anyone connected with a specific bill.

We have told God how great Nebraska is, how good our team is (guess which sport), that we are a fine people (even noble), that there is sin in the world, what a blessing the pastor's own church is to the children in a state-sponsored program, how good it was for God to sacrifice (kill?) Jesus and how many people are going to hell because they do not believe God killed Jesus. We are expected to believe something like that? One wonders, when they get so oratorical, do they want a law to enforce their opinion of God?

One of the more curious words to be used a great deal is "just." It is meant to imply God is so great and I am so small, so "I just pray that..... (Therefore, I am very humble as I pray)." Somehow, when the concept comes two or three times in a sentence it does feel like humility on parade. It has certainly become a theological proposition.

One senator prayed: "God, we are just here and we just are not sure just what to do." Understood. 2-B

Assorted instructions to God

We are prone to instrucf God on rain making, hurting our enemies, providing miracles in disaster, and on and on.

Regarding prayer, several readers noted the offense of a pray-er implying that God "likes" us better than someone else, even our enemies. Agreed. A prayer meeting where we share blunt thoughts about prayers would be helpful, but most "prayer meetings" this pastor was invited to were heavy on pious and light on prayer.

The prayers this week would receive high ratings. One described the qualities of God and then related them to gifts we can use. "We seek to reflect your grace and love."

Other request phrases: courage to speak the truth, peace in the world <u>and</u> in our hearts (amazing -- we would rather pray for peace in distant places), guidance in complex decisions, penitence for times we should have worked longer and with more patience, appreciation for each other, and help to listen to a new idea in order to understand its possibilities. 2-5

Suffragettes
At Prayer

One of the pray-ers this week acknowledged that God had charged us with heavy responsibilities. So <u>God</u> is the one who caused all this?? Did not God get rid of chaos in creation? My neighbor whispered, "That is o.k. as long as God does not try to collect on the charges."

Another pastor complained to God that "(We teach) that we are here for no reason and human life means nothing more than any other life; that we will never face a Judgment Day. We've put our children into the same category as other mammals, and we wonder why sometimes they act like animals. Forgive us for sowing the seeds of anarchy in the hearts of children."

He was not praying to God, but trashing his political adversaries. There are many theological questions here. Do we assume God is done creating? Or is defeated? Can any one of our theories or opinions capture all of Godness, box it and block other thoughts of God? However, it would be a mistake to get serious working from his shaky platform.

Compare his putdowns with the wonderful creation story in the mosaic on the floor of the rotunda, weaving the account of God's creation and preparation for us. Is it Christian or Jewish or partisan in any way? It is an affirmation of 'God with us' and we need that.

Lord, it isn't fair that some of the members of my church go South for the Winter and I have to stay here and scoop snow . . . Nevertheless, not my will . . . .

Pastors receive clear instructions as they are invited to come and pray for our state. These include not being political. One pastor said he was not political because he did not mention Republicans or Democrats. Well. Also, this is the way he prays in private and he should be able to say in public what he thinks in private. Now there is a novel thought! We do hope it does not catch on. Chambers quoted scripture he should read: when you pray go in a closet. "Do not pray in public like Pharisees and other hypocrites." –Matthew 5:5-6 Without a public audience he would be free to pray what he thinks.

Prayer in public places, when it resonates in a voice that God would envy, is sometimes referred to by devout souls as "the voice of God"." Then it cannot be prayer! The 'voice of God' is a metaphor, but it is misleading for a legislator to ever assume to hear the voice of God. We are surrounded by voices. Singular, loud, dulcet, deceptive, authoritative, gentle. God is a presence, not a voice. We have a sense of place, providing the arena in which the voices may be heard -- and measured. We do not need a stained glass voice or words in Old English script. We need support to have the confidence of being a child of God, unafraid to listen and ready to evaluate every voice.

Will close this book, which is basically on faith in action, and this chapter on prayer, with prayers from the legislature. They illustrate the role of prayer as an excellent way to center people of faith at the beginning of a new day.

Gracious God, thank you for another beautiful day. We welcome the sun. Life is good. However, we are looking at an intimidating agenda. It has a complex variety of subjects. Not one of us understands them all. We hear commenting voices from outside the chamber, from persons who do not have to comprehend the network which laws become.

From some voices we hear complaints about taxes but not about services. Other voices complain about services without comment on taxes. We hear voices from the young and happy, voices of hurt and despair, of hope and trust, of anger and frustration. Not one of us knows all of these persons or fully understands them. Help us to listen as we hear. Amen."

"God our creator, in this place we have colleagues who do understand complex legislation, with someone who has expertise on each subject. We have staff members who research the connections and we welcome persons who will raise a flag when a potential conflict emerges. We gain unexpected support in discussion. We have colleagues who truly care, which is what counts most. Thank you. Amen

God we remember those who have always been here – the Native Nations, who were displaced, yet whose proud heritage and unyielding spirit live on.

We thank you for those who with incredible courage left known lands and family and came to build new lives in a new land.

We remember those who had no choice in coming here, their bodies stolen and placed on slave ships.

We thank you for all who bring their own rich gifts to the rich diversity of this land. Gracious God, help us to celebrate all that makes us different, but to never forget all that boinds us together as one people, in one nation. Amen.

Lord, keep us alert to your presence and wisdom. Help us to be the body that will produce what you can bless. Amen.

May a Psalm teach us. A paraphrase of Psalm 130 by Walter Percy is clear writing that communicates to people who would like guidance in prayer.

Do you read? Do you read?
Are you in trouble?
How did you get in trouble?
If you are in trouble, have you sought help?
If you did, did help come?
If it did, did you accept it?
Are you out of trouble?

What is the character of your consciousness?
Are you conscious? Do you have a self?

Do you know who you are?
Do you know what you are doing?

Do you love?
Do you know how to love? Are you loved?
Do you hate?

Do you read me? Come back.
Come back. Come back. Come back.

POSTLUDE

Got a broom? To sweep back the ocean?

We will wrap up with a review of long term trends -- what the states are doing -- the feds -- opinion makers – other shakers and movers. It is not divine revelation, just a listing of what is fairly clear. Here is a part of our future, no matter what we do.

This is not prophecy, but the flow of the ocean. On each, there are folks who are sweeping against the current and some who sweep with it. You will probably want to sweep both ways. Personal preference is not a factor in the selection of items. Our individual and group actions can affect the timelines, but will not change the eventual outcome. There are many other parts we of course will affect.

Immigration of cheap labor. Some will huff and puff, but enough businesses want it that government efforts to stop it will fail. We built our country on cheap immigrant labor.

World Trade. Here again we have a lot of brooms out. However, you may know someone who has recently purchased an item made in China. (!) With instructions in five languages.

Concern over global warming. Some political types cried "Traitor" when Evangelicals recently stated that they are beginning to worry. Get used to it. People care about their planet's health and will care more. Whether the planet is warming is a side issue. How human activity affects the climate will be the eventual focus.

Concern over mercury in the air. So called "Clean Air Acts" are labels for more polluted air and there is a beginning backlash. Mercury from coal burning plants affects the intelligence of children. The more we talk, on either side, the more people will be concerned. Change will be controversial and slow, but we will do it.

Loss of privacy. The government has a flurry of proposals, as do many of the state legislatures, to protect our privacy. They will help, but will not protect you. You will have to do that.

Improved health care will reduce costs. This will take years of tug of war, but we are so far behind other countries we can learn how to do better. So far, for example, we know that we can use fewer tests and do so much more in prevention. One agreement: we <u>must</u> do it.

Increased cost on education, K-12 through college. Two factors guarantee this one for Nebraska. First, we have some of the lowest salaries in the nation and are trying to catch up. Salaries are the big item in school budgets. Second, it is clear education is the best economic development we can do. Nebraska will not get more people, so we have to grow the ones we have.

Increased care and costs for child abuse and neglect. We passed several bills with almost no objection. The same is happening in other states. It is a movement.

Kindergarten and pre-school will gain attention, improving quality. People want it, but there is also clear evidence that we will get the money back down the road, with better-prepared students.

More federal power/control and less state options. Do you know someone who has sent an email across state lines? Should state regs control that? Recently we argued at length about how to control phone service. You may know someone who phones other states, connects to a cable service with nationwide tentacles, or is intrigued with computer service that will be plugged into an electric wall socket. States rights are diminished by our new technologies.

Stable Social Security benefits. A few keep playing with the idea of cutting benefits for those who are now under 45. Or 40. Or 35. Cannot happen. Will not happen. Any politician who messes with benefits for our elderly neighbors is dead meat. Personal accounts with tax advantages? It's here, called a 401K or IRA, and is a good deal in the long haul.

Trash on TV. Increased violence in our culture. We grumble but there is no effective way to diminish it, except to change ourselves.

A new standard of personal/family values. People really care about that and when we quit shouting at each other we will build a solid base. For example on the warmest debate there is, when gay families are accepted as families we can increase talk about family -- what it means, how we can grow, how we can change the dialog. It is already happening.

Gay respect and rights. It is just a matter of time, like the tide. (To be clear, passion by a minority who fear gay persons will continue pretty much like it is. We will continue to kill one gay each week, as we have done for years.) The passion comes from inner fears of the accusers -- fear of their own thoughts and feelings. Without fear the subject is an afternoon conversation, with little passion.

A culture of teamwork. States are giving up on agency top-down authority in order to get more efficient use of tax dollars. Gallup University, in Omaha, is making big money by bringing in leaders from around the globe to learn how to do this. It is a wave.

We all had something to celebrate in a recent year: that the world shows resounding respect and great admiration for the Pope, a man who centered on peace, love and goodwill, and who gave that message in simple, unadorned language without profuse illustrations or eloquent soaring rhetoric. Amazing. And wonderful. 5-11

What wonderful gifts we have to share. This writer is an optimist. We are better than we appear. Much of the above indicates higher attention to one another, to community. We are in better agreement on what needs to change and we are moving as fast as we can. Perhaps too fast. Public consensus is slow to form and no change counts until that happens. Leaders of today are good listeners as well as thinkers, and know how to apply what they hear. That is also our future!

Partisanship in politics.

NOTES

A. "Omaha: Paradise on the Prairie" --book by Lowen Kruse, Paradise Publishing, 2001

B. "History of the Catholic Church in Nebraska" – series of books by Henry W. Casper, S. J., 1966

C. "Liberty" – magazine published the the Seventh Day Adventists, features academic articles on Freedom of Religion. "Liberty" is a remarkably disciplined collector of research on diversity and religious freedom, reaching back thousands of years. It has provided a broad background of writers, and is excellent in stimulating thought. 2004, June, p 10 ff., plus several others

D. "What is Patriotism?" -- Address by A. T. Jones to the Seventh Day Baptist convention in 1896. Published by "Liberty."

E. "Washington Post" -- Op-Ed by Michael Gerson, 2008

F. "Honey from the Rock" --book by Rabbi Lawrence Kushner

G. "God's Politics" -- (book, and address at Creighton University) Jim Wallis, Editor of "Sojourners" -- 2006

H. "The World That Isn't" – book by Frank Tashlin, Simon and Schuster, 1951

I. "Liberty" -- copy of address by Ebrahim Rasool, Premier of South Africa, to the General Assembly, 2007

J. "The Progressive Revolution" -- book by Michael Lux, Wiley, 2009, pp. 32-35

K. "New York Times" -- Op-Ed by David Brooks (2004?)

L. "Newsweek" -- article following the death of William Buckley 3/10/8

M. "Nebraska History" – magazine/journal of the Nebraska Historical Society, Winter, 2007. "Nebraska History" has provided background for several pieces in the book.

NOTES

N. "Nebraska History" -- Vol 90/1 Spring 2009. Dr. John Sautter wrote "Social Trnasformation and the Farmers' Alliance Experience" page 6, ff.

O. :Doorway to Freedom" -- book by William Ramsey and Betty Dineen Shrier, 2008. The book centers on David Kaufman of Grand Island, known personally by the author, who provided safe passage for Jewish persons escaping Nazi Germany and provided funds for their opportunity to start over in the United States.

P. "Nebraska History" -- Spring 2009, page 56

Q. Hymn based on Micah 6:8 is by David Haas.

R. Matthew 22:1-10. Cf, Luke 14:12-24

S. "Paradise on the Prairie" – book by Lowen Kruse, 1986

T. Omaha World-Herald -- column on 11/13/08

U. Pogo cartoons are mostly from "The Jack Acid Society Black Book as told to Walt Kelly," 1957.
Other titles are "The Pogo Papers," 1952, "I Go Pogo," 1951, "The Incompleat Pogo," 1952, and "Potluck Pogo," 1954.
All are by Walt Kelly.
History notes are from "Pogo Files for Pogophiles," Kelly and Thompson, 1992.

V. Several line drawings and the "Revener" cartoon are from "We Are The Church." by Lowen Kruse, 1995

Index

Index